PRE-INDUSTRIAL KOREA AND JAPAN IN
ENVIRONMENTAL PERSPECTIVE

HANDBOOK OF ORIENTAL STUDIES

HANDBUCH DER ORIENTALISTIK

SECTION FIVE
JAPAN

EDITED BY

MARK BLUM · R. KERSTEN · M.F. LOW

VOLUME ELEVEN

PRE-INDUSTRIAL KOREA AND JAPAN
IN ENVIRONMENTAL PERSPECTIVE

PRE-INDUSTRIAL KOREA AND JAPAN IN ENVIRONMENTAL PERSPECTIVE

BY

CONRAD TOTMAN

BRILL

LEIDEN · BOSTON

2004

This book is printed on acid-free paper.

Library of Congress Cataloging-in-Publication Data

The Library of Congress Cataloging-in-Publication Data is available on
http://catalog.loc.gov

ISSN 0921-5239
ISBN 90 04 13626 6

PRINTED IN THE NETHERLANDS

For Michiko
Companion of Fifty Years

She has crossed oceans,
bridged chasms,
shouldered mountains,
weathered storms,
and been there despite it all.

CONTENTS

LIST OF ILLUSTRATIONS

Plates

 1. Korea: lowland vista, near Seoul
 2. Japan: mountain ridges, in Tōhoku
 3. Japan: wet rice maturing amidst other vegetation, near Tokyo
 4. Japan: the port of Hirado, in Kyushu
 5. Korea: atop Mt. Kwanak, near Seoul
 6. Japan: Edogawa at flood stage, near Tokyo
 7. Korea: agricultural landscape, near Seoul
 8. Japan: valley and low hills, in Tōhoku
 9. Japan: paddy terrain, in Tōhoku
10. Korea: paddy fields in harvest, near Taegu
11. Japan: Hōryūji, near Nara
12. Korea: paddy fields ripening, north of Seoul

PREFACE

From its beginning down to the present the elemental story of humankind has been one of growth: of swelling numbers, expanding global presence, rising per-capita demand for goods and services, and as a consequence intensifying pressure on the broader ecosystem.[1] During the past century or so the beneficiaries of that experience have commonly celebrated it as an estimable story of "progress," of continual betterment wherein "a rising tide lifts all boats."

When viewed from a broader perspective, however, that elemental story appears to be less one of progress or gain than of trade-offs among and within living species. Those trade-offs are now in the process of unbalancing both marine and terrestrial biomes of the planet Earth so severely as to invite speculation about "broad-spectrum" global extinctions, the ecological impoverishment that would follow them, and the massive contraction in human affairs—the collapse of industrial society as we know it—that would result.[2]

This present-day fear for the global future is a recent development for good reason: over the past century or so industrialization has enhanced spectacularly the human capacity to manipulate, fabricate, exploit, and destroy not merely other humans but much of the entire earthly biosystem. It is easy to imagine, therefore, that the story of human-environment relations, whether viewed as progress or as unbalancing and ecological impoverishment, merits our attention only as evinced in recent decades.

In fact, however, the story of that relationship traces back through pre-industrial millennia to a pre-agricultural age when our few forebears foraged, fed, fought, and fornicated to survive in rather simpler ways than we do now. What has changed with industrialization to create these unprecedented fears for the earthly biosystem's future is not the fact of human injury to it, which traces far back in time,

---

[1] For a wide-ranging examination of these themes and a good bibliographical listing of earlier works, see Chew, 2001. [For full source citations, see Bibliography.]

[2] For a recent set of opinions on the question of present and future extinctions, see the report, "Life on the Edge," in *Science News* 160-11 (Sept. 15, 2001): 168–70.

but the particular types and magnitude of injury and its consequences. Knowledge of the pre-industrial story will, therefore, sharpen our understanding of what specifically is different or destructive about our performance today.

In its entirety, from origins to the present, the human story can be treated in terms of three basic historical "stages," each characterized by a distinctive pattern of human-ecosystem relations. The timing of the three differs from place to place, of course, and everywhere the three lack clear termini, the "transitions" from one to another being ill-defined and revealing many forms of overlap. Nevertheless, the basic sequence and distinctions are clear enough. The first stage is that of forager society, when the naturally recurring yield of the surrounding biosystem sustains human life. Second is that of agricultural society, when humans collaborate with an assemblage of "domesticated" plants and animals to sustain one another. Third is that of industrial society—our own day—when humans reach beyond the living ecosystem to exploit past generations of life, most notably that stored in fossil fuels. That strategy gives people an immensely expanded and flexible energy base, making possible radical chemical and physical manipulation of their material surroundings, as epitomized by humankind's record during the twentieth century.

We are most familiar, of course, with the present-day industrial segment of the story, and with the story as it is unfolding in our own society. We have easy access to information about its problems of rapid and ill-managed population growth, urban sprawl, environmental pollution and despoilation, bio-habitat loss, species endangerment, escalating per-capita demand for material goods, the resulting depletion of natural resources, and the consequent intensification of disputes over the use of air, water, land, biota, and subsurface materials.

The way the story has unfolded in other times and places we know less well. But while, depending on time and place, the particulars vary in wondrous ways, there remains a basically shared narrative that merits our attention because it helps remind us of the commonality we have as humans making our way through life in the distinctive ecosystem of the planet Earth.

This volume looks at the pre-industrial stages of this larger human story as they played out from "pre-history" down to about 1870 in the areas we know today as Korea and Japan.[3] For reasons noted in the Introduction, scholars rarely examine these two societies together. Rather, they treat them separately or as parts of a larger ecumene called East Asia, in which China is the main element. This study examines the two together because, while each is certainly distinct and the chronologies and content of their histories do not fully coincide, there is, from an environmental perspective, a high level of commonality in both the timing and dynamics of their experience. And that shared quality speaks clearly of our common passage here on Earth.

---

[3] The industrial segment of Korean and Japanese history, from about 1900 to the present, has essentially the same attributes as it does in other societies that have industrialized. The topic is sufficiently well documented, however, so that it merits treatment in another book.

ACKNOWLEDGEMENTS

As the appended notes and bibliographical listings indicate, this overview of Korean and Japanese history could not have been written without the uncountable years of dedicated research and writing pursued by scores of scholars. To thank them properly would mean listing them all, from A to Z, or at least from Ahn to Yoshida. That listing could be so long, moreover, only thanks to years of tireless work by librarians at Yale University who acquired, catalogued, and cared for so many, many journals and books, enabling me to find and use them. I thank also the anonymous press reader whose comments helped improve the text.

Since this is my first written foray into Korean history, I'd like to express thanks to Edward Wagner, who introduced me to Korean history during the fall semester 1959. And particular thanks to Shannon McCune, geographer of Korea.[1] While serving as Provost of the University of Massachusetts in Amherst, he encouraged me as an undergraduate during 1956–58 to pursue Asian studies. In the end I focused on Japanese history rather than Korean geography, but his fascination with geography and his appreciation of Korea finally asserted themselves, shaping the structure, content, and emphases of this volume. I wish both men were still here; hope they'd approve; and trust they'd forgive me the myriad things I've gotten wrong.

A Note on the Illustrations

The Plates in this text are selected from the author's personal collection. Those showing Korean scenes are pictures taken during August 1954–February 1955, while the author was assigned to a medical laboratory near Seoul cataloguing information on mosquito specimens. Most of the scenes of Japan were taken during March

---

[1] For detail on McCune, see Han-Kyo Kim, "Shannon McCune and His Korean Studies," *The Journal of Modern Korean Studies* 4 (May 1990): 9–12, and the personal data in McCune's *Views of the Geography of Korea* (Seoul: The Korean Research Center, 1980), 227 pp.

1955–May 1956, while the author worked as a military sanitation inspector in Japan. A few, however, were taken during the early 1960s and 1970s, while he did research on Japanese history.

Most of the population numbers in the two Figures derive from Colin McEvedy and Richard Jones, *Atlas of World Population History* (N.Y.: Penguin Books, 1978), pp. 177, 181, 342. Additional numbers for Korea and Japan are assembled from diverse sources.

Except as noted elsewhere, the several maps are based on the following sources:

Matsuda and Mori, 1966. Matsuda Sumio and Mori Shikazō, comps. *Ajia rekishi chizu* (Tokyo: Heibonsha, 1966), 148 pp.

MSTS, *Korea Japan*. MSTS, *Korea Japan* (Seattle: Northwest Mapping Service, for Department of the Army, Military Sea Transportation Service, ca. 1950), 2 sheets.

Nihon annai, 1965. *Nihon annai bunken chizu* (Tokyo: *Shōgakkan*, 1965), 277 pp. (a volume in *Nihon hyakka daijiten*).

Nihon rekishi, 1961. *Nihon rekishi chizu* (Tokyo: Kawade shobō shinsha, 1961), 178 pp. (a volume in *Nihon rekishi daijiten*).

Ōsaka-fu, 1992. *Ōsaka-fu to/shi chizu* (Tokyo: Shōbunsha, 1992), 156 pp.

Rand McNally, 1982. *Rand McNally Universal World Atlas* (Chicago: Rand McNally & Co., 1982), 269 pp.

Replogle, 1954. *Replogle Comprehensive Atlas of the World* (Chicago: Replogle Globes, Inc., 1954), 376 pp.

Sanseidō, 1941. Sanseidō henshūsho, comp. *Saikin sekai chizu* (Tokyo: Sanseidō, 1941), 108 pp.

Tōkyō kaiseikan, 1941. Tōkyō Kaiseikan henshūsho, comp. *Shōwa Nihon chizu* (Tokyo: Tōkyō kaiseikan, 1941), 125 pp.

Finally, please note that the customary diacritical marks are used for all place names except those few Japanese cases where, by customary practice, they are omitted; namely, Kyoto, Osaka, Tokyo, Hokkaido, Honshu, Kyushu, and Ryukyu islands.

CHRONOLOGY

byBP = billion years before the present
myBP = million years before the present
yBP = years before the present
BCE = before the Common Era
CE = Common Era

13.7 byBP	"Big Bang" creation of this universe
5–4 byBP	Earth coalesces in Milky Way galaxy
2.5 byBP	Plate tectonics activity commences
400–250 myBP	Continental plates collide to form Pangaea
200 myBP	Pangaea starts to disaggregate
by 65 myBP	the areas of future Korea and Japan adjoin
45 myBP	collision of Indian and Eurasian plates commences
30–17 myBP	Sea of Japan forms; Korea and Japan separate
2 myBP	Pleistocene "Ice Age" commences
400,000 yBP	humans (*Homo erectus*) probably in Korea-Japan area
by 30,000 yBP	*Homo sapiens sapiens* present in Korea-Japan area
24–15,000 yBP	Final Würm glaciation
15–10,000 yBP	Glacial melt-off; Yellow Sea is restored; "land bridges" to Japan disappear; mega-fauna die off
12,700 yBP	pottery in use in Japan, precursor of *jōmon*
12,000 yBP	*yunkimun* pottery probably in Korea
10,000 yBP	(= 8,000 BCE); Holocene (current interglacial period) commences
6,000 BCEff.	residents of Korea and Japan live in pit dwellings, more and more in small hamlets
5,000 BCE	millet and wet rice (paddy) culture appear in China
4–2,000 BCE	*chŭlmun* pottery use spreads across Korea
3,000 BCE	Shang rulers in northwest China
3–2,000 BCE	global cooling spurs "incipient agriculture" in Korea and Japan
2,000 BCE	bronze metallurgy in northwest China
2,000 BCE	millet cropping and *mumun* pottery appear in northwest Korea, then diffuse southeastward

1,200 BCE	by this date paddy culture appears in Korea
ca. 1,000 BCE	Zhou rulers displace Shang in China
700 BCE	bronze artifacts present in northwest Korea, then diffuse southeastward
600 BCE	iron metallurgy in China
400 BCEff.	iron artifacts present in northwest Korea, then diffuse; communities enlarge; social structure becomes more elaborate; evidence of local polities and warfare
400 BCEff.	paddy and millet culture appear in southwest Japan, with Yayoi pottery and, shortly, iron and bonze implements; then diffuse eastward, along with larger, more complex social organization; evidence of local polities and warfare; a millennium of sustained immigration from continent
206 BCE	Han Dynasty established in China
108 BCE	Lelang commandery established in northwest Korea
100 BCEff.	Koguryŏ develops in Manchuria; Paekche, Silla, and Kaya in Korea; numerous small polities in Japan
222 CE	collapse of Han Dynasty; replaced by political disorder
230s–240s CE	Himiko heads Yamatai in southwest Japan
313	Koguryŏ in Manchuria pushes southward, overruns Lelang
300s–400s	heyday of mounded tombs in Korea and Japan
300s–700s	diffusion of Chinese elite culture to Korea and Japan
370sff.	recurrent warfare in Korea
390s	heyday of Kwanggaet'o, ruler of Koguryŏ
by 400s	Yamato leaders in Kinai Basin expand westward
427	Koguryŏ headquarters relocated southward to northwest Korea
by 450s	Yamato rulers acquire horse-riding technology
400s–500s	Yamato rulers consolidate power eastward across Kantō
532–62	Silla conquers Kaya vicinity in stages
by 560s	smallpox introduced from China to Korea and Japan

618	Tang Dynasty established; spurs self-strenthening reform activity among regimes in Korea and Japan
663	Silla allies with Tang, then destroys Paekche, routs Yamato forces in Paekche; defeats Koguryŏ in 668
660s–670s	King Munmu of Silla builds capital city at Kyŏngju
by 680	Silla controls all Korea south of P'yŏngyang vicinity
708–20	Genmei, ruler of Yamato, builds capital city of Nara (Heijō); promotes use of coins
700s–800s	conquest and settlement extend Yamato rule into northeastern Japan
713	Koguryŏ survivors establish Parhae regime
794	construction starts on capital city of Heian (later Kyoto)
800s	use of coinage in Japan disappears
830s–840s	Chang Po-go dominates Silla maritime trade
850s–1050s	major Fujiwara aristocratic lineage dominates Heian politics
907	Tang Dynasty collapses; disorder follows
926	Parhae collapses
935	Silla falls; Koryŏ founded, with capital at Kaesŏng
960	Song Dynasty established
1050s–1150s	retired emperors dominate Heian politics
1170s	military rule established in Koryŏ
1180s	military rule—Kamakura *bakufu*—established in Japan by Minamoto no Yoritomo
1196	Ch'oe Ch'ung-hŏn implements military coup in Koryŏ; Ch'oe lineage dominates politics
1200sff.	signs of agricultural intensification appear in Japan; renewed use of coins in trade with China
1218ff.	Mongol invasions and conquest of Korea
1220sff.	*waegu* (pirates) become active in Japan-Korea vicinity
1232	Ch'oe regime moves to Kanghwa Island
1258	last Ch'oe military ruler is slain
1270	Koryŏ rulers return to Kaesŏng
1271	Mongols establish Yuan Dynasty in China
1274, 1281	two Mongol attempts to invade Japan; both fail
1330s	Kamakura *bakufu* is destroyed; Go-Daigo attempts a restoration of monarchy; Ashikaga (Muromachi) *bakufu* is established in Kyoto by Ashikaga Takauji; *nanbokuchō* period of civil war ensues

1356	King Kongmin ousts Mongols from Korea
1358	Ming Dynasty displaces Yuan Dynasty in China
1392	Yi Sŏng-gye establishes Chosŏn Dynasty, takes reign name T'aejo, makes Seoul his capital
1390s	Ashikaga rule stabilizes in Japan
1390sff.	*waegu* piracy is suppressed
1400s	estimate about one-third of Koreans are legal slaves
1400sff.	signs of agricultural intensification appear in Korea
1400sff.	lively commercial economy develops in central Japan; imported coinage used in domestic trade
1419	"Six Licensed Stores" are established in Seoul
1420sff.	cotton produced in Korea; exported to Japan as part of foreign trade
1460sff.	cotton produced in southwest Japan
1467ff.	Ōnin War and endemic civil strife in Japan; Ashikaga become impotent
ca. 1515	syphilis reaches Korea and Japan from Europe, via Southeast Asia
1550sff.	Europeans trade with Japan
1580s	major daimyo consolidate their domains in Japan; end of endemic civil strife
1592–98	Toyotomi Hideyoshi, dictator of Japan, invades Korea in attempt to conquer China; fails
1600	Tokugawa Ieyasu defeats rivals, founds Tokugawa *bakufu*, with headquarters in Edo
1600ff.	Chosŏn leaders reinvigorate their regime
1600ff.	copper coinage standardized in Japan; economy flourishes
1609	diplomatic relations and trade restored between Korea and Japan
1627	first Manchu invasion of Korea
1636	Chosŏn rulers accept Manchu suzerainty
1660s	Manchus defeat last Ming holdouts, found Ch'ing Dynasty
1670sff.	regular use of copper coinage spreads through Korea
1678	first rough but usable census figures for Korea; later ones depict demographic stabilization in 18–19th centuries
1721	first rough but usable census figures for Japan; later ones depict demographic stabilization in 18–19th centuries

1700s–1800s	wide-ranging signs—demographic, economic, fiscal, environmental—of ecological stress in Korea and Japan
1720sff.	sweet potatoes grown in Japan
1760sff.	sweet potatoes grown in Korea
1791	"Six Licensed Stores" of Seoul are abolished
1801ff.	Chosŏn releases most central government slaves; slavery generally is in sharp decline
1821–22	cholera introduced from India to Korea and Japan
1860sff.	European imperialism precipitates turmoil and change in Korea and Japan; industrialization follows

INTRODUCTION

As mentioned in the Preface, scholars rarely treat the histories of Korea and Japan together. In environmental terms, however, there is good reason for doing so, and the logic of that proposition was suggested a century ago by a distinguished agronomist, F. H. King. When writing of his recent trip across eastern China, Korea, and Japan (see Map 2-1), he noted the similarities of Korean and Japanese agriculture:

> Coming from China into Korea, and from there into Japan, it appeared very clear that in agricultural methods and appliances the Koreans and Japanese are more closely similar than the Chinese and Koreans, and the more we came to see of the Japanese methods[,] the more strongly the impression became fixed that [either] the Japanese had derived their methods from the Koreans or the Koreans had taken theirs more largely from Japan than from China.[1]

This shared agricultural regimen and its environmental ramifications are the central foci of this study. As we shall see, however, the commonalities of pre-industrial Korea and Japan reached well beyond agriculture to include geography, climate, biota, and much of the human experience.

In terms of the three-stage forager-agriculture-industry formulation, nearly all of the known history of Korea and Japan falls within the middle stage, that of agriculture. However, that stage subdivides into early and later periods, with each marked in turn by phases of growth and stasis. In all cases, the transitions are ill-defined, and they do not occur in the two places at quite the same time or pace. But these vagaries notwithstanding, a shared narrative does unfold.

We shall examine briefly the development of forager society to around 3,000 years ago (1,000 BCE). Over the next several centuries,

---

[1] King, 1911, p. 374. King was a retired "Professor of Agricultural Physics" in the University of Wisconsin and Chief of Divison of Soil Management, USDA. In the sentence quoted here, King placed "either" after "methods," rather than after "fixed that."

Map 0-1. *Korea and Japan.*
Based on map of Japan and Korea in Rand McNally, 1982, p. 37.

fairly simple agricultural practices gradually spread across Korea and, later, Japan, becoming sufficiently developed by 700 CE (AD) to support consolidated ruling elites in both places. The "early" horticultural arrangements that sustained those regimes lasted for another five or six centuries with only modest change in agronomic technique or scale. But from around the thirteenth to fourteenth century, this early agricultural order changed as forms of horticultural "intensification" began spreading across the two realms, doing so in Japan somewhat sooner than Korea. These changes gave rise to a more productive agronomy that expedited substantial social growth and remained the basis of society until the advent of industrialization, which can be dated to the decades around 1900 (see Fig. 0-1).

This overall narrative developed irregularly in both societies, earlier in southerly regions than northerly for the most part. It was ever shaped by the particulars of environmental context (geography, climate, biota), local human culture and society, and external human influence (from one another and from elsewhere, notably China and Northeast and Central Asia). In this volume we shall look at these basic variables to see how they interplayed over the centuries, shaping both social and material technology and producing the particular Korean and Japanese expressions of the larger global story of human historical growth and change, with its associated stories of environmental costs and complications and occasional attempts at remediation.

When noting chapter titles, readers need to bear in mind the vagaries, irregularities, regional differences, and temporal disjunctions of this history. The dates in all four chapter headings are only crude indicators of the time when trends began or faded. The "round number" 1350, in particular, is an awkward compromise: for Japan 1200 or 1250 might be better; for Korea 1400. The year 1870 could be 1850, 1880, 1920, or some other moment. Even if Korean and Japanese history—and that of all regions within each—moved in close synchronicity, the dates would still be approximations, more satisfactory by some criteria than others for dating the gradual processes of complex change that we are examining.

* * *

Korean and Japanese history are rarely presented together for a number of reasons. Most obviously the twentieth century was an age of rampant nation-state-ism, and the historical discipline everywhere treated nations as the units of consequence, pointedly distinguishing "our" history from "theirs," and asking such questions as when did "our" national group appear, from what antecedents, and with what distinctive qualities and rightful realm, etc. etc.[2] When larger integrative

---

[2] Pai, 2000, explores this matter in the case of Korea with exceptional thoughtfulness. Hudson, 1999, treats it for Japan.

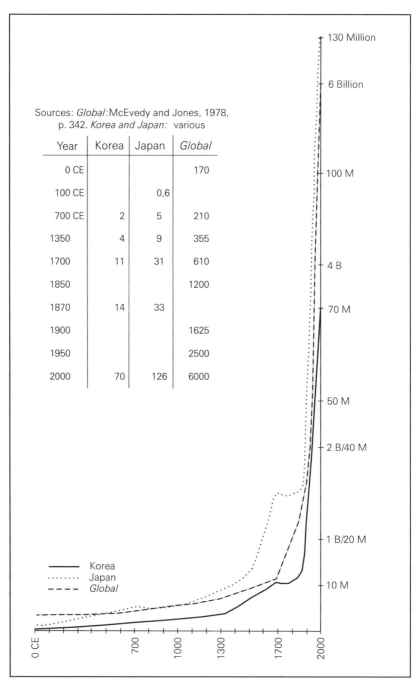

Figure 0-1. *Demographic Trends, 0–2000 CE.*

units were sought in the Korea-Japan vicinity, the pre-eminent choice of both indigenous scholars and outsiders was an imagined collectivity called "East Asian civilization," which was in essence China writ large, extending from Annam to the Amur River and Tokyo to the Tarim Basin (see Map 2-1).[3]

Secondly, the global social upheaval associated with industrialization found harsh expression after 1895 in the establishment of Japanese political control over Korea. The ill-will engendered by that experience has been well reflected in Korean- and Japanese-language historiography in some mix of distrust, dismissal, denunciation, and distancing that is only slowly abating.[4] Moreover, because we outsiders who write Korean or Japanese history must read the relevant language and rely on the corpus of secondary scholarship, and because mastery of either language is extremely difficult, most of us have ended up utilizing almost exclusively one or the other corpus. Willy nilly the agendas and inclinations of that scholarship have tended to be reflected, sometimes quite belatedly and on occasion in exaggerated form, in the works of outsiders.

Finally, much of the scholarship has focused on elite political and cultural history—the subjects that are most richly documented—so core agendas of the elite, notably political power and authority, higher "national" culture, and socio-economic "progress," have remained central topics of study. These are areas in which the hurts of colonialism were felt deeply and have lingered painfully. They also are areas in which it is comparatively easy to disregard underlying historical commonalities and particularly gratifying to emphasize separateness and dissimilarity. Because of this focus most historians of Korea and Japan have found little reason to treat the two together and considerable grounds for doing otherwise.

*   *   *

In short, the political and historiographical legacies of the twentieth century make it difficult to write any form of Korean and Japanese history together. Other problems add complexity for the writer seeking to focus on environmental matters.

---

[3] A classic statement of this perdurable formulation is Reischauer and Fairbank, 1958. See pp. 395–96, for example.

[4] A fine example of the new trends in Korean historiography is Shin and Robinson, 2000.

A basic problem for such a writer is imbedded in the old ecological truism that "everything is hitched to everything else." Because
one cannot include everything, one must select, and wise selection
requires appropriate criteria. In practice this means that much of
what is most thoroughly documented and most central to the existing historical scholarship—the details of political process and higher
culture in particular—falls by the wayside while one scavenges for
pertinent information among the random references to plants and
animals, disease and demographics, patterns of primary production,
and so on.

This observation in turn suggests the second great problem: scarcity
of the most relevant and necessary information. For both societies,
but especially for Korea, satisfactory documentation often is lacking. Records were not kept or have been lost or overlooked. Only
a fraction of those that are available have been used by scholars
because they are not pertinent to research agendas. Also, the English-
language corpus, on which this introductory survey is based, contains only a small portion of the findings available in Korean- and
Japanese-language works.[5] Happily, however, a number of those
Korean and Japanese scholars who are interested in issues pertinent
to environmental history have made their findings available in foreign languages, and their work has proven helpful here.

Finally, we should note that the historiographical legacy of industrial-age Korea and Japan, as it stands today, may well lead one to
overstate the degree of similarity in the two histories when viewing
them in environmental perspective. To explain, historical scholarship in the two societies has evolved over the past century in ways
that are basically similar, even though the rise and evolution of an
industrial-age historical discipline occurred in Korea a bit later than
in Japan, with emphases, agendas, and changes therein tending to
appear somewhat later.

During an initial phase—down to mid-century or thereabouts—
much of the writing highlighted the above-noted ethnic issues of
"national" uniqueness and accomplishment. A second, Marxian-
inspired approach, which gained favor from the 1920s onward, treated

---

[5] The present author does not read Korean and has examined only select parts
of the environmental literature in Japanese, notably that on forest history. In addition, he is not young and hears the clock ticking loudly.

the evolution of society in terms of economic class conflict, using that criterion to explain problems of the past and present. During the latter half of the century these two bodies of scholarship metamorphosed into a predominant interest in the issue of "modernization," by which authors meant the socio-economic and cultural changes associated with what this volume calls "industrialization." For scholars who saw modernization as a Good Thing, that interest commonly included a search for "indigenous roots" of the process. For those who saw it as a Bad Thing, scholarship often included a critique of the ways modernity was allegedly damaging the ethnic self. Unsurprisingly, those themes have also cropped up in the English-language corpus.[6]

Thanks, perhaps, to this interest in the putatively universalistic theme of modernization, which muted the earlier emphasis on uniqueness of the national legacy, by century's end historians of the two societies seemed often to hold similar perceptions of the past. The dynamics of history were seen as leading both Korea and Japan in the direction of modernity, the beginnings of that process being evident by the 1700s or even earlier. The effect of this shared perspective has been, then, to create bodies of scholarship that have much in common, even when they imply, or sometimes emphasize, national singularity. To some degree, surely, the extent of historical commonality that is described in the following pages is a reflection of those common historiographical experiences. Later scholars may find much to say differently in that regard.

*   *   *

As the appended Bibliography and Bibliographical Essay indicate, this volume is based almost exclusively on secondary sources in the English language. (NOTE: a number of valuable but specialized works that do not appear in the Bibliographical Essay are cited in footnotes.) For telling much of the story, the English corpus has provided a sufficient, and in places a wonderfully rich, foundation. In

---

[6] In the Japanese case, the modernizationist theme first found voice in 1960s American scholarship as a reflection of the Cold War. It was absorbed into the Japanese scholarly community as the post-1950s boom validated the course of contemporary Japanese history. More recently there have emerged, in addition to the nascent interest in environmental issues, bodies of work focused on minority and gender problems.

some areas, however, the literature has proven weak, a weakness that often reflects limitations in the Korean and Japanese literature or even in the primary sources. In a general sense the literature on Japan has been more adequate because the modern-day historical profession there is larger and has been active for a somewhat longer time. But scholarship in Korea is thriving, and with each passing year researchers produce new works that improve our understanding. In both, moreover, as the environmental problems of our own day gain greater visibility, more and more scholars focus on the history of such matters, producing a small but growing corpus of works that directly address environmental history. One may hope, therefore, that this introductory overview will soon be rendered obsolete by richer, more solidly based studies.

Finally, a comment on terminology. Words often carry multiple meanings, and in an age of roiling ethnic sensibilities and political instability, they can serve passionate purposes. In this volume the words "Korea" and "Japan" will denote identifiable present-day geographic areas. The former denotes the Korean peninsula and adjoining continental region north to the Yalu and Tumen rivers, together with the large southerly island of Cheju and the peninsula's numerous nearby islets. "Japan" denotes essentially the four major islands of Hokkaido, Honshu, Shikoku, and Kyushu, together with the offshore islands of Oki, Sado and Tsushima, the innumerable islets close by the main islands, and, when occasion requires, the associated Bonin and Ryukyu island chains. The few islands in the region whose political identification is a continuing source of controversy need not detain us.

The adjectives "Korean" and "Japanese," when applied to language, people, government, culture, or society will denote, respectively, the predominant languages of people living in the two areas, native speakers of the language who are resident therein, the governments that exercise authority over them (including "North" and "South" Korea where applicable), and the cultural and social configurations of the human populations in the two areas.

Please note also that the text follows current international usage in identifying geographic places. Thus the rivers Yalu and Tumen, rather than Amnok and Tuman, the Korean readings. Also Tatar Strait rather than the Japanese Mamiya Strait. And Yellow Sea, East China Sea, and Sea of Japan, rather than Western, Southern, and Eastern Sea, the Korean usages.

CHAPTER ONE

PALEOGEOGRAPHY AND PRE-AGRICULTURAL SOCIETY (TO 1,000 BCE)

Geological Background
Geographical Context
Pre-Agricultural Society
  A. *People of the Pleistocene Epoch*
  B. *Adjusting to Holocene Conditions*
  C. *Holocene Society*

Korea and Japan today are temperate-zone neighbors perched on the far eastern edge of the Eurasian land mass.[1] They are densely populated, middling-sized countries, with Korea's population numbering about 70 million while that of Japan is a bit over 125 million.[2] The land surface of Korea covers some 221,000 km^2 (slightly larger than England and Scotland combined) and that of Japan, about 377,000 km^2 (somewhat larger than Germany), giving Korea a population density of 317 and Japan 332 people per km^2. Of Korea's land surface about 20 percent is arable, the rest too hilly, while in Japan about 15 percent can be cultivated, the remainder too mountainous. Both, moreover, are advanced industrial societies (North Korea less so), highly urbanized and closely integrated into the global economy and its worldwide resource base.

The two differ, however, in that Korea is a geologically stable land, marked by no active volcanism and comparatively little earthquake activity. Japan, by contrast, and easterly Japan in particular, experiences almost ceaseless tremors, most being inconsequential in magnitude. Moreover, the archipelago contains some 60-odd active volcanoes, about ten percent of the world's total. These dissimilarities,

---

[1] A richly detailed collection of essays on Korea's geography is Kim and Yoo, 1988. A more concise, richly illustrated study is McCune, 1956. On Japan, see the detailed collection of essays by the Association of Japanese Geographers, 1980. An older but still useful work is Trewartha, 1978.
[2] Kim and Yoo, 1988, p. 150, gives 60 million, ca. 1985.

together with the fact that Korea is a peninsula of Asia and Japan an archipelago situated close offshore, betray basic differences in the geological origins of the two areas, differences that helped shape their present-day geography and their recent history as realms subject to human exploitation.

Geological Background

For our purposes it will suffice to skip over the first two billion or so years of plate-tectonics history and commence rather late in the story.[3] Some two hundred million years before the present (myBP), as the Mesozoic era (230–65 myBP) was commencing, the grand clustering of continental plates known as Pangaea began to break apart, its fragments being pushed out across the great Panthallasic Ocean.[4]

Sidestepping huge uncertainties and glorious complexities, it appears that the area we know today as northeastern Japan was situated near the northwest corner of what became the North American Plate, which headed northwestward as Pangaea broke up (See Map 1-1).[5] The area we know as Korea evidently was situated near the North Pole on the northeastern face of the larger Eurasian Plate, and it was propelled southeastward as that plate commenced a grand clockwise rotation. The area that became southwest Japan probably was situated adjacent to Korea and accompanied it on the journey: at least, massive rock formations that extend from southern Korea into southwest and central Japan suggest the two to be part of a single geologic formation that acquired its distinctive character before the two continental plates collided.[6]

---

[3] For a concise, nicely illustrated treatment of the earlier geologic history, see Bambach, 1980. On the later story, see Dietz and Holden, 1970. A more recent, more detailed treatment with good guidance to earlier works is Burchfiel, 1993.

[4] A handy reference for geological terminology is Watt, 1982.

[5] This formulation is currently favored by the Geological Survey of Japan (see their "Fact Sheet D-3," 1998). Older works have placed all of Japan with Korea on the Eurasian Plate or have treated northeast Japan as a marginal chunk of oceanic plate thrust up by its collision with Eurasia. For the former see Uyeda and Miyashiro, 1974. For the latter see Chough, 1983, especially map, p. 135.

[6] Hiroi, 1981, examines the linkages of Korea and Japan west of the Fossa Magna. Two general works that treat the geology of the two countries are the richly detailed, beautifully illustrated volume by Lee D-s, 1987 and the concise work by Yoshida, 1976. Neither volume, however, employs the framework of plate tectonics.

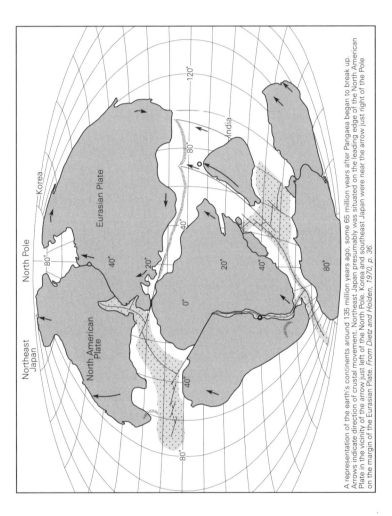

A representation of the earth's continents around 135 million years ago, some 65 million years after Pangaea began to break up. Arrows indicate direction of crustal movement. Northeast Japan presumably was situated on the leading edge of the North American Plate in the vicinity of the arrow just left of the North Pole. Korea and southeast Japan were near the arrow just right of the Pole on the margin of the Eurasian Plate. *From Dietz and Holden, 1970, p. 36.*

Map 1-1. *The Breakup of Pangaea.*

Driven by seafloor spreading in what became the Atlantic Ocean, the fragments of Pangaea slowly but relentlessly made their way around the globe, overriding plates of the Panthallasic Ocean. At some point, perhaps a hundred million years ago or thereabouts, the leading edge of the North American Plate began ramming into the Eurasian, which dragged the former in a more southerly direction. That collision set in motion a process of tectonic interaction involving the newly proximate areas of Korea and northeast Japan. By 65 myBP the constituent elements of Japan were squeezed up against the Eurasian continental margin, hard by the eastern edge of the future Korea and Siberian Maritime Provinces, which lay just to Korea's northeast.

In succeeding millennia the processes of grinding confrontation between the two continental plates, together with their southward advance over northwest-moving oceanic plates, kept rock surfaces moving up and down. In addition, beginning around 30 myBP (the Oligocene epoch), intense volcanism at several points along the east coast of the present-day Korea and Maritime Provinces appears to have caused the collision point of the two continental plates to buckle, pivoting southwestern Japan away from the continent by pushing it in a southeasterly direction while pushing the northeastern regions and Sakhalin eastward. That movement, which occurred in two major phases down to about 17 myBP, formed the Sea of Japan, with its complex structure, steep slopes, and great depth, some areas being in excess of 3,500 meters deep. By 10 myBP the process had established the basic geographic relationships of Northeast Asia that we see today (see Map 1-2).[7]

This is not to say, however, that Korea and Japan had acquired today's form. Korea was largely in place, but over succeeding millennia its eastern coast continued rising, producing the high T'aebaek Mountains, which descend abruptly to the water's edge, where they front a narrow coastal shelf and sharp dropoff into the depths of the Sea of Japan. The south and western coasts, on the other hand, slowly sank, shrinking the peninsula and giving it an overall east-to-west tilt and the exceedingly convoluted ria coastlines of today. Meanwhile, erosion gradually wore down mountain surfaces, filling

---

[7] Curiosity about the origins of the Sea of Japan has provoked substantial geological study. Shimazu, 1989, exemplifies the work and lists earlier publications.

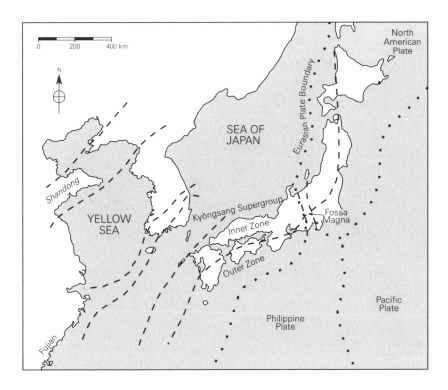

Map 1-2. *Major Tectonic Elements of Korea and Japan.*
As an integral part of the continental plate, Korea's mountainous regions are linked across the Yellow Sea Basin to those of northeast China, notably the Shandong and Fujian massifs. The Kyŏngsang Supergroup underlies Korea's southeast corner and extends to the Inner Zone of southwest Japan. There the Outer zone is the section most powerfully uplifted by the adjoining oceanic Philippine Plate. The Fossa Magna lies at the juncture of southwest and northeast Japan, being a tortuously mountainous area produced in the aftermath of the buckling that created the Sea of Japan. The Outer Zone of northeast Japan has been uplifted since Pangaea's breakup by its confrontation with today's Pacific Plate. Based on map at Lee, D-s, 1987, p. 440, and Trewartha, frontispiece foldout map in 1963 edition.

in valleys to create the lowlands of the peninsula's western side (see Plate 1) and adding thick layers of sediment to the shallow Yellow Sea, producing the extensive tidal flats for which it is known.[8]

For Japan those millennia were far more hectic. The orogenic

---

[8] A careful study of the seas around Korea is Chough, 1983.

activity that had sculpted the Sea of Japan and elevated portions of
Japan during Oligocene-early Miocene times eventually gave way to
widespread subsidence, erosion, and oceanic transgression. By about
15 myBP much of the future archipelago was gone, sunk below sea
level. The largest surviving land mass was the southern part of southwest Japan, where continuing collision with oceanic plates evidently
offset the effects of erosion and subsidence.[9] During the Pliocene
epoch (11–2 myBP) mountain-building renewed, continuing into the
Pleistocene (2 myBP–10,000 yBP). That orogony almost entirely separated the Sea of Japan from the Pacific Ocean. Rapid uplift, sieges
of subsidence, widespread faulting and folding, and intensive volcanic activity produced the towering ranges of the Fossa Magna, the
great cordillera that marks the interface of southwest and northeast
Japan. Those processes also elevated many other areas and spotted
the archipelago with a host of spectacular volcanic peaks. By a million years ago Japan had acquired the shape it has today, an archipelago of intricate mountain ranges (see Plate 2) interspersed with
narrow valleys and small sedimentary plains that front the sea on
all sides.

With the Pleistocene epoch we enter the "this morning" of historical geology, prelude to the "this minute" of the Holocene (10,000
yBP-present)—which probably is best understood as the most recent
inter-glacial phase of the Pleistocene. During the Pleistocene, Korea
and especially Japan continued to experience modest tectonic activity. Korea's western coastline continued settling, many of Japan's
mountain arcs kept on rising briskly, some coastal patches subsided,
and volcanic activity continued vigorously in the archipelago, producing several new cones, of which Mt. Fuji is the most celebrated.

A more notable aspect of the Pleistocene, however, was the recurrent
phases of cooling and warming. Major periods of warming, with
associated marine transgressions (flooding of coastal regions) and
changes in vegetation and animal populations, occurred some 2.4
myBP and much more recently around 300,000 yBP, during 100–
70,000 yBP, 39–24,000 yBP, and most recently around 13–8,000
yBP.[10] Evidence of the earlier transgressions has largely been erased,

---

[9] On the Outer Zone, see Trewartha, 1978, pp. 10–13. A sketch map of Middle
Miocene Japan can be found on p. 19 of Yoshida, 1976, or in reproduced form
on p. 14 of Totman, 2000.
[10] The four earlier dates are given in Wang, 1984, p. 175. For slightly different
dates, see Whyte, 1984, Vol. II, p. 928.

however, by the later sequences of cold and warm, during which sea level again dropped, old coastlines eroded, and new expanses of lower-lying coastal plain formed, only to be re-flooded and buried under new layers of sediment.

The obscurity of the Pleistocene's first million and a half years poses little problem for us, however, because the key point of consequence requires only a general paleogeographical knowledge. Specifically, thanks to the general topography of East Asia, the cycles of glacial-age cooling and warming did not permanently strip the Korea/Japan region of its earlier biological vitality.[11] Rather, when compared to other temperate-zone regions, western Europe most notably, the area retained an exceptionally lush and diversified floral and faunal repertoire (see Plate 3). By one count, for example, Korea today numbers some 4,500 plant species, more than twice the diversity of England.[12] Japan's flora is similarly varied.[13] This matters because biotic diversity has enabled the region to support a dense human population during recent millennia by strengthening its capacity to adapt to and recover from sieges of excessive human exploitation.

The reasons for this biotic richness seem straightforward. First, even during the Pleistocene's coldest phases, the highlands of Korea and Japan were subjected to only local field glaciers while lower-lying areas remained open, ranging from tundra in far northern spots to boreal forest and, further south, mixed forests of coniferous and deciduous growth. More importantly, during those cold phases sea level dropped, forming broad coastal lowlands that extended from Sakhalin to Southeast Asia (see Map 1-3). Because so many mountain ranges in the region trend more or less north-to-south, plant populations were able to migrate as ambient temperatures gradually fell, with successive generations of seedlings sprouting as far southward as a species' distribution system permitted and climate change required. Subsequently, as weather warmed again, they could trek northward, uninhibited by intervening mountain ranges or inhospitable deserts, thereby restoring to Korea and Japan the rich temperate-zone flora and fauna that have served human settlers so well over recent millennia.

---

[11] On earlier vegetation in the region, see Song Z, 1984.

[12] *Handbook*, 1993, p. 24.

[13] Muntschick, 1995, p. 800, reports over 6,000 species of plants in Japan. How many of these present-day Korean and Japanese plant species are industrial-age introductions is unclear, but surely only a small percentage of the total.

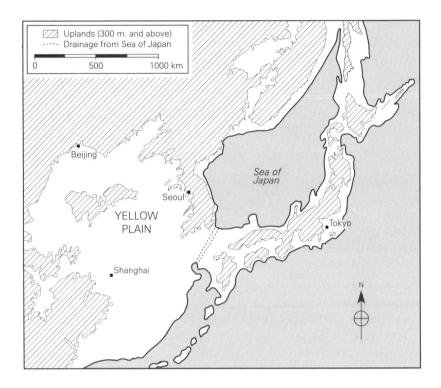

Map 1-3. *Northeast Asia, ca. 18,000 yBP, an Approximation.*
This map suggests the coastline during the final glacial maximum by following the present-day 200-meter marine elevation. Probably the actual
coastline was somewhat further inshore, especially in the lowland between
Kyushu and southeast Korea. The darkened areas, 100 meters or more
above present-day sea level, denote mountainous uplands. The intervening
regions are lowlands, most notably the vast "Yellow Plain" nearly encircled
by highlands of China and Korea. It was extensively cut by the many rivers
that flowed across it to the sea. Moreover, the land-locked Sea of Japan
would have maintained a major river, or perhaps a substantial strait, linking
it to the ocean southeast of Korea. Also, tidal action may have continually
scoured the strait between Hokkaido and Honshu, keeping it open, at least
some of the time. Based on Map #1 of Tōkyō kaiseikan, 1941, pp. 1–2.

Geographical Context

During the geological "today" of Korea and Japan, meaning the
recent millennia of human habitation, the two areas have been ver-
dant lands, thanks to their combination of temperate-zone location
and ample precipitation. Through the centuries this verdure has to

considerable extent been protected by the mountainous topography, which has supported a wide range of plant species and affiliated birds, animals, and other biota while obstructing human efforts to exploit or displace them. At southerly latitudes both Korea and Japan sustain subtropical forests of evergreen broadleafs and tropical grasses (the bamboos) while far northerly highlands are clothed in boreal spruce and fir. The broad heartland between these extremes sports a richly variegated forest cover of deciduous hardwoods, several species of pine and other conifers, and a wide array of other shrubs, forbs, and grasses.

Both, moreover, have long enjoyed rich marine fisheries. The broad tidal flats of Korea's west and south coasts have supported modest populations of shallow-water fish and shellfish while the waters of its east coast, with their great depths and intersecting warm and cold ocean currents, have sustained a much more lushly diversified marine life. Japan, with its similarly deep ocean trenches and inter-mingled warm and cold currents, has enjoyed equally dense and diversified fisheries. Today, of course, thanks to marine pollution and industrial-age fishing technology, all these fisheries have been severely depleted. But until the human assault of recent decades, coastal geo-graphy gave the region great richness of maritime life and main-tained that richness through scores of centuries of human utilization.

These similarities of Korea and Japan notwithstanding—their shared temperate-zone location, similar biota, modest amounts of flat land, ample coast lines, and rich fisheries—the geographical differences are equally noteworthy. Because Japan is more fully embroiled in the ongoing collision of continental and oceanic plates, it experiences much more tectonic instability—damaging earthquakes, volcanism, and geothermal activity—with its implications for architecture, engi-neering, and other human endeavors. That tectonic activity has, on the other hand, given Japan an uncommonly large number of well sheltered, deep-water ports (see Plate 4) whereas Korea, with its extremely shallow seas west and south and its abrupt transition from mountain to ocean depths on the eastern coast has relatively few such ports.

Of broader and more enduring consequence are differences in land forms because of Japan's more recent, more rapid, and more stressful formation. Neither country has much arable land—20% of Korea's total; 15% of Japan's—but an appreciably larger proportion of Korea's total land surface is accessible to human exploitation and has been put to use in the support of agriculture. This has been possible because while the peninsula is mountainous, its mountains are relatively old and in many regions are worn down, giving it lower hills with gentler slopes, more weathered features, and more accessible intermontane valleys, especially in its westerly regions.

Weather patterns, on the other hand, have favored agriculture in Japan more than Korea. Both, as we note more fully in Chapter 2, are exposed to southerly, summer monsoon rains that facilitate rice cropping. Korea, however, is directly subject during winter months to the frigid continental winds that blow out of north-central Asia, giving it appreciably colder and drier winters than comparable latitudes of Japan, where surrounding seas meliorate temperature and add moisture (see Plates 5, 30). In consequence Korea's precipitation, especially in northerly regions, is heavily concentrated in the summer months, which has presented two types of difficulty.

First, when irregularities in the monsoon air flow produce insufficient summer rain, Korea can experience severe droughts, crop failure, famine, and tax shortfalls, circumstances that have for centuries made drought a recurrent problem for rulers and ruled alike.[14] In addition, the highly seasonal distribution of rainfall has reduced the capacity of Korea's long-term mountain erosion to sustain the nutrient level of lowland soils. Because the precipitation in Korea is so seasonal—and in recent centuries because so much of Korea has been severely deforested—river beds that stand nearly dry during other months turn into "raging torrents during the rainy season, sweeping many tons of soil, gravel and boulders along their beds and out to sea," thus adding nutrient-rich sediments to the Yellow Sea rather than to the peninsula's lowlands.[15]

On the other hand, these seasonal flood surges have regularly scoured the long estuaries of Korea's larger rivers, keeping them deep enough to permit boat traffic, at least during the daily hours of high tide. In consequence, the estuaries have served as major arteries of commerce and travel. The scouring has also reduced the risk of destructive flood damage to adjacent settlements and arable land, although lowlands in the peninsular southeast do periodically

---

[14] Kim and Yoo, 1988, p. 128.
[15] Nelson, 1993, p. 19.

experience serious flooding. Moreover, thanks to human effort the sediments swept out to sea have not, in the end, been entirely lost to human exploitation. In many coastal areas, villagers, entrepreneurs, and governments have over the centuries erected sea walls around parcels of tidal flat created by this riverflow, thereby forming arable plains that today constitute an appreciable portion of the country's total lowland.

Japan's mountains are much younger, rise more steeply, and stand higher than do Korea's. These conditions have meant that through the centuries of human occupancy, many intermontane areas of the archipelago have been poorly accessible, minimally hospitable, and hence nearly unexploited, a situation found in Korea only in the mountainous interior of the northeast. Most of Japan's mountainsides are sheathed in a stoney, immature forest soil that, when dislodged by landslide or erosion, washes into fast-flowing streams and thence down to the flatland below. Because Japan's rainfall is spread somewhat more evenly through the year than is Korea's, however, riverbeds tend to accumulate more sediments and detritus that interfere with stream flow, causing flood waters to back up and overflow adjoining lowlands, oftimes damaging nearby arable and settlements. On the other hand, that same overflow adds material to the land's surface—stones, gravel, and other debris on alluvial fans but, further downstream, finer, more nutrient-loaded materials (see Plate 6). These deposits periodically give many of Japan's small sedimentary plains a new coating of rich loam. In some areas, moreover, fallout from volcanoes has added fine ash deposits that have gradually matured into deep and productive topsoils.

These differences have meant, in essence, that Korea's basic topography has been more favorable to agriculture than has Japan's, but Japan's climate has provided compensation. In consequence, insofar as residents adapted their agricultural regimens and settlement patterns to their surroundings, both places were capable of supporting fairly dense populations despite their mountainous character. But the differences in topography have also meant that fewer areas of Korea have been insulated against human predation, should circumstance drive occupants to exceed the land's sustainable productive capacity.

Finally, it is frequently noted that throughout recorded history Korea has been attached to the continent whereas Japan has not, and that as a result Korea's people have experienced longer and fuller interaction with neighboring societies. This difference is then used to explain differences in political, cultural, and socio-economic experiences of the two. There surely is merit in observing this dissimilarity, but perhaps it should not be emphasized too strongly. Throughout most of Korea and Japan's human history, occupants of both places have interacted with people of nearby continental regions, a situation evident even during the final Pleistocene ice age, and the commonality of that experience, rather than differences in the degree of its intensity, may be the more noteworthy consideration.

Pre-Agricultural Society

Slender evidence indicates that humans were present in the Korea/Japan vicinity for tens of thousands of years during the Pleistocene ice ages. The Final Pleistocene melt-off and Holocene emergence opened the way for a substantial expansion in their numbers and for marked changes in their living arrangements.

A. People of the Pleistocene Epoch

While the repetitive Pleistocene story of warming, cooling, and biotic flux was unfolding, creating the conditions that humans found when they reached Korea and Japan, those humans gradually made their appearance in the region, with the oldest reliable evidence dating to some 130,000 yBP.[16] Whether humans were present in the area before that date is unclear.

Suffice to note that early humans (*Homo erectus*) are known to have been in northern China more than a million years ago.[17] During periods of maximal cooling (such as the Riss glaciation around 5–400,000 yBP) they would have found much of the Yellow Plain a grassy steppe land supporting a rich array of large animals. If the humans ventured eastward toward the shore, they would have encoun-

---

[16] Yasuda, 1990, whch draws together earlier scholarship and links changes in human culture to changes in environment, reports evidence for human presence in Japan back to about 130,000 yBP. A reported find dating to about 400,000 yBP subsequently proved to be a silly bit of fossil fakery.

[17] For a recent analysis, see *Science News* 160–13 (Sept. 29, 2001): 199, citing a report in the September 27 issue of *Nature*.

tered mixed forest that offered its own bounty of game, nuts, fruit, other edible materials, and, in rivers and coastal waters, fish and shellfish of diverse sorts. So, depending on the flux of glacial ages and accompanying changes in coastlines and biota, they could well have penetrated the Korea/Japan vicinity, perhaps occupying lowland areas long since covered by sea and sediment. In any case, there is no evidence that they had an impact of consequence on the biosystem there nor that residence there led to any noteworthy changes in human behavior in East Asia.

There is clear evidence of a human presence in Korea and Japan some 50,000 years ago, during the coldest millennia of the Early Würm (Wisconsin) glaciation. Where the people originated and whether they were *Homo sapiens* of the *Neanderthalis* or *sapiens* subspecies is unclear, as is their number and permanence. Any humans present in Hokkaido or northeastern coastal Korea may have reached there by following the shoreline down from the Maritime Provinces and Amur River regions of Siberia as game followed the steppe land southward. Those found in areas facing the Yellow Plain may have approached from a westerly or southerly direction.

Whatever their provenance, by thirty to twenty thousand years ago, as a warmer and wetter period gave way to Earth's most recent glacial maximum (the Later or Main Würm), the human population (*H. s. sapiens*) in Korea and Japan became larger and more settled. At some sites people continued to live in caves; at others, in constructed huts. The types of stone tools they produced and used suggest that they were mobile hunters who relied heavily on the region's big game, such as the woolly mammoth in Hokkaido and other northerly areas and bison, giant deer, horses, bear, and other mammals throughout the region.[18]

By 18,000 years ago, at the Würm's coldest point, evidence suggests that the Korean region was cold and fairly arid and that its occupants sustained themselves primarily by hunting cave bear, wild ox (auroch), giant deer, and smaller species of deer, supplementing the game with fruit, nuts, berries, fish, and other seafood as opportunity allowed. Surrounded by mixed steppe and forest, they lived

---

[18] A recent, broadly arched, richly illustrated interpretive treatment of East Asian archaeological history is Barnes, 1993. On Korea, see Nelson, 1993. On Japan, see Yasuda, 1990. An older but still valuable treatment of Siberian prehistory is Chard, 1974. On the Manchurian region, see Wa, 1992.

in huts equipped with a cooking hearth and supported by framing poles, some of which were set in post holes.

One suspects that their lives resembled those of the more richly evidenced occupants of Japan. The "arcland" of the latter, which flanked the southern and eastern shores of the Sea of Japan, was only modestly more moist and somewhat warmer than Korea. It is estimated to have had about one third the present-day rate of precipitation and an average annual temperature about 7–9°C. lower than today.[19] There, it appears, people commonly lived in small groups of ten or so people. They occupied clusters of three or four huts that were framed with branches, elephant tusks, or large bones and covered, one supposes, with animal skins. They used these huts, whether on a seasonal or longer-term basis, as dwellings or as work sites for processing food, weaving fibers, producing stone and bone tools, or pursuing other tasks. These included the creation of simple stone "art work" that presumably had ornamental or amuletic functions and the production of goods for other groups to be exchanged for needed items, such as the high-quality stone used in tool-making.[20]

B. *Adjusting to Holocene Conditions*

The final Pleistocene melt-off seems to have produced major changes in the living arrangements of humans in Japan, and probably Korea as well, although a satisfactory archaeological record of the latter is still lacking. Major changes in diet and transportation, and thus in the relationship of people to the surrounding biome, seem to have occurred as a result of human moves to cope with their warming environment.

One needs to keep in mind the slowness of sea-level change. Even when global climate changed abruptly, as it evidently did in the final Pleistocene warming, the process of glacial melting—and hence sea-level rising—still proceeded slowly, taking "many thousands" of years, perhaps ten thousand, to reach the levels of the most recent several millennia.[21] Few people would have noticed it as it occurred. If it

---

[19] Yasuda, 1990, p. 123.
[20] Reynolds and Kaner, 1990, summarize information on Korea and Japan.
[21] Alley, 2000, pp. 94, 162. On warming at ca. 15,000 and 11,500 yBP, see p. 118. Alley's bibliographical references will guide one to many earlier works.

took 5,000 years for sea level to rise 150 meters, after all, the average annual rise would have been three centimeters—half the length of your thumb. Even in an abnormally long lifetime of fifty years, the rise would total only 150 centimeters, about five feet.

The rate of sea-level rise probably was much faster during the centuries around 15,000 and 11,500 yBP. However, for most of these millennia scores of generations of residents would have come and gone, scarcely able to tell their grandchildren how patches of dry land had over the years slowly grown more soggy, decades later evolved into swamp, where the trees gradually died off, their hulks eventually toppling into the brackish muck, finally being fully covered by sea water. Nor could they have told the likely story of how ancestors had year after year splashed across the increasingly soggy spots, later walking on fallen tree trunks, their descendants eventually using parts of tree trunks to ferry themselves across wider patches of water, in due course lashing logs together for more satisfactory transport over wider inlets, and finally using stone choppers to shape their vessels so as to carry people and goods and employing poles and paddles to propel and steer them.

The gradual mastery of rafting and boating was important to residents of the region. As the Yellow Sea re-filled, the ria coastlines of Korea were restored, creating myriad inlets, tortuous peninsulas, and numerous islands, between which water transport was essential. Furthermore, the rise in sea level restored the long estuaries of Korea's rivers, making them convenient avenues of ingress to the inner regions of the peninsula's lowlands. And in Japan, what had been a unitary realm gradually fragmented into the four main islands and countless islets we know today, and only by traversing open waters could people move between them. That they did so is clear from the evidence of stone tool distribution, with rock derived from formations in central Honshu showing up in archaeological deposits scattered widely about the region and its nearby islands.

More broadly, while Korea remained solidly anchored to the continent, Japan was severed from both Siberia in the north and Korea in the south. In the north the Tatar Strait between Siberia and Sakhalin is very shallow and would have remained dry well into Holocene times. But Soya Strait at Hokkaido's northern tip is much wider and deeper, and Tsugaru Strait between Hokkaido and Honshu is deeper yet. By 12–10,000 yBP or even earlier, they likely were restored to open sea. In the south, Korea Strait is deeper still and likely was the first to revert to a fully marine condition, probably doing so by 13,000 years ago.[22]

Siberian continental contacts with Sakhalin could therefore have been sustained quite easily. And in later millennia people negotiated all three northerly straits by boat, probably Siberian-type, animal-hide vessels, thereby maintaining Siberian continental influence in these regions into historical times.[23] Of greater ultimate consequence, however, was contact across Korea Strait and its adjoining waters. There the open sea became broad enough and the shallow water choppy enough to impede travel. It is reasonable to suspect, therefore, that after about 13,000 yBP or so contact between peninsula and island arc became appreciably less frequent, which may explain divergences in stone tool and pottery assemblages. But some purposeful crossing between the two via Tsushima and Iki islands did continue, as evidenced by pottery and other items—probably trade goods—that appear to have originated on one side of the Strait and been used on the other.[24]

Besides intentional traffic in both directions, other people surely found themselves driven to the western shore of Japan by storm, wave, and ocean current. Some of them originated in China itself, but most arrived from or via southeast Korea.[25] And doubtless some of those castaways who reached the islands settled there, contributing something to the corpus of native culture. Even so, it was not until some 2,500 years ago, as we note in Chapter 2, that broader continental developments spurred unprecedented numbers of people to undertake the hazardous crossing to Japan, in the process initiating major changes in the archipelago's human culture and society.

However, we have gotten ahead of our story. Back during the Pleistocene melt-off, changes in vegetation and wildlife also occurred, probably more rapidly than fluctuations in sea level. Eventually, however, the latter abetted the former. As the Yellow Plain shrank, so

---

[22] Yasuda, 1990, p. 139. Properly speaking Korea Strait lies between Korea and Tsushima; Tsushima Strait between Tsushima and Iki islands, and Iki Strait between Iki and northwest Kyushu.

[23] A fine treatment is Kikuchi, 1986.

[24] Nelson, 1993, pp. 72, 106–07.

[25] Maritime travel directly from China would have been difficult because of the distance. As recently as 7,000 yBP Shandong was still an island in the Yellow Sea because East China's broad coastal plain was still only partially re-established following the initial Holocene rise in sea level. Nelson, 1990, p. 245.

too did the many areas of broad lowland that flanked the mountain ranges of Korea and Japan. With them went much of the grassy vegetation that had sustained large mammals, along with the flat expanses where they had lived, able to nurture their young and hide from or outrun predators. Restricted to increasingly forested and ever narrower coastal strips at the foot of steep hillsides, they probably found reproduction more difficult and predators, including man, more able to corner them on soggy spits of land and in dead-end valleys.

By about 13,000 yBP the "mega-fauna"—the woolly mammoths, giant deer, bison, Newman's elephant, and others—had become extinct. Their passing forced occupants of Korea and Japan to turn to other sources of food and to develop the means of securing them. Evidence from Japan suggests two main types of adaptation. One was diversification of stone tools, which enabled users to exploit more varied food supplies.[26] In particular, smaller, finer stone points made better arrow heads and spear tips for hunting the deer, boar, and other smaller, fleeter game that still survived.[27] The points also facilitated spear fishing in the growing expanse of shallow inshore waters.

The other, more transformational development was the invention of pottery (or perhaps its introduction by migrants from some yet-to-be-identified place). Pots offered two great benefits. First, they enabled people to store for later use foodstuffs that otherwise would have been lost to decay or other animals. Second, the pointed base found on some pots allowed users to set them into the ground, encircle them with kindling and fire wood, and use them to boil food. Such boiling enabled people to convert numerous indigestible plants and seafoods into palatable meals. In the short run these changes equipped residents to offset the loss of big game and to supplement their fish, small game, and nut supply with various new shellfish and plant foods, thus giving themselves a more nutritious diet as well as a food supply that was more diversified, more reliable, and hence more able to sustain the larger population that better nutrition probably fostered. In the longer run utilization of ceramic ware for storage and cooking made plausible the development of food-crop cultivation (whereas pots had little value as storage for

---

[26] See Bleed, 1992; Yasuda, 1990, pp. 139–41.
[27] A careful study of stone tool types, materials, and provenance is Yamamoto, 1990.

most orchardry or for herding—which was in essence a form of "living storage"—and were not needed in preparing most fruit and meat for consumption).

During the millennia of Pleistocene melt-off and Holocene warming, one sees the changes in stone projectile points and associated changes in game occurring in Japan. And from about 12,700 yBP onward (by evidence to date) more and more people there began adopting a simple ceramic ware that was precursor to *jōmon* ("cord marked") pottery. *Jōmon*, so-called because the surface of many pots was decorated by impressing or rolling a strip of twisted or braided fiber across it, was a hand-molded, low-fired ware that remained in use for the next 10,000 years.

Meanwhile, Korea was experiencing similar environmental changes, and one suspects that people there made comparable adaptations. At least, a few sherds of raised-design pottery (*yunkimun*) that seem to date from early Holocene millennia have been found at sites on the south and east coasts. Their location, together with similarities to pottery found in the adjacent regions of Siberia and Japan, seem to indicate contacts among seafaring people, contacts that became less frequent after sea level had risen.[28] It is possible, however, that enough of the peninsula's residents chose to migrate northward or westward as the biome changed so that most of its small surviving population could get by on existing technology. In any case, until more complete Holocene archaeological sites older than about 7,000 yBP are discovered, the puzzle of early Holocene humankind in Korea probably will remain unsolved.

C. *Holocene Society*

By 7,000 years ago, occupants of Korea were using pottery widely in the processing of nuts, shellfish, and other foods. Their *yunkimun* pottery was gradually displaced—in the northwest initially, throughout the peninsula later—by a ware known as *chŭlmun* ("comb-patterned"), which commonly was decorated with incised surface lines of geometric design. Its users developed and adopted more varied stone and bone tools to aid them in food processing, cloth-making, and construction tasks. They produced decorative objects and engaged

---

[28] Nelson, 1993, pp. 58–59, 70–72, 106–07.

in exchange of items, such as pots, baskets, and stone products, that were produced by people with specialized skills.

Mostly these people, who relied heavily on fish and shellfish for sustenance, lived in small clusters of pit dwellings along streams and near the coastline. The marine harvest remained particularly important to residents along the east coast, and as centuries passed, people there improved their fishing gear, developing or acquiring "detachable toggle-head harpoons" and other more effective devices.[29] Moreover, and especially across the mountains on the lowlands to the west, where the sea was less bountiful, villagers supplemented their catch with game—mainly boar and deer—nuts, and other forest growth, some of which they stored in underground storage pits for later off-season consumption. And they used stone mortars and pestles to grind food, probably nuts and grains, into meal. Initially the grain came from wild growth, mainly "millet" of some sort. As we note in Chapter 2, however, more elaborate tillage practices gradually developed during the later Holocene. Although the demographic effects of these pre-agricultural developments are not clear, one scholar estimates that Korea's population numbered in the tens of thousands before the introduction of cultivation.[30]

In Japan, meanwhile, the several millennia down to about 5,000 yBP appear to have been relatively comfortable ones for human residents. People improved their food-gathering techniques by employing hunting dogs, pit-trapping for boar, and using weirs, nets, improved hooks, and harpoons for catching fish. For maritime travel they employed dugout vessels that were large enough—some two feet wide by twenty feet long—to carry several people or a substantial cargo.[31] They stored food more carefully in jars and, at some places, in raised storage sheds. And they appear gradually to have begun nurturing select plants, such as chestnut trees, that would flourish in sunlit areas cleared of competing growth.

In the northeast, furthermore, people were consuming the seeds of more and more wild grasses, notably foxtail millet, buckwheat, and the sturdy, well-seeded barnyard grass. They also seem to have

---

[29] Barnes, 1993, p. 76. Choe, 1990, sees the east-west distinction as so pronounced that it denotes two separate cultural complexes.

[30] Kim B-m, 1987, p. 51.

[31] Farris, pending-I, a ms. currently in submission for publication, p. 7. With permission of the author.

begun increasing yields by gardening: disturbing the soil and sup-
pressing unwanted growth.[32] As food supplies expanded and diversified,
settlements proliferated and many grew larger, with the archipelago's
total population rising to perhaps a quarter million.[33]

Housing also improved. Hut size increased and floors came to be
set a half meter or so below ground level to give more shelter from
wind and cold. Sturdier framing supported thatch roofing that provided further insulation against the elements. Meanwhile, Jōmon pots
diversified, and their decoration became more elaborate. Stone and
clay ornaments and figurines became more common, and burial practices seem to have become more systematic and respectful of the
deceased. Finally, more and more signs appeared of regional trading arrangements that offset local material disadvantages: thus coastal
folk in the Kantō vicinity produced sea salt and other products that
they exchanged with central highlanders, who responded with stone
for tool making or other uses, or perhaps edible nuts or other highland goods.

These enhancements notwithstanding, life in Jōmon Japan was still
difficult. Periodic famines occurred, and people commonly died in
their thirties. In Korea, it appears, life was even more austere, with
food resources less diversified and dwelling groups smaller and more
scattered. Archaeologists have thus far discovered on the peninsula
fewer evidences of variety in stone and pottery work and less elaboration of decorative, or amuletic artifacts.

Beginning some 5,000 years ago, moreover, renewed global cooling
dropped temperatures enough to modify woodland composition, in
the process making life even more difficult. This was especially so
in highland Japan, where it appears to have led to scarcity of game
and a substantial decline in population. Along the coasts, on the
other hand, sea level dropped a few meters, creating in bays and
estuaries strips of sunlit, well-watered shoreline that developed into
reedy, grassy, brushy plains. On these, wild grains were able to
flourish, and this change, along with the presence of pottery, facilitated—in both Korea and Japan—a gradual increase in grain consump-

---

[32] Crawford, 1992, pp. 120, 126.
[33] Koyama, 1978, pp. 56–57. The frequently repeated number of 260,000 derives
(in English) from this source. Koyama suggests for Japan some 22,000 people ca.
8,000 yBP, rising to 260,000 by 4,500 years ago, dropping to 160,000 by 300 BCE,
and swelling to 600,000 by 100 CE.

tion and the diffusion of simple nurturing practices that foreshadowed a much more full-blown cultivating economy. Particularly in southwest Japan, where broadleaf evergreen forests had supported only a sparse human population, one sees growing evidence that locals were nurturing foxtail millet, barley, and probably broomcorn millet.[34]

Whether the cropping activity in Korea and Japan arose locally or was introduced by migrants from the north, south, or west is unclear. In the case of Japan, however, by 3,000 years ago (or 1,000 years BCE in the more familiar calendrical system) residents were utilizing a wide range of vegetable products, including by one account gourds, beans, *shiso*, *egoma*, hemp, mulberry, colza, burdock, and peach.[35] Some degree of nurturing seems to have been involved in at least some cases, but a fully developed system of tillage—purposefully breaking soil, scattering seed, and nurturing the sprouts to grow seasonal crops of choice—was yet to develop. When it did, it did so in conjunction with substantially expanded contact between the archipelago and continent. By then, contact with neighboring regions had already begun to transform human life on the Korean peninsula, especially in the northwest.

*   *   *

As of 1,000 BCE, then, humans had lived in the Korea/Japan region for thousands and thousands of years. As millennia passed, they had acquired more and more skill at exploiting their surroundings, learning how to combat cold weather, how to broaden and strengthen their resource base, how to improve their diet, how to travel over water, and how to exchange valued goods to mutual advantage. Nevertheless, by the present-day standards of industrial society's beneficiaries, their lives had not been easy: their numbers always were few, their life spans short, and their material standard of living modest in the extreme.[36]

It is also worth noting, however, that while they may well have played a secondary role in the final destruction of the region's mega-

---

[34] Crawford, 1992, p. 121.
[35] Pearson, 1992, p. 68. Hudson, 1999, p. 106, offers a similar but somewhat longer list.
[36] A thoughtful and instructive discussion of subsistence dynamics in Jōmon Japan is Koike, 1992, pp. 53–57.

fauna, and while their fires doubtless broke free on occasion to burn nearby areas of grass or woodland, their numbers were so modest and their material demands so simple that by and large they had no enduring impact on their ambient biosystem. Unable, that is to say, to impose onerous burdens on their environs, they could expect their descendants to continue living in the region for as many future millennia as the underlying determinants of climate and geology would permit.

CHAPTER TWO

THE RISE OF EARLY AGRICULTURAL REGIMES
(TO 700 CE)

In Korea and Japan, as elsewhere, two major developments in human-environment relations ended forager society, ushering in a new era of human affairs. One was the adoption of crop cultivation, which constituted a radical systematizing of technique for manipulating and exploiting the terrestrial biosystem. The other was mining of ore for use in metallurgy, which was the first sustained exploitation of sub-surface resources.

The cultivation of grain (millet and rice) appeared in China around 5,000 BCE. Metallurgy came millennia later, bronze around 2,000 and iron around 600 BCE. Cropping entered Korea around 2,000 BCE, metallurgy some centuries later. The former reached southwest Japan around 500 BCE or earlier, metallurgy probably a couple of centuries later.

The tillage-bronze-iron sequence was thus much more compressed in Korea than in China and even moreso in Japan. In both Korea and Japan, however, the adoption of tillage and metallurgy and the consequences thereof—growth in human population, organization,

and stratification, intensified social conflict, and environmental dis-
ruption—played out quite similarly, along with the emergence in
each of a more integrated elite culture that reflected the interplay
of indigenous tradition and new influences from abroad.

In both Korea and Japan the processes of initial political consolidation, social elaboration, and elite cultural development were largely
completed by about 650–700 CE. For centuries thereafter, however,
peripheral areas of both did remain beyond the political pale. And
as we note in later chapters, these agrarian-based regimes subsequently witnessed recurrent political crises, collapses, and reconsoli-
dations as well as gradual changes in elite culture, the broader society
and economy, and the human-ecosystem relationship.

Cropping, Metallurgy, and Their Impact: An Overview

Crop cultivation enabled people to increase both their productivity
per capita and the "useful" output of any potentially arable land
they controlled. Even when they used stone tools, as most did for
centuries, their efforts led to major changes. They fostered population growth, the spread of cropping techniques (by mimesis and
migration), and inter-group conflict over land-use rights. More basically they achieved a gradual transformation of the landscape and
its biota as domesticates and parasites (weeds and pests) gained promi-
nence at the expense of other flora and fauna.

The development of metallurgy improved cropping efficiency and
allowed much more elaborate construction and engineering work. Its
direct environmental effects, however, were much less profound than
those of agriculture. It produced patches of noxious detritus at mining and smelting sites. More importantly, it fostered deforestation
and downstream damage as wood was consumed in mine construction and smelting. On occasion, too, it surely led to accidental outbreaks of destructive wildfire.

Compared to those environmental impacts, the social effects of
metal use were transformational. Metallurgy facilitated a striking
increase in conflict, conquest, warfare, and its paraphernalia; the rise
of powerful ruling elites and elite culture; a huge expansion in the
producer populations that particular elites controlled; the emergence
and celebration of elaborate social stratification; and the develop-

ment of greater institutional complexity—in a phrase, the rise of the early state.

As centuries passed, population growth and escalating elite demands overloaded local ecosystems, spurring migration as producers fled tribute takers and as both sought more or better land to till and tax or other resources to exploit. This migration extended geographically the ongoing contest for living space and essential resources that pitted humans and their domesticated collaborators (both plants and animals) against non-domesticates. It destroyed more and more natural habitat, altered biotic composition (see Plate 7), reduced biodiversity on ever more lowland sites, and denuded more and more hillsides. These changes in turn increased the risk of wildfire, and they intensified erosion, flooding, drought, and soil depletion.

On the other hand, in the case of Korea and Japan, because of their mountainous character, the opening ·of land to tillage created miles and miles of forest edge (see Plate 8). Moreover, irrigated rice (paddy) culture established numerous patches of seasonal wet land. In many areas these changes probably increased the populations of shrubs, grasses, and forbs, as well as select wading birds, frogs, various insects—mosquitoes most notably—and other fauna.

Agriculture and Metal Use in Korea and Japan to 100 BCE

In Korea and Japan, as noted in Chapter One, indigenous techniques for nurturing desired food plants (and possibly for domesticating boar and dogs as sources of meat) gradually appeared during *chŭlmun* and later *jōmon* millennia. Subsequently two major forms of horticultural practice—dry-field millet and paddy culture—became established, having been introduced, it appears, from regions now known as northern and east central China.

A. Dry-Field and Paddy Culture: Some General Issues

In East Asia the earliest full-scale cultivation of foxtail millet as a dry-field crop seems to have occurred on the hilly western edge of the broad lowland that extends westward from the Yellow Sea. The cultivation of rice as an irrigated crop appears to have arisen on lowlands south of modern-day Shanghai. Millet culture probably reached Korea before irrigated rice did, and in both Korea and Japan millet appears to have remained the more important crop for general consumption. Eventually, however, because of the high value that ruling elites attached to it, paddy tillage acquired the greater visibility in both historical records and modern scholarship.

At first glance Korea and Japan seem highly implausible sites for paddy culture: they are too northerly and surely too cold for it. In fact, paddy culture was possible there because of the particular way in which the great super-continent of Pangaea broke up and re-configured during the Mesozoic Era. As Pangaea disassembled (see Map 1-1), the Indian Plate, a wedge of land on its southeastern side, broke away and commenced a long, northward journey that caused it to crash into the underbelly of the rotating, consolidating Eurasian Plate. That collision, which started late in the Mesozoic, some 45 myBP, and is still underway, produced the Himalaya Mountains and their associated highland mass (see Map 2-1).[1] This towering upland shunts westerly winds southward across India and the Bay of Bengal, enabling them to warm and pick up moisture before swinging back northward as they round the eastern end of the Himalayas. During summer, when the westerly winds over Siberia are light and dry, these muggy "monsoon" winds from Bengal are able to push north-ward in an arc that curves up across eastern China to encompass most of Korea and Japan south of Hokkaido. In consequence, its northerly latitude notwithstanding, this entire region of East Asia became fit for paddy culture.[2]

It could do so, however, only after the original Asian wild rice—which evidently was a sub-tropical perennial—had been modified by centuries of cultivation, eventually developing two main types of annual domestic cultivars (*Oryza sativa indica* and *O. s. japonica*).[3] Of these the latter, the "short-grain" or *japonica* type, was particularly suited to cooler climates. Over the millennia, and especially in recent centuries, breeders have developed a grand diversity of both types of rice, and numerous varieties of *japonica* now flourish in both Korea

---

[1] Burchfiel, 1993, pp. 12–14, 18–19. Earlier works that exemplify the close study being given to the India-Eurasia collision are Molnar & Tapponnier, 1975, and Allègre, 1984.

[2] On the long-term influence of monsoons, see Yasuda, 1990.

[3] A third category of cultivar, *O. s. javanica*, developed later; it is noted in Im, 1992, p. 158.

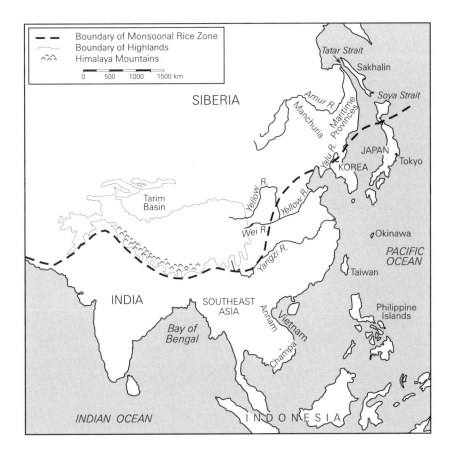

Map 2-1. *Continental Asia.*
Based on map of Eurasia in Rand McNally, 1982, p. 33.

and Japan, as well as in many other regions, most commonly uplands, of East and Southeast Asia.[4]

Even after one explains why this northerly region of Asia was capable of sustaining paddy tillage, however, a host of uncertainties surround its appearance. Rice, after all, can be grown as either a dry-field or an irrigated crop. Moreover, the term "irrigation" can refer to systems of varying complexity, ranging from simple techniques for steering hillside runoff onto one's rice (or other) fields all the way

---

[4] A richly informative collection of essays on rice is Association of Japanese Agricultural Scientific Societies, 1975.

to elaborate systems of dams, dykes, and ditches designed to regulate both the intake and outflow of water as well as its depth in one's fields.

Agronomists note that in paddy culture's fully developed form, with carefully regulated water intake and outlet (which provides nutrients, stabilizes ambient temperature, and suppresses competing growth), rice cultivars can yield much richer harvests per hectare than do dry-field grains, including dry-field rice. However, achieving those higher yields requires land that is table-top flat, access to a dependable water supply, and considerable engineering skill (see Plate 9). The larger the contiguous acreage under such cultivation, moreover, the more complex the technical demands and the greater the need for reliable communal collaboration and a large supply of disciplined labor. Not until the fourteenth century or thereabouts, as we note in Chapter 4, do Korea and Japan appear to have developed the organizational arrangements necessary for large-scale, fully articulated systems of paddy tillage.

On the other hand, although dry-field farming is a much simpler task, the regular application of fertilizer materials appears not to have become widespread in either Korea or Japan until the fourteenth century or so. Before then, dry field soils, which lacked the added nutrients furnished by incoming irrigation water, became exhausted after a few years of cropping, forcing farmers to fallow them (allowing them to revert to "wild" growth), which helped rejuvenate soil vitality, enabling cultivators to reclaim the fields for cropping a few years later. Even simple irrigation helped obviate fallowing, permitting farmers to keep fields in production year after year, thereby eliminating the need to seek new fields and invest energy and time in clearing forest and brush growth.

In both Korea and Japan it seems likely that rice was from the outset grown as both a dry-field and crudely irrigated crop. And in both, the systems of irrigation became more complex as centuries passed. For the first millennium of agriculture's presence in the region, however, attempts to determine the extent, character, and role of paddy culture ensnare us in unanswerable questions about the relative yields of simpler rice-cropping and dry-grain practices and about the roles of land scarcity, labor availability, record keeping, rulers' preferences, and social coercion in shaping agricultural choices. It may well be, however, that until the fourteenth century or thereabouts only a quarter to a third of grain acreage in Korea and Japan was devoted to paddy tillage.

In any case, both dry field and paddy culture did become established in Korea and Japan, followed in a few centuries by the adoption of bronze and iron technology. Precisely how, why, when, and by whom these practices were introduced is still unclear. But the process seems to have been inextricably linked to political changes in northeast China (meaning the region extending from the Yangzi River northward to the plains of southern Manchuria and the southeastern reaches of the Mongolian Plateau) that accompanied the adoption of tillage and metallurgy there. The process affected Korea first, Japan later.

B. *Korea*

By 3,000 BCE or so a ruling elite known to us as the Shang Dynasty enjoyed a control of sorts over a substantial millet-growing region west of the Shandong Peninsula. As centuries passed, local elites formed and competed in and around the Shang area, and to advance their interests they seem to have promoted millet culture, along with its associated livestock: pigs, chickens, dogs, cattle, horses, and—on the Mongolian Plateau—goats and sheep. Most pertinent here was the emergence of millet-based local elites on the Manchurian Plain, in the watersheds of the Liao and Sungari rivers (see Map 2-2). The deceased rulers of these elites were buried in substantial cist-type graves, and by about 2,000 BCE, it appears, groups who employed these cist burials, as well as a plain style (*mumun*) ceramic ware, were moving eastward across the Yalu River into northwest Korea, in the process introducing millet culture to the area.

Whether these migrants were propelled by political turmoil, land hunger, environmental change, or other factors is unclear. As they moved into Korea, however, they seem to have settled in uplands, leaving lower, flatter areas available for conversion to cropland. Initially that pattern left local users of *chŭlmun* pottery in possession of their coastal and streamside settlements, but gradually land clearance impinged on them, even as it reduced the area of woodland available for their exploitation. So while spatial segregation may for a time have helped reduce the level of conflict between tillers and locals, sooner or later competition for resources ensued and violence did occur, as suggested by the considerable number of stone swords, spear points, and mace heads found at settlement sites.

Doubtless there were other, more peaceable forms of interaction

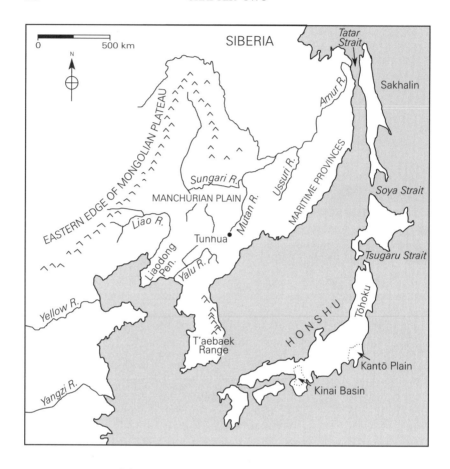

Map 2-2. *Northeast Asia: Principal Rivers.*
Based on maps of Northeast Asia in Replogle, 1954, pp. 74, 85.

too. Indeed, one can argue that the general cooling of climate that decimated Japan's population some four to five thousand years ago, as noted in Chapter 1, may well have spurred *chŭlmun* users to adopt new methods of sustenance by making life more difficult on the peninsula, especially in the west where seafood was less ample. That cooling altered the faunal repertoire and led to changes in the human diet, including heavier reliance on indigenous cereals and more harvesting and storage of food for later consumption. Villagers appear to have practiced some basic gardening to nurture millet, which may well have predisposed them to seize upon any new tillage practices that seemed to offer a bigger and/or more sure harvest.[5] In any case, as generations passed, pottery and stone-tool styles were modified, diverse forms of *mumun* pottery came to prevail, and a swidden type of dry-field farming slowly spread across the peninsula, with fields opened to use, tilled until their fertility gave out, and then fallowed for a few years until the soil could again produce a harvest.

The introduction of dry-field agriculture was, however, only a part of the tillage story. In the Yangzi region of east central China, paddy culture had for centuries been spreading in all directions.[6] As *japonica* rice varieties became more cold-resistant, their use moved northward, eventually to the Shandong Peninsula. At some unknown moment, but probably several centuries after millet first reached Korea, this rice was introduced to the peninsula's west and south lowlands, where it fitted the climate.

Political turmoil in Shang China may have been the key factor behind this development. Ruling elites there continued to jockey and battle for advantage, and under these turbulent circumstances rice-growing villagers (or vanquished members of a local elite) might have circled the Yellow Sea via Manchuria to reach Korea. More plausibly, perhaps, residents of the Shandong coastal region, or even south or west of there, with lives ravaged by warring armies, sneaked supplies onto small boats and set out along the coast in search of safe haven. Some doubtless would have been blown out to sea by offshore winds, the luckier ones ending up in southwestern Korea.[7] As they became established there, they could have introduced rice culture to new neighbors, gradually enabling rice cropping to spread throughout southern Korea.

Whatever the route of its introduction to the peninsula, there evidently was rice consumption, and probably cultivation, in Korea by about 1200 BCE, and perhaps earlier.[8] The prevalence of paddy tillage should not be overstated, however. As late as ca. 1400 CE, it is reported, only about a third of Korea's grain acreage was

---

[5] Choe, 1990, develops this thesis very nicely.

[6] For a brief outline of rice origins, see Sasaki, 1991, pp. 35–38.

[7] The case for introduction of rice via northern China to northwest Korea and thence to southern Korea and Japan is nicely made by Chon, 1992.

[8] Nelson, 1993, p. 163, mentions new reports of rice in Korea before 2,000 BCE. Choe, 1990, p. 11, says simply late *chŭlmun*, meaning 2–1,000 BCE.

producing rice, the rest being dry grains.[9] During earlier centuries the portion in rice likely was even lower.

Even after millet and rice cropping were established, they did not abruptly displace the older systems of seafood gathering, hunting, and forest-yield consumption. Rather, depending on the particulars of location, they supplemented and only slowly and partially supplanted them. However, because land dedicated to tillage will, under appropriate climatic conditions, yield much more human food per hectare than does natural vegetation, this addition of cultivated grains to the diet increased substantially the total food supply available to residents of Korea. It thus opened the way for unprecedented population growth and the influx of more migrants while also laying a foundation for the sort of social stratification and elite cultural development that northeast China had experienced over preceding centuries.

That potential was heightened when residents of the peninsula began using and producing metal—bronze and later iron—tools, weapons, and ceremonial goods. As with grain cultivation, their introduction seems to have reflected political conflict in and around China.

To elaborate, by 1,000 BCE the rulers of Shang had fallen to challengers who went on to found the Zhou Dynasty. Zhou rulers had only modest success in controlling their realm, but by striking bargains with local strong men, they were able to claim a suzerain role over a much larger region than had the Shang. Their sway extended southeastward to encompass rice-growing regions along the Yangzi and northeastward nearly to the edge of Manchuria, where the frontier was in the hands of a regional strongman, the ruler of Yan.

By 700 BCE regional regimes such as the Yan were powerful enough, and warfare punitive enough, so that a host of defensive walls, mostly made of reinforced mud, were being erected between and around more and more domains and headquarters settlements. The warfare extended beyond Zhou territory, reaching farther southward into rice-growing areas and northward to involve groups of mounted fighting men on the Mongolian Plateau and other peoples and polities on the plains of Manchuria. Artifact finds, most notably daggers of a type found in the Liao-Sungari region, suggest that around 700 BCE, or perhaps earlier, weapons and other goods made of bronze were introduced to northwestern Korea from the territory

---

[9] Yi T-j, 1983, pp. 34, 40–42.

controlled by Yan or other groups battling west of the Yalu. Whether they were brought by conquerors, refugees, or possibly even traders is unclear.

As the use of bronze items spread across Korea, more and more weapons, ornamental items, and tools for agriculture, woodworking, and other crafts were imported and produced locally. Also, a more elaborate dolmen-type burial practice appeared in which leaders' tombs were covered by huge flat stone slabs whose transport and placement required immense amounts of labor.[10] Eventually the wall-building practices of Zhou also appeared, with headquarters towns being encircled by defensive earthen and stone walls, initially in the northwest and during later centuries elsewhere on the peninsula.[11]

Then armed violence was raised to new levels by the introduction of iron-working. Iron manufacture (smelting, forging, and casting) and use emerged in the Zhou realm around 700 BCE, and, for a time at least, the rulers of Yan seem to have benefited from it. Through warfare and trade they expanded their reach onto the Mongolian Plateau and eastward across the Liao River Basin and Liaodong Peninsula, overwhelming some polities in the region and probably striking bargains of convenience with others. It evidently was through this Manchurian connection that iron, like bronze, was introduced from Zhou China to northwest Korea, probably by 400 BCE, later spreading through the rest of the peninsula.[12]

In Korea, as in China, the adoption of bronze and iron fostered more violent, larger scale political processes. Political consolidation ("state building") on the peninsula is ill-recorded prior to about 100 BCE, but the mastery of metal technology had by then surely enabled some rulers to equip and deploy more dangerous armies, overrun less well-armored neighbors, and thereby gain control of more producers and production sites.

The use of metal would have had environmental consequences, as well. One suspects that fuelwood demand and accidental wildfires

---

[10] These dolmen continue to mystify archaeologists, some of whom suspect that they functioned as markers by which local leaders asserted their claims to "ancestral land" in the dolmen's vicinity. See Nelson, 1993, pp. 147–50.

[11] On archaeological evidence for "walled towns," see Barnes 2001, pp. 152–78, which is based on two articles she wrote in 1988 and 1991.

[12] On iron in Korea see Yoon, 1989 and Taylor, 1989. Their bibliographies will lead one to earlier works.

led in places to deforestation, with its injury to local biota and its downstream complications of flooding, drought, and damage to settlements and arable land. Generally, however, these hurts were incurred by the biosystem and villagers, not by ruling elites, for whom the benefits of metal use clearly outweighed any costs. Moreover, the magnitude of the environmental hurt should not be exaggerated. For centuries metal use in Korea (and also in Japan) remained largely an elite perquisite. Bronze and iron implements were available to few villagers, most of whom continued to rely on stone, bone, and wooden tools for their daily-life tasks of chopping, woodworking, digging, cultivating, harvesting, butchering, and burying. Furthermore, while population likely was growing at an unprecedented rate, it was still very modest, well below the peninsula's carrying capacity for even a non-intensive agricultural order.

As of 100 BCE, then, the horticultural and metallurgical ingredients involved in the displacement of Korea's forager society were solidly in place. And the political and social ramifications of that change were becoming visible all across the peninsula.

C. *Japan*

Even as the use of metals was spreading through Korea, in China the scale and frequency of warfare kept growing until around 200 BCE, when a new dynasty, the Han, established solid control over the region that Zhou had claimed as its realm. By that time continental agricultural and metallurgical practices were reaching beyond Korea into western Japan, where their transformational influences were already being felt.

The means and moment of paddy culture's introduction to Japan are as obscure as they are for Korea. Archaeologists have recovered evidence of rice grains in Kyushu that date roughly to 1,000 BCE, but whether the rice was grown in Japan or brought from elsewhere is unclear. The remains of paddy fields dating to about 600 BCE have been found in northwest Kyushu, and from about 500 BCE onward paddy tillage and dry-field cropping spread eastward, together with associated "wooden and stone agricultural tools and a variety of other continental influences."[13] The initial appearance of paddy

---

[13] Hudson, 1999, p. 112.

culture in northwest Kyushu, and the timing of its spread eastward strongly suggest that it came from southern Korea, perhaps as a byproduct of the political turmoil surrounding Zhou disintegration and the spread of metal-using polities across the peninsula.[14]

Ambient circumstances within Japan are similarly uncertain. Because Kyushu was heavily forested with evergreen broadleafs, it supported a relatively sparse Jōmon population that could offer little resistance to immigrants. Moreover, local experience with wild-grain nurturing, plus the occasional contact with mainland castaways, traders, and migrants that had occurred during preceding centuries, may well have predisposed residents there, as in Korea, to find the new provisioning system attractive. Also, the people of southeast Korea and northwest Kyushu may in fact have shared a common language or otherwise been cultural or genealogical kinsmen, among whom the diffusion of new practices was a relatively simple process.[15]

With political turmoil continuing to wrack the China-Korea region, it seems likely that a substantial and sustained influx of people from the mainland continued, with the immigrants gradually settling farther eastward.[16] By 100 BCE communities cultivating paddy fields were established eastward all along the Inland Sea littoral and adjacent lowlands as far as the vicinity of present-day Nagoya. Paddy tillage was also practiced at a few sites along the Sea of Japan coast in northerly Honshu.[17] But for most of Japan east of the Nagoya

---

[14] On the Korean route to Japan see Chon, 1992, pp. 167–68. Sasaki, 1991, pp. 38–41, favors the idea of migrants dislodged from the Yangzi region by the political turmoil of ca. 470–300 BCE, who escape by boat to Cheju Island and the south coast of Korea and thence to Japan. This formulation, however, doesn't deal with the prior centuries of rice culture in Korea.

[15] The linguistic and physical anthropological character or identity of the populations of early Korea and Japan, and the nature of their relationship to one another and to others, are topics that have generated a great deal of heat, and a bit of light. A splendid examination of this topic, as it relates to Korea, is Pai, 2000. See also Kwon Y-g, 1990. For Japan, see Hudson, 1999; Farris, 1998a, Ch. 2, and items cited in his bibliography, notably Kirkland, 1981. Archaeologists commonly treat pre-historic Japan in dyadic terms of pre-agricultural Jōmon and agricultural Yayoi society, viewing them as separate cultural, linguistic, and genetic groups, and that approach tends to preclude more complex and ambiguous patterns of interplay between residents, new arrivals, and their descendants. Hudson, 1999, attempts to make room for these complexities and ambiguities within this dyadic framework.

[16] The source and scale of Yayoi immigration are matters that have provoked much scholarly—and even more quasi-scholarly—writing. See, for a thoughtful example of the former, Hanihara, 1987.

[17] Hudson, 1999, p. 198.

vicinity, where mixed deciduous forest had long supported a more
dense population, the bearers of wet-rice culture, or at least the
tillage practices themselves, appear to have encountered more resistance, and older Jōmon forager customs persisted, enduring in the
northeast for several more centuries.[18]

Whatever the particulars of immigrant/resident relations—and
here, as on the peninsula, they probably involved conflict, cooperation, segregation, and intermixture—the immigrants introduced rice
culture along with a simpler, *mumun*-like pottery style known today
as Yayoi. With these developments came metal tools and weapons,
communal defensive structures, and burial arrangements that suggest
social stratification and the presence of local elites. In short, the
socio-political changes previously evidenced in China and Korea
played themselves out in Japan as well.

Elite presence was marked by larger buildings and warehouses,
more elaborate burial practices, and the spread of warfare. This last,
as evidenced in archaeological sites, entailed more extensive fortifica-
tions and the proliferation of swords, arrow heads, halberds, and
skeletons that display wounds and dismemberment. Communities
grew larger, and rulers regularized the tribute obligations of their
producer population. For those producers, both diet and the routines of daily life changed as tillage work gradually displaced hunting and foraging. The rhythms of famine also changed, with a fairly
regular "spring hunger," which followed depletion of the prior year's
food reserves, replacing the older pattern of irregular hunger associated
with vagaries of nut, berry, or wild grain harvest, marine catch, or
the hunt. Whether the producers' material standards of living or
sense of well-being improved or declined seems impossible to say.

Clearly, however, in Japan, as in Korea, major change was occurring in the ecosystem. In location after location, patches of forest
and mixed growth were cleared and burned off as acreage was
opened to sunlight and converted to tillage. Although tillers may
have tried to create grain monocultures, in fact their fields supported
a sufficiently diverse population of "weeds" so that harvesting was

---

[18] On the development of agriculture in northeast Japan, see Crawford, 1992,
and Crawford & Takamiya, 1990. Concerning marine foraging and agriculture on
the Kantō coast during the "Jōmon-Yayoi transition," see Aikens and Akazawa,
1992.

done by sorting out and snapping off heads of the desired grain rather than by cutting handfuls of stalk at the base. And while land clearance and deforestation had diverse malign consequences for the biosystem, they also created new opportunities for some biota, as earlier noted.

Whether on balance the early centuries of crop growing and metal use in Japan and Korea increased or decreased species diversity or biomass volume is probably impossible to say. But it did shift the balance in favor of the human-centered biotic community of cultivators, domesticates, and parasites. And it equipped the humans as never before to manipulate their environment and one another. Only time would tell how the distribution of gains and losses from that empowerment was to work out.

Political Ramifications (100 BCE–700 CE)

In both Korea and Japan, then, by the start of the Common Era (0 CE), the adoption of agriculture and metallurgy had wrought far-reaching changes. In both places, moreover, the particulars of the process were strongly influenced by other developments in the region, of which the most extensively recorded are changes in Chinese politics. Over the next several centuries to 700 CE a complicated and erratic process of political consolidation in the Korea/Japan vicinity itself transformed a realm of hamlets and petty local groupings into a political arena dominated by three moderately large, elaborately structured, aristocatic states—Parhae, Silla, and Nara—that dominated society all the way from central Manchuria to northeastern Japan.

This process of consolidation can be treated in terms of two stages. During the first, ca. 100 BCE to 300 CE, a number of small, ill-defined polities arose in the region. Most notable in the end were Koguryŏ, Paekche, Silla, and Kaya in Korea, and Wa (or Yamatai, in Kyushu) and Yamato (in the Nara Basin) in Japan. During the second stage, ca. 300–700 CE, leaders of these small polities battled and bargained until only the three larger ones of Parhae, Silla, and Nara still survived as autonomous, much more highly articulated, and much more powerful regimes. Parhae, which was larger than Great Britain, stretched from the Liaodong Peninsula northeastward across northern Korea and central Manchuria well into the Maritime Provinces of Siberia. Silla, larger than Denmark, controlled all of peninsular Korea.[19] Nara, about the size of Great Britain, claimed a realm that stretched eastward from Kyushu to middle Tōhoku (see Map 2-3).

A. *Forming Initial Regimes, 100 BCE–300 CE*

We can pick up this story of political consolidation around 100 BCE, when leaders of the century-old Han Dynasty in China were energetically enlarging their realm. One expansionary thrust sent their armies into southern Manchuria and the plains of northwest Korea, overrunning local rulers and establishing so-called commanderies, of which the most famous was Lelang, situated near present-day P'yŏng-yang in the fertile Taedong River basin.[20]

These commanderies were essentially frontier garrison headquarters whose function was to keep the empire's borders tranquil.[21] Over the next four centuries their configuration changed on occasion, but from start to finish their basic managerial strategy consisted of bargaining in mutually advantageous ways with those local elites that would cooperate. In a *de facto* system of trade, local leaders on the empire's perimeter would send to the commandery in their region (Lelang in the case of Korea and Japan) items of interest to China's rulers—foodstuffs, minerals, other local products, handicrafts, and slaves most commonly—offering them as "tribute." In return they received diverse material "gifts," notably Chinese cultural artifacts and "prestige goods," titles of office, and on occasion diplomatic or military assistance.[22] Around this official tribute system then developed supplemental, *ad hoc* entrepreneurial trading arrangements that involved Chinese traders and residents in Lelang and such Korean or Japanese traders or leaders as were in a position to deal with them.

---

[19] A dated but detailed treatment of the Korean aspect of this political history is Lee K-b, 1984, Ch. 2–4, a translation of the 1967 revised edition of a work Lee originally published in 1961. An updated version of that text is Eckert, 1990.

[20] Of the "local rulers" who were overrun, the most celebrated were those of Wiman Chosŏn, a regime that was reputed to control a trans-Yalu realm. See, for example, Ch'oi, 1992.

[21] The antecedents, character, and role of these commanderies have at times been a subject of considerable debate among Koreans interested in their society's history. The issues are vigorously addressed in a set of essays in *Korea Journal* 27–12 (December 1987).

[22] An extended treatment of this exchange is Pai, 2000, Ch. 5–6. A concise discussion is Pai, 1989.

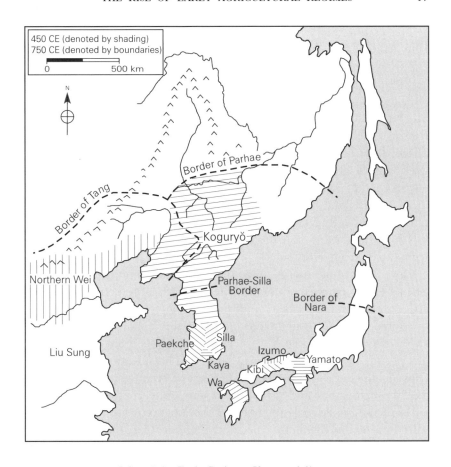

Map 2-3. *Early Regimes: Korea and Japan.*

In 450 CE East Asia was in turmoil. China was divided, with the Liu Sung controlling much of the south and the Northern Wei much of the north. Korea was divided among four ruling elites: the large realm of Koguryŏ, the smaller ones of Paekche and Silla, and the cluster of very small entities known as Kaya. Southern Japan was divided among a number of small, ill-defined polities, of which Wa, Kibi, Izumo, and Yamato are the best documented. By 750 CE substantial political consolidation had been achieved. The Tang Dynasty controlled China; Parhae dominated much of Manchuria as well as continental Korea and the southwestern Maritime Provinces; Silla controlled peninsular Korea, and Nara controlled Japan from Kyushu to the southern portion of the northeast. Based on Lee, K-b, 1984, pp. 39, 70, and Matsuda and Mori, 1966, pp. 15, 19.

The commandery system may have worked to the satisfaction of Han leaders, but it did not stop political change on the empire's periphery; indeed, it may have accelerated it by giving the locally ambitious more reason to enhance their power, thereby acquiring official recognition and access to the tribute system of exchange. Most pertinently here, ruling groups in the Mongolia-Manchuria region, which were sustained by animal-herding fully as much as by tillage, sporadically employed mounted warfare to invade more productive agricultural areas of China and Korea so as to extract tribute from the communities they overwhelmed. This strategy pitted them against both one another and Han authorities, leading to continual maneuvering and recurrent warfare, and it was through victory in such ventures that they positioned themselves to receive official recognition from Han rulers.

One of the most successful of these northern mounted ruling elite groups was Koguryŏ, which appears to have benefited from a special combination of place and time. Koguryŏ rulers were headquartered some 200 kilometers north of the Yellow Sea in narrow valleys along the middle Yalu, where tillage was limited to "numerous pockets of rich alluvial farm land."[23] That location placed them between horse-riding herders of the North Asian interior highlands and the cultivators and fisherfolk of temperate coastal lowlands. In consequence, while male members of the Koguryŏ elite were mounted warrriors of the highland type, and therefore capable of projecting their power forcefully over long distances, they also were well placed to extract tribute from the more densely populated and productive sedentary lowland populations that lay just to their south.

The timing of Koguryŏ's rise proved advantageous because it occurred after the Han Dynasty had passed its peak. From the first century BCE onward, Koguryŏ leaders managed to outmaneuver and outlast other regimes on their inland periphery, which enabled them to expand into the Sungari and Liao River basins. Their horsemen also rode eastward across Korea's mountainous interior to coastal lowlands in the vicinity of today's Hamhŭng, where they established tribute-collecting arrangements. Exemplifying Koguryŏ's extractive system, tribute from this last region included "sable, cloth, fish, salt, and seafood."[24]

---

[23] Rhee, 1992, p. 193.
[24] Nelson, 1993, p. 170.

Then, around 220 CE the Han Dynasty collapsed, to be followed by four centuries during which diverse strong men strove with only sporadic, partial, and transient success to impose order on the realm of China. With no overpowering neighborhood policeman to pound the uppity into line, Koguryŏ leaders were able to expand in more directions. By the fourth century they were pressing southward into the Taedong River basin, overrunning the enfeebled Lelang commandery in 313 and establishing control over the productive lowlands thereabouts.

By then the political scene throughout Korea was changing rapidly. Locally organized communities with their defensively walled headquarters had proliferated on the peninsula during earlier centuries, but gradually the more successful among their leaders gained control over more and more neighboring localities. Whether competition for tribute benefits intensified this neighborly conflict and accelerated the process of regional consolidation is unclear. But by 300 CE the process had eventuated in the emergence of three clearly identifiable political units on the peninsula south of Koguryŏ.

Just south of Lelang, astride the agriculturally productive river basins of western Korea was Paekche (see Plate 10), whose ruling elite developed an opulent aristocratic culture.[25] East of Paekche, along Korea's mountainous eastern coast, there gradually emerged a second polity, the spartan regime known as Silla. It arose in the vicinity of today's Kyŏngju (see Fig. 3-2), but the logic of its emergence is unclear. Its rise may well have been spurred, one way or another, by horse-riding immigrants from the north, and the archaeological evidence of nearby iron works suggests that people in that vicinity produced iron goods for exchange, perhaps with neighboring groups in Japan as well as on the peninsula.[26] Despite the limited agricultural capacity of their small, fertile valley, local leaders may have been able to turn this iron provisioning capacity into control over neighboring peoples, in the process forming a regional polity.

Finally, on a wedge of fertile territory in south central Korea, which embraced the Naktong River valley and the coastal strip west of today's Pusan, was Kaya, a collaborative cluster of farming-fishing-maritime trading communities.[27] Kaya leaders used the good iron

---

[25] On Paekche, see the forthcoming study by Jonathan Best.
[26] Barnes, 2001, pp. 218–24.
[27] On the archaeological evidence for Kaya, see Barnes, 2001, pp. 179–200.

mines in their area, together with their strategically advantageous
location between Lelang, Paekche, Silla, and southwestern Japan, to
carry on a lucrative entrepreneurial trade with their neighbors. They
handled it with enough skill, and defended themselves with enough
iron weaponry, so that these neighbors were for centuries content
to let the affluent but politically unconsolidated "city states" of Kaya
retain their autonomy.

The political disorder in and around China and the disruptions
that accompanied consolidation in Korea had effects that reached
beyond the peninsula into the islands of Japan. The turmoil appears
to have sustained human movement through Kaya and on across
the straits to western Japan. There small polities also arose, some of
them probably formed by locals and others by immigrants who seized
or developed their own agricultural-tribute bases. Leaders of these
communities then jockeyed for position, at times seeking recognition
and support from mainland authorities. The most famous of these
nascent regimes, commonly called Yamatai, was headed during the
230s–240s by a woman known as Himiko. Her regime was probably situated in northwestern Kyushu, and it seems to have functioned as the main element in an unstable political confederation
that mainlanders knew as Wa.[28] Other small polities also existed in
Kyushu, and additional ones arose along the Inland Sea, the Sea of
Japan littoral, and the lowland areas of central Honshu, some probably founded by locals, others by migrants from within or beyond
the archipelago.

By 300–350 CE, that is to say, locally organized elites existed all
across the Korea-Japan region, the major regional polities being
Koguryŏ, Paekche, Silla, and the "confederated" groupings of Kaya
and Wa. Developments of following decades then entangled the five
in harsh warfare that spurred yet more change.

B. *Regional Consolidation, 300–700 CE*

The escalation in warfare was triggered by Koguryŏ's southward
advance, which had by the mid-fourth century brought it into contact with the emerging states of Paekche and Silla. The resulting

---

[28] A vigorous argument can be made for Yamatai's location being in the Nara
Basin. See Edwards, 1996): 53–79. Also see Farris, 1998a, Ch. 1.

confrontations reshaped the political face of Korea and had ramifications that reached far across the straits to the center of Japan.

During the 370s Paekche leaders responded to Koguryŏ's advance by launching major assaults intended to drive their new neighbor out of the Taedong region. Their effort precipitated decades of fierce struggle that entangled Silla, Kaya, and Wa in recurrent warfare and a series of unstable alliances and alignments. The mounted forces of Koguryŏ continued to prove superior, however, especially under the command of Kwanggaet'o (r. 391–413), Koguryŏ's most celebrated ruler. Reputed to have conquered "sixty four fortress domains and 1,400 villages" in his two decades of rule, his battling extended Koguryŏ's domain further northeastward to the margins of Siberia and southward toward the Han River basin.[29]

Cumulatively Kwanggaet'o's battlefield triumphs served to shift the core of his dominion southward, and in 427 his son and successor moved Koguryŏ headquarters from the mountains of Manchuria down to P'yŏngyang, site of the former Lelang commandery headquarters. These developments spurred further political consolidation on the peninsula and prompted regional elites to form defensive alliances.

Most notably, leaders of Silla had for some decades been tightening their control of lesser "walled-town" regimes on the eastern side of Korea. In 433 they responded to Koguryŏ's encroachment by allying with Paekche and seeking ties to leaders in northern China. In following decades they continued to strengthen themselves, improving their military system and arranging their central government organization and district administration in ways akin to those already adopted by Paekche and Koguryŏ.

Silla's efforts notwithstanding, during the 470s Koguryŏ leaders again defeated their allied rivals in battle and extended their rule yet farther south by driving Paekche forces out of the Han River basin and confining the residual regime to a smaller area, essentially the Kŭm River watershed and southwest corner of Korea. By then, a half century after its move south from the Yalu, Koguryŏ seems to have lost much of its original character and become a more fully agriculture-based regime in the manner of its peninsular neighbors.

---

[29] Lee K-b, 1984, p. 38. A careful study of the Kwanggaet'o stele in Manchuria, source of these numbers, is Takeda, 1989.

However, its military successes had inspired decades of emulation, as evidenced in the southeastward spread of mounted warfare and its associated iron weapons and equestrian goods.

This peninsular turmoil continued to produce migrations across the straits to Kyushu, contributing to processes of regional consolidation in the islands. Most importantly, a regime that arose in the upper reaches of the Yamato River (in the Nara Basin, see Map 3-2) gradually extended its sway across adjoining areas. By 400 CE it was projecting power westward via waterways in the vicinity of present-day Osaka (see Map 2-4) and the Inland Sea. It seems to have done so primarily as a means of securing access to iron, which was produced and purveyed by figures in Kaya.[30] Yamato rulers could assure themselves the iron they needed for both military and productive purposes only if they could bypass or subdue regional rulers in Kyushu, probably the leaders of Wa. Their efforts sufficed: by the 450s they had acquired Koguryŏ's horse-warfare technology, and during following decades they extended durable control all across central Japan, westward into Kyushu and eastward into the Kantō region.

While Yamato was extending its sway, so too was Silla. Despite setbacks at the hands of Koguryŏ, its leaders continued to centralize their political organization, enlarge their military forces, and promote agriculture and trade to fund their expanding operations. In 532 they conquered part of the Kaya region and during the 550s launched broader conquests that by the mid-560s extended their control northeastward across the Hamhŭng Plain while also giving them control of the rich Han River basin and the rest of Kaya.

For a while thereafter the turmoil eased as the established regimes of Koguryŏ, Paekche, Silla, and Yamato pursued internal consolidation, diplomatic maneuvers, and quotidian governmental management. During the 580s, however, things began to change. In China a new unifying regime consolidated its position, ending some 350 years of political fragmentation, and by 620 that process had eventuated in formation of the Tang Dynasty. Tang was a behemoth whose hegemony reached from the Liao River basin in the

---

[30] A recent summary of trans-Strait material influences on Japan ca. 350–700 CE is Farris, 1998a, Ch. 2. Access to bronze also may have been an objective. Pearson, 1990, p. 921, reports that prior to about 600 CE all bronze originated on the continent.

northeast all the way southward into modern-day Vietnam and westward into the highlands of southwest China and the upper reaches of the Yellow River on the southern fringe of the Mongolian Plateau.

The reappearance of a super-power in the region created new dangers, tensions, and opportunities for leaders in Korea, and within decades the implications of this situation were realized. During the 660s Silla and Tang jointly mounted an attack on Paekche, defeated it in 663, and destroyed Koguryŏ five years later. When Tang moved to restore Han-style commanderies, however, Silla leaders recruited supporters from among their erstwhile rivals and succeeded in ousting Tang.[31] By 680 they had consolidated their control over all Korea south of the P'yŏngyang-Wŏnsan vicinity.

Silla's triumph had entailed the destruction of both Paekche and Koguryŏ, but while that outcome placed nearly all of peninsular Korea under one regime, it did not end the presence of a large regional power to its north. Rather, following their defeat by Silla, some Koguryŏ survivors are said to have retreated northward into the Manchurian part of their old dominion, where they established a new regime, in 713 giving it the name Parhae. Over the following century Parhae leaders bargained and battled with their neighbors, and by 800 they controlled a large swath of land that, as noted above, reached from the Liaodong Peninsula to the Siberian Maritime Provinces. Theirs was a substantial regional regime that amounted, in effect, to a latter-day Koguryŏ, but its center of gravity lay outside Korea.

China's reconsolidation and re-engagement in Korean affairs in the early 600s also had an impact on Japan, presenting Yamato rulers with some painful diplomatic choices. For generations they had maintained trade and diplomatic connections with the elites of Paekche and Kaya, and during the 530s–560s they were particularly dismayed when Silla overran Kaya. They took no effective action to prevent that outcome, but thereafter they tended to regard Silla as an unfriendly, or at least dangerous, force. Then, after a newly reconsolidated regime arose in China, Yamato leaders dispatched emissaries to gather useful information, learn the secrets of Chinese power, and establish advantageous connections. As Paekche-Silla relations worsened again during the 650s, however, Paekche's rulers

---

[31] The ambiguities of the Tang-Silla alliance are explored in Jamieson, 1970.

turned to Yamato for assistance, which eventuated during the early 660s in Yamato rulers despatching naval forces to assist Paekche in its resistance to the Silla-Tang alliance.

As noted above, Paekche went down to defeat in 663, and in the process the Yamato expeditionary force was smashed. That outcome compelled the survivors to flee back to Japan, together with members of the Paekche ruling house and other refugees. For nearly a decade after that rout Yamato leaders devoted their energies to defense preparations in anticipation of an invasion by Tang, Silla, or a combination of the two. In the end, however, that invasion did not occur, and from the 670s onward Yamato rulers turned their attention to domestic reform and consolidation, a project whose most visible symbol was the construction during 710–20 of a grand capital city at the site we know today as Nara.[32]

* * *

From time to time, then, this centuries-long process of political consolidation in Korea and Japan was shaped by the intrusion of powerful outside politico-military forces. For the most part, however, it seems to have been a process of local, piecemeal consolidation in which the relatively more able, fortunate, or ambitious managed— by one or another combination of weapons and wiles—to subordinate their neighbors, thereby acquiring a position as *primus inter pares*. Reflecting this situation, the political order that took shape in both areas involved a great deal of delegated power, with local strongmen commonly being confirmed in their control of particular populations and places in return for performance of specified obligations.

As centuries passed, the levels and expressions of political subordination grew more elaborate, gradually becoming systematized as hereditary aristocratic hierarchies. Much of the political history after 700 CE, as we shall see in Chapter 3, is a story of attempts by central rulers to impose more complete control over their hereditary subordinates and attempts by the ambitious among these latter to enhance their own positions at the expense of their betters or others in the ruling elite.

---

[32] A recent, detailed study of political consolidation in Japan, with a good bibliography of earlier works, is Piggott, 1997. On the issue of continental danger, see Batten, 1986.

Society and Environment to 700 CE

In both Korea and Japan the broader history of these centuries is poorly recorded, and much of our understanding must be inferred from artifacts that are basically remnants of elite culture. A smattering of evidence derives from written sources; most is archaeological, and the bulk of that comes from tombs of the favored few. The evidence sheds light on the character of ruling elites, and it reveals aspects of the cultural diffusion and material exchange that shaped social change during these centuries.

It sheds only the most tentative light, however, on broader issues of social structure and process, social well-being, and human-ecosystem interactions. For example, one could—but need not—infer that the gains in productivity that tillage and metallurgy yielded were almost entirely consumed in enhancing the material well-being of the ruling elite and in enabling its members to engage in ever more warfare, perhaps leaving the mass of producers in worse condition than before. The slender evidence, mainly from Japan, also suggests that in localities where ruling elites assembled, they surrounded themselves with such large populations of menial service personnel that as regional consolidation advanced, they overloaded local ecosystems. Excessive deforestation and land clearance produced early instances of erosion, flooding, wildfire, and soil depletion. And heightened population density, together with changes in patterns of travel and mingling, gave rise to early instances of pollution and epidemic disease.

A. *Elite Culture: Basic Aspects*

In both Korea and Japan two trends in elite history are evinced with particular clarity by the surviving cultural artifacts.[33] One is the formation of ruling groups and the celebration of their privileged position. The other, essentially a facet of that celebration of privilege, is a process commonly called Sinification, meaning adoption by the favored few of cultural attributes that they associated with China's rulers.[34] In combination the two trends fostered the social

---

[33] Cultural historians could rightly point out that the aesthetic qualities of these artifacts—the beauty of copper, gold, and glass creations, of ceramics and lacquerware—merit comment.

[34] For a recent and thoughtful exploration of "Sinification," see Holcombe, 2001.

and cultural distancing of ruling elites from the general population under their sway.

The former trend accompanied consolidation of regional states and was most strikingly evidenced in the construction and equipping of giant tombs whose size was roughly proportional to the power and glory of their occupants. While one can find evidence of cele-bratory tomb-building in earlier centuries, the heyday of large mounded tombs came around 300–500 CE, occurring first in Koguryŏ, later in southern Korea, and later yet in Japan. Although there was con-siderable regional variation in tomb materials and style and in their contents, in general the largest tombs became more grand as regimes waxed powerful and as the use of giant mounds to glorify rulers moved eastward from Koguryŏ to Silla and on to Yamato. The most stupendous mounded tombs were constructed in the Kinai Basin, being attributed to Yamato rulers of the early fifth century, most notably the Daisen Tomb (Nintokuryō), which survives as a low, man-made, moat-enclosed, 486-meter-long hill on the coastal plain south of present-day Osaka (see Map 2-4).

Decorated in diverse ways, equipped with various systems of inter-ment, and filled with varieties of goods to accompany the one or more deceased, these great tombs reveal the material elegance of the elite and their pretensions to grandeur. More stunningly, they stand as mute testimony to the tremendous amount of corvée labor that rulers were able to mobilize and put to work for months and months of manual exertion that had no real value for the laborers, their kinsmen, or neighbors. To what extent this capacity to mobilize labor reflected increased social productivity and to what extent a more complete exploitation of the subordinate populace is unclear.

Sinification—the emulation and adaptation of cultural practices derived from the elite of one or another Chinese regime—was a shadowy process that dates back at least to the era of Lelang. Essen-tially it was but one manifestation, by far the most visible, of the more general process of multi-directional cultural diffusion and inter-penetration that had long been occurring in northeast Asia, as it did (and still does) everywhere in the world.

This process, which elites pursued with varying degrees of zeal and thoroughness, became pronounced from about the time regional rulers began utilizing Chinese systems of administrative organization. Along with these systems they appropriated methods of official rank-ing and reward, embraced Chinese styles of architecture and urban

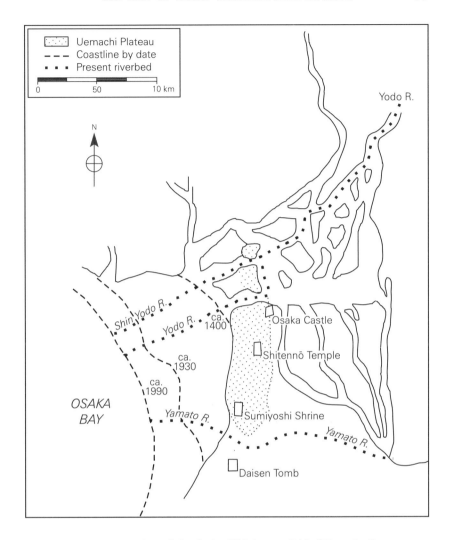

Map 2-4. *Formation of the Osaka Vicinity, ca. 700 CE to the Present.*
During post-Pleistocene millennia coastal waters in the Osaka vicinity gradually filled with sediments. The region east of Uemachi Plateau (a strip of
coastal dune about 3×12 kilometers in area) was largely filled in by ca. 700
CE, as both the Yamato and Yodo rivers deposited debris in the remaining shallows east of today's Osaka Castle (#A). By 1400 most of the area
was filled out to the west flank of Uemachi (coastline #a). During following centuries the silt-line moved farther west, especially during the twentieth
century when aggressive land-filling for industrial purposes extended it all
along the nearby shore (to coastline #c). Based on Map #3 in McClain
and Wakita, 1999, p. 4, Map #31–3 in Tōkyō kaiseikan, 1941, p. 42, *Nihon
annai*, 1965, pp. 62–63, and *Osaka-fu*, 1992, frontispiece.

design, adopted Chinese art, garb, and finery, subscribed to Confucian ideas of government, and started promoting Chinese Buddhist and other religious notions as an aid to governance and personal well-being. These trends were evident in Paekche and Koguryŏ before 400 CE, and during the following century they spread to Silla and Japan. By 700 CE large rectangular capital cities that surrounded fine palace enclosures were established or were in process of development on both the peninsula and archipelago, along with grand Buddhist temple compounds, elaborate hierarchies of government officialdom, written rules and regulations for officials to follow, and schools to teach Chinese-language literacy and promote Confucian, Buddhist, and other teachings.

B. *Trade*

In both Korea and Japan, as noted in Chapter 1, trade—meaning here the purposeful exchange of material goods and services with people beyond one's communal group—long antedated the development of agriculture and metallurgy. From the outset it appears to have had a symbiotic relationship with technology and social arrangements, both shaping and being shaped by them.

During the terminal Pleistocene melt-off, the desire to trade may well have encouraged the devising of techniques for maritime travel, specifically the use of dugout vessels and rafts, the latter consisting of logs lashed together with vines to form wider and longer floating platforms that were propelled and steered by oar.[35] It subsequently contributed to the diffusion of other types of technology, knowledge, and elite culture, changes of life style and material standards of living, and changes in the form and scale of human dealings with the environment.

Conversely, during that final melt-off, this maritime technology enabled commerce in stone points, salt, and foodstuffs to continue despite the resubmergence of coastal Korea and Japan, and it permitted the later broadening of trade to include ceramics, sea-shell products, and more diverse stone and bone items. This trade embraced the myriad islands and islets of Japan and the islands, estuaries, and convoluted coastlines of Korea, and it reached as far afield as Siberia,

---

[35] Farris, pending-I, p. 8.

continental China, and the Ryukyu chain. Millennia later, when the mastery of metallurgy enabled craftsmen to develop and use saws, axes, chisels, hammers, nails, and metal clamps, mariners began to enlarge their dugouts by attaching planks atop their walls. And eventually they began using constructed plank vessels that could carry larger cargoes and travel more swiftly and surely over long distances.

The development of trade was also fostered by the earlier-noted Chinese diplomatic system of tribute relations, which bound elites together through mutually advantageous transactions. This mechanism was then adopted by regimes in Korea and Japan when dealing with one another. Doing so was not always easy because tribute relations were grounded in the notion of suzerain and vassal rather than that of peer relations, and those regional polities were in fact more equal than unequal; none was suzerain vis à vis the others.[36] It appears, however, that polite fictions obscured this awkwardness sufficiently to permit regimes and their collaborators to engage in exchange. More importantly, perhaps, elites in the Kaya "city states" may have used their central position and non-threatening political status, as well as their control of iron resources, to play an important role as entrepreneurial intermediaries. This may help explain why rulers in Paekche, Silla, Wa, and later Yamato dealt so extensively through Kaya leaders, for generations leaving the communities there independent despite their apparent vulnerability to easy conquest.

In any case, recurrent political disorder notwithstanding, trade persisted during the centuries to 700 CE, growing in scale together with the general population and the ruling elites. It played a role—along with conquerors, refugees, and mendicants—in the dissemination of stone, metal, and other technology, innumerable luxury items, slaves, foodstuffs, textiles, and other craft goods, and eventually books, religious icons, and works of art. Much of the trade, like much of the artisanal work, was handled by government agencies, but entrepreneurial activity was also present, and that pattern of mixed sponsorship continued to be evident in the commerce of later centuries.

Finally, one should note that by contributing to the spread of relevant knowhow and technology, and by enabling producers to dispose of goods and consumers to obtain them, trade contributed to

---

[36] Tōno, 1995, looks at the awkwardness of the tribute system in the Japanese case. Rogers, 1961, reveals it in the later case of Koryŏ. Lewis, 1985, notes it in the post-1600 period.

environmental change. It facilitated the spread of mining, logging, land clearance, water management for paddy culture, and their environmental ramifications of habitat modification and loss, biotic change, soil erosion, flooding, drought, and wildfire.

C. *Population and Environment*

The key human variable in human/ecosystem relations is the scale of demand that people make on the biosystem.[37] The two key determinants of this demand are population size and the level of consumption per capita. Unfortunately, we have satisfactory figures or information for neither of these factors in early Korea and Japan.

Regarding demand per capita, that ruling elites constituted an ever-greater burden is amply evidenced in data on the volume and variety of their goods and the scale of their construction and war-making activities. For the vast majority of people, however, we have only a minimal amount of evidence suggesting that their housing improved a bit, their diet became more varied, and their ornamentation increased somewhat. It was primarily through their productive activities that the general public increased its demand per capita. Specifically the adoption of tillage and metallurgy increased sharply the burden that an individual producer made upon his or her surroundings, regardless of whether the resulting yield benefited producer or political master.

Demographic information is no more satisfactory, not even establishing the size of ruling elites in the region. Back in the 1970s, however, the authors of a statistical study of global population made educated guesses at the populations of early Korea and Japan, basically by employing general principles of demographic change to calculate backward to the beginnings of agriculture from plausible figures of recent centuries. On that slender basis they suggested that until about 500 BCE Korea held some 10,000 people and Japan around 400 BCE some 30,000.[38] With the spread of agriculture, they estimated, the numbers grew as Figure 2-1 indicates. By 700 CE, the

---

[37] Human demand is perhaps best calculated in terms of the portion of a biosystem's energy-cycling activity that is redirected to human purposes or otherwise disrupted by human conduct. But one can also approach it in terms of habitat destruction, biomass loss, biodiversity decline, or a combination of these.

[38] McEvedy and Jones, 1978, pp. 176, 179.

Fig. 2-1. *Population Estimates, 200 BCE–800 CE*

YEAR	KOREA	JAPAN
200 BCE	100,000	100,000
0 CE	200,000	300,000
400 CE	500,000	1,500,000
600 CE	1,000,000	3,000,000
800 CE	2,000,000	4,000,000

Source: McEvedy and Jones, 1978, pp. 177, 181.

human population was thus approaching 1.5 million in Korea and 3.5 million in Japan.

Today these numbers pose some problems. Most pertinently here, more recent scholarship indicates that the introduction of agriculture, and hence the onset of rapid population increase, occurred, particularly in Korea, a few centuries earlier than these authors assumed. That re-dating would raise the postulated population for several centuries thereafter, and while estimates do differ, scholars now place Japan's population ca. 700 CE at some 5 million and that of Korea at perhaps 2 million.

Even those estimates perplex, however. Given the earlier onset of agriculture in Korea, one would expect it to become and remain the more populace area, at least into the early centuries CE. Although the archipelago is larger than the peninsula, the latter has perhaps 70% as much arable, and as of 700 CE much good crop land remained unopened in both places. Perhaps Korea's population remained smaller due to the climatic differences noted in Chapter 1, which could have led to more frequent crop failure and famine on the peninsula.

Or perhaps Korea's population remained smaller because residents there were more exposed to imported epidemic disease than were the islanders to their east, with the resultant illness and mortality restraining demographic growth. One can only speculate, however, for a couple of reasons. Most obviously, records are scanty, and those few report mainly on affairs of the favored few, shedding little or no light on the condition of the general populace. Less obviously, symptomology is, at best, a profoundly inexact science. Random references to sweats, coughing, sore throat, respiratory difficulties, bodily swelling, boils or other skin eruptions or lesions, diarrhea, bloody stools or urine, poisons, plagues, contagions and so on are crude guides to particular pathologies and hence to estimates of probable mortality rates.[39] And finally, the interplay of disease, famine, and other variables is intricate, and cause-and-effect often ambiguous. When members of a famine-ravaged populace succomb to influenza, for example, should we credit the hunger or the pathogen with the outcome? Or, when villagers die from malaria, should we blame the pathogen, the paddy culture, or a ravenous tax collector?

There may, however, be another, ultimately socio-political explanation for Japan's relatively more rapid population growth. Scholarly studies suggest that a substantial and sustained migration moved people from Korea to Japan throughout these centuries. Indeed, one scholar has suggested that the rate may have averaged well over 1,000 migrants per year.[40] Such a continuing exodus from Korea could explain the archipelago's more rapid demographic increase. And while migrants might have fled to escape starvation, one should perhaps look not to the issue of crop failure so much as the level of elite exploitation or the magnitude and persistence of political violence during these centuries for an explanation of the continuing emigration and such demographic consequences as it had.[41]

In the future, scholars doubtless will continue to recalibrate their population estimates, but perhaps the important point for us is that in neither Korea nor Japan did populations of this—or even much greater—magnitude pose a serious threat to the overall ecosystem. In subsequent centuries, using basically similar but more intensive agricultural and metallurgical techniques, the producer populations in Korea and Japan were to reach several times these levels. And they did so while supporting much larger and more self-indulgent elites and the proliferation of intermediate status groups. Yet they continued to function tolerably well, only gradually and irregularly precipitating environmental troubles of one sort or another that suggested by the 1700s a more basic trend to ecological overload, as we note in Chapter 4.

---

[39] A convenient source of information on disease in pre-industrial Korea and Japan is the sections by Lois N. Magner (on Korea) and W. Wayne Farris and Ann Bowman Jannetta (on Japan) in Kiple, 1993, pp. 376–408.

[40] Hanihara, 1987, pp. 394–96. Hanihara offers a range of estimates, from about 100 to 3,000 immigrants per year, arguing that the higher end of the range is more compelling.

[41] The sense of a violent political history that could well have slowed population growth and prompted flight of this magnitude and duration is nicely suggested by Lee K-b, 1984, Ch. 2–4.

Insofar as population growth to 700 CE posed an environmental problem, it surely did so because it was overly concentrated in particular localities. And even there the crux of the issue may have been the high level of elite demand per capita more than the large number of local residents. The Taedong River basin, for example, supported for centuries the elegant life style of the Chinese immigrants and collaborating Korean locals of Lelang as well as the bare-bones lives of the minions who serviced them. Deforestation of hills in that region could well have precipitated substantial erosion and downstream flooding. The Kaya vicinity sustained centuries of busy trading and iron producing and provisioning activity, and it could well have experienced considerable deforestation and wildfire in conjunction with the metal work.[42]

Across the straits, northwest Kyushu, which was the major settlement site for emigrants from Korea and probably the core area of the Wa confederation, experienced a rapid spread of land reclamation and conversion to paddy culture, and that trend entailed substantial changes in the region's biotic composition. Further east the Nara Basin supported the pretensions of the fifth-century Yamato elite, those celebrated builders of gigantic tombs. By 700 AD their land-clearance activity, construction work, and fuel-wood demands appear to have stripped most of the region's lowland of good timber, spurring the logging of steep hillsides with malign downstream consequences.[43] In particular areas such as these, one can imagine appreciable amounts of deforestation, soil erosion, and terrestrial biotic disturbance. And those developments foreshadowed the future fully as much as did the rise of competing regional elites or an elegant aristocratic culture.

It is worth noting, moreover, that terrestrial disturbance also affected marine biosystems. In Korea, as mentioned in Chapter 1, sedimentation slowly intruded on, relocated, and modified coastal wet lands, especially on the peninsula's shallow western seaboard. In Japan similar processes were at work, building shoreline and rearranging wetland near river mouths, especially after the commencement of agricultural land clearance. Thus, as Map 2-4 indicates, much of the

---

[42] Unfortunately, these speculations are just that, to my knowledge having no foundation in recorded evidence.

[43] Totman, 2000, pp. 84–86.

interior area of Osaka Bay was already built up as delta deposits by 700 CE. In subsequent centuries sedimentation completed the filling-in of what are today the eastern reaches of Osaka city. The coverage of wetlands then continued to the west, doing so most rapidly after the commencement of industrial-age landfill operations.

Recapitulation

Centuries of horticulture and metal use wrought striking changes in Korea and Japan. The human population grew briskly and experienced substantial stratification. Ruling elites emerged and created powerful regimes that enjoyed considerable success in securing their hereditary privilege. Whether for the populace as a whole material standards of living or a sense of well-being rose or fell is perhaps impossible to say. But clearly the basic rhythms of life changed as foraging gave way to farming and as one's labor output came under the fuller control of higher authority.

Looking at the realm more broadly, by 700 CE most coastal lowlands and valley bottoms of peninsular Korea and the southern half of Japan had been at least partly opened to tillage. In those areas a mix of cultivated crops, diverse weeds, and opportunistic growth on fallowed land had replaced high forest and its understory. Doubtless some fauna had been displaced, but other birds, small animals, insects, and other creatures found agreeable habitat in the miles of forest edge and paddy fields that had appeared. Certainly the biological composition of lowland areas had shifted in favor of the human-centered biotic community, but as a whole the lowland biosystem may well have gained rather than lost in terms of both biodiversity and biomass production.

On the other hand, in the vicinity of the new political centers, with their dense populations and higher rates of consumption per capita, it seems likely that excessive land clearance and deforestation were beginning to promote hillside deterioration, soil erosion, downstream flooding and drought, and increased likelihood of wildfire. At least, these trends became clearly evident in later years, as we shall see in Chapter 3.

CHAPTER THREE

THE EARLY AGRICULTURAL ORDER (700–1350 CE)

The centuries from 700 to around 1350 CE witnessed the flourishing and failure of early agricultural regimes that are today celebrated primarily for the political and cultural accomplishments of their ruling urban elites. In both Korea and Japan, as noted in Chapter 2, forceful regional chieftains had by 700 battled and bargained their way to supremacy, establishing three unified hegemonial regimes that spanned the region (see Map 2–3). Manchuria-centered Parhae controlled the northern continental portion of today's Korea while Silla, headquartered near the southeast coast at Kyŏngju (called Kŭmsŏng at the time), controlled all of the peninsular portion. In Japan a government known as the *ritsuryō* ("penal and civil codes") regime, which originally was headquartered at Nara and after 794 in Heian (the later Kyoto), controlled a realm that reached from Kyushu well into northeast Honshu. The areas beyond there remained politically unconsolidated, although local forms of communal organization likely existed in the far northeast.

For a century or two these regimes flourished, but by the year 900 all were experiencing difficulty. In Korea, both Parhae and Silla collapsed, Parhae in 926 due to foreign assault and Silla in 935 due mainly to regional and intra-elite rivalries. Koryŏ, the successor regime, was headquartered at Kaesŏng (called Kaegyŏng at the time), among Korea's western lowlands. It took over all of Silla's territory and the most productive part—the Taedong River basin—of Parhae, leaving a gradually shrinking corner of northeast Korea in the hands of successive Manchurian regimes. For more than two centuries Koryŏ leaders managed to control their enlarged realm, but during the 1170s internal tensions culminated in a coup by military leaders, followed by decades of martial rule and then domination by Mongol invaders until 1356.

In Japan, meanwhile, the *ritsuryō* regime, which slowly extended its influence northeastward, outlived Silla. From about 900 onward, however, it underwent substantial changes in its ruling arrangements as members of the elite and would-be-elite grew more numerous, more diverse, and more fractious in their competition for advantage. By the 1150s, military men were acquiring decisive roles in settling factional quarrels among aristocrats, and by 1200 the old elite of Heian was sharing power in a clumsy and unstable manner with a military regime headquartered at Kamakura in eastern Japan, an arrangement that lasted into the 1330s.

For the producers who sustained these ruling elites, affairs were also changing. In both Korea and Japan tillers reclaimed more and more land, gradually putting more acreage into paddy fields and enlarging total output. Elite demands for tribute always seemed to keep pace, however, contributing to a generally difficult living situation. As long as unreclaimed and uncultivated lands were available, the disgruntled and destitute could—and did—abscond to new locations or become "wanderers," evading tribute levies by drifting about, peacefully for the most part, until they died or found a place to set-tle or a master to serve. As unopened land became scarce, however, flight became less and less of an option. Instead, as arable came to be more fully utilized and the squeezing by elite tribute takers inten-sified, one sees the rise, especially from the 1100s onward, of diverse forms of sedition, including tax evasion, banditry, piracy, and local insurrection. And one begins to see, in Japan at least, the first signs of that intensifying of horticultural practice that came to character-ize the later agricultural order, which we examine in Chapter 4.

Whereas the stories of elite politics and culture are richly docu-mented, the broader topic of social process is recorded only spo-radically, and much must be inferred. The yet larger subject of human-environment relations is even less evidenced, especially for

Korea, and we rely heavily on the Japanese side to construct a tentative story of environmental change.

A concise reconstruction of the overall history of these centuries is difficult in part because evidence is slender but perhaps in greater part because, while the Korean and Japanese stories are similar in their basics, they differ in some noteworthy particulars. It may help, therefore, to approach this topic in terms of an era when the regimes functioned reasonably well, roughly during the years 700–1150, and an era when they were wracked by disorder and disintegration, roughly 1150–1350.

The Heyday of Aristocratic Bureaucracy (700–1150)

The elite politics and culture of these centuries are intrinsically interesting. They also warrant attention because they have broader social and ecological significance: policies and performance of the rulers bore directly and heavily on the lives of the general populace and had both direct and indirect impacts on the ecosystems of Korea and Japan. Conversely, needless to say, the broader social and environmental contexts also influenced elite affairs.

A. *Political Structure and Process*

The political experiences of Silla, Koryŏ, and the Nara/Heian *ritsuryō* order command our attention. Parhae, however, need not.[1] Although it was a sprawling, diplomatically influential northeast Asian presence during its heyday, it was at heart a Manchurian regime, with its headquarters on the Mutan, a branch of the Sungari River in the mountains of eastern Manchuria near today's Tunhua (see Map 2–2). Most of the Korean area it controlled was a relatively unpopulated and undeveloped highland, which it seems to have treated as a marginal, tribute-bearing hinterland. Most of agricultural Korea lay within Silla's sphere, and nearly all came under control of Koryŏ, with the consequence that the longer-term story of Korea's history played out around the vicissitudes of those two regimes and the area they dominated.

---

[1] On Parhae, see Song K-h, 1990a and 1990b.

The regimes of Silla, Koryŏ, and Nara/Heian can be called "aristocratic bureaucracies," a label that suggests their "hybrid" character. In part they were centralized monarchies with elaborate bureaucratic structures whose designated realms of authority reached from palace to paddy field. But in part they were consociations of aristocratic, landholding patrilineages that collaborated or competed with one another and with the monarchy and its core functionaries, depending on what policy seemed most advantageous to lineage leaders at a given moment. The semi-complementary, semi-competitive relationship of monarchial households and aristocratic lineages was reflected in both the way these regimes organized systems of rank, office holding, and land control and the way domestic political conflict and disorder waxed and waned as decades passed.

This basic similarity of the three regimes notwithstanding, there also were differences among them. And needless to say all three changed as decades passed. The differences among them reflected dissimilarities in how the monarchial lineages won their supremacy, dissimilarities that shaped the particulars of the regimes' internal structure and function, patterns of conflict, and eventual dissolution.

In the case of Silla, during the 660s, as noted in Chapter 2, its kings suddenly faced the challenge of repelling Tang and absorbing into their political system large new territories; namely, the well organized area of former Paekche and the fertile southern end of former Koguryŏ. To that end they (most notably King Sinmun during the 680s) adopted more elaborate forms of administrative organization, strove to incorporate elites from the conquered areas, and attempted to transfer Silla's capital from its isolated Kyŏngju site to a more central location.

Silla's kings won acceptance of their new administrative arrangements in part by incorporating aristocratic lineages at mutually acceptable levels. They evidently were unable, however, to persuade Silla grandees to move westward from Kyŏngju, even to Taegu in the upper reaches of the Naktong River basin (see Map 3-1).[2] Accordingly they settled for the creation of branch headquarters, a strategy that helped perpetuate the influence of lineage leaders from outlying areas, notably the former Paekche and Koguryŏ regions. To offset this concession to local power, the kings promoted a sort of hostage system

---

[2] Eckert, 1990, p. 49.

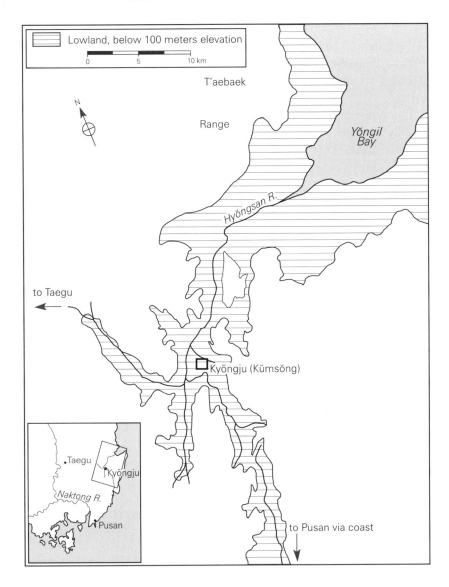

Map 3-1. *The Kyŏngju Vicinity.*
Kyŏngju was established at the confluence of three small branches of the
northward-flowing Hyŏngsan River. Narrow river valleys lead westward to
Taegu and southward via the coast to Pusan. Based on Barnes, 2001, maps
at pp. 207, 225.

by inviting regional grandees to settle in Kyŏngju. As a whole this arrangement surely facilitated the incorporation of elites from the conquered areas, but it also provided a foundation for regionalist political movements, should changing circumstances seem to invite them.[3]

By comparison the external threats to creators of the *ritsuryō* regime usually seemed distant, and the process of territorial expansion was more gradual. By the early 700s they, too, had developed an "aristocratic bureaucratic" structure that proved serviceable. But their regime, like Silla's, still had weaknesses that eventually led to major change. Specifically, although they managed to subordinate regional elites to the center, their polity contained a small cluster of powerfully entrenched patrilineages whose chiefs used their very closeness to the throne to manipulate government in their own favor, thereby accumulating great autonomous wealth and power. Main lines of the celebrated Fujiwara family did this with the most spectacular success for several generations, but from about 1050 onward members of the monarchial family itself became the most energetic builders of landed estates under household control.

This scramble for estates undercut the treasury's control of the tribute supply, and Heian leaders tried to counter the trend by granting provincial governors more authority, in effect converting them into tax farmers. But that policy served to shift more power into the hands of local grandees even as it capped treasury receipts. The competition for landed assets also led to intensified inter-lineage rivalries that entangled Buddhist temples and professional military forces, which lineage leaders recruited and paid to defend their interests. By 1150 the rivalries were getting severely out of hand, and within a generation key military figures had acquired substantial autonomous power and authority, which they exercised after 1185 through their "shogunal" regime (*bakufu*), headquartered at Kamakura.

In Silla, meanwhile, the lines of political fracture were somewhat different. There regionalism resurfaced during the late 800s in breakaway attempts to found a "Later Paekche" and "Later Koguryŏ." It was the latter venture that ultimately led to the founding of Koryŏ.[4]

---

[3] Standard texts note the regional issue in Silla. See also Salem, 1975. For Japan, where *ritsuryō* leaders faced periodic but far weaker breakaway threats in Kyushu and northeast Honshu, see Totman, 2000, p. 612, under "regional secessionism."

[4] A careful study of the Koryŏ political system is Duncan, 2000, which will lead

From the outset, however, this new regime followed much the same path as early Silla, with consolidation entailing a mixture of confirming aristocratic lineages in their land-holding and status privileges while drawing them into the new regime's bureaucratic structure and building marriage alliances with as many of them as possible. Only gradually and in a piecemeal fashion did early Koryŏ kings extend effective central control outward from Kaesŏng into the former heartland of Silla, in the outcome reaffirming the basic pattern of aristocratic bureaucracy.

Whereas the *ritsuryō* order fragmented along the lines of major lineages and Silla realized its regionalist breakaway potential, Koryŏ developed yet a different set of fault lines. Facing recurrent armed attacks from Manchurian groups that sought to establish control over the former Parhae territories north of Kaesŏng, Koryŏ gradually acquired a substantial military elite. At the same time, the civil aristocrats who dominated the bureaucratic order were enhancing their own power and cultivating the anti-military prejudices embodied in Confucian political thought. From around 1000 onward, professional resentments and rivalries for power, prestige, and privilege waxed and waned, culminating in the coup of 1170 that placed military men in control of the dynasty.[5] By 1200, then, Korea and Japan had, via dissimilar paths, reached similar outcomes of military-dominated governments.

The variations in particulars notwithstanding, leaders of these aristocratic bureaucracies had succeeded in elaborating administrative systems that lasted for generations. They delineated formal status hierarchies that reached from princely household to peasant hut, and they fitted this system of ranks to the staffing of government. In all three regimes, small groups of highly ranked, richly landed, handsomely stipended aristocrats and monarchial kin held the topmost positions in the capital cities while large numbers of much less well treated officials held lower posts in subordinate central, provincial, and district offices. Regulations spelled out how the chains of command thus staffed were to reach from the throne downward through layers of officialdom to lands and people in the hinterland. The regulations also sorted out civil and military functions, assigning

one to earlier works. On its founding, see also Kang H, 1974 and 1977, and Rogers, 1983.

[5] Shultz, 1979; also Shultz, 2000, Ch. 1.

the latter to appropriately subordinated posts in the hierarchies of command.

In both Silla and the *ritsuryō* order rulers developed durable tribute-collecting mechanisms by conducting censuses of village populations and surveys of land, trees, and other valued assets.[6] They drafted and implemented regulations that spelled out how much tribute—rice, cloth, other local products, and corvée labor—each surveyed village was to provide and how it was to be delivered, stored, and distributed to recipients. They built storage warehouses in the hinterland, at provincial and regional offices, and in their capital cities, and they promoted the development of roads and waterways to expedite shipment of tribute goods and people.

Reflecting the three regimes' origins in the interplay of consolidating monarchs and resistant local grandees, land-control regulations identified several categories of land, thereby accommodating both the land-control claims that monarchs had successfully asserted and the concessions they had made to secure aristocratic acquiescence to reform.[7] The categories of land varied greatly among the three; furthermore, their application changed as decades passed. And everywhere diverse forms of concealment and deception persisted. In essence, however, regulations identified three categories of lands and producers: those whose tribute payments went to provincial and central warehouses to support the monarch, his (or her) household, and the governing apparatus; those whose payments went (whether via government warehouse or directly) to aristocratic officialdom as office stipend or merit reward; and those whose payments went directly to aristocrats—and increasingly to Buddhist monasteries and professional soldiers—as hereditary household income.

One way or another, that is to say, tribute was funneled upward to the social elite, doing so in a manner that served the interests of both monarch and aristocrat. Together with the other aspects of aristocratic bureaucracy, these land arrangements enabled ruling elites of the day to erect handsome capital cities, and they facilitated the rise of flourishing elite cultures that even today continue to command the admiration of afficionadoes.

---

[6] The *ritsuryō* system for registering land and people is treated in standard sources. See, for example, Torao, 1993. The few remaining village registers for Silla are discussed in a valuable essay by Kim C, 1979.

[7] Standard texts discuss the Korean and Japanese land-control systems. See also Palais, 1982–83, on Koryŏ.

B. *Elite Culture*

The higher culture—arts and letters—of aristocratic bureaucracy was basically an urban culture of the favored few, and it was centered in the successive capital cities of Silla, Koryŏ, and the *ritsuryō* order. From about 700 onward these ruling elites lived in cities laid out in the rectangular manner then favored by Chinese monarchs. In both Korea and Japan these cities gathered into a single integrated space influential lineages that previously had been only semi-clustered in the vicinity of royal households. Their number was supplemented with landholding grandees lured from the hinterland and with the large service population that sustained their newly urbanized betters.

In pre-660s Silla, the ruling group appears to have clustered along the edges of the small but salubrious, gently vista'd, low-lying, and fertile valley of the Hyŏngsan River, some twenty kilometers upstream from Yŏngil Bay on the Sea of Japan (see Map 3-1). King Munmu (r. 661–681) laid out on the valley floor a rectangular capital that covered, by one scholarly calculation, some 80 hectares of land.[8] Within its boundaries he placed an enclosed palace ground, while major temples and the numerous mansions and other buildings of the aristocracy, together with the undistinguished dwellings and work sites of the supporting population of lesser folk, filled the rest of the site and probably sprawled out into the nearby valleys.

Compared to contemporary Chinese capitals, Kyŏngju was a modest creation. Built in a small valley and poorly accessible to major sources of rice and other necessities, it could have sustained only a small fraction of the one million inhabitants that older scholarship once envisioned.[9] But compared to earlier political headquarters in Korea, it was huge and stunning in its opulence and grace. It was said that within Kyŏngju there was, "not a single thatched roof house but instead unbroken lines of tiled houses with enclosed courtyards, while the never-ending sounds of music and song filled the streets night and day."[10]

---

[8] Barnes, 2001, pp. 207, 217–18, 224–27. For comparison, Central Park in New York City covers some 340 hectares; the Yoshiwara entertainment district in Edo covered 12 hectares.

[9] Nelson, 1993, p. 244, is a recent iteration of this figure.

[10] Lee K-b, 1984, p. 78. The words appear to be Lee's paraphrasing of an original source.

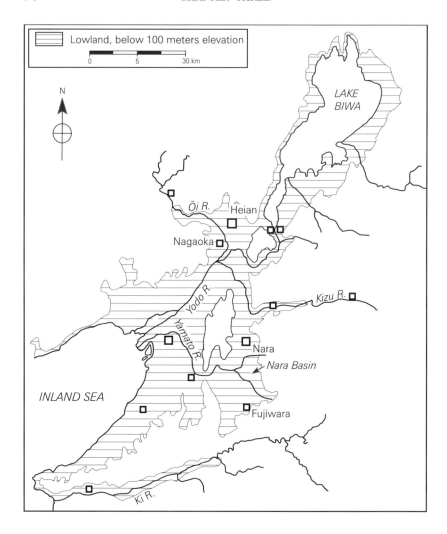

Map 3-2. *The Kinai Basin.*
Yamato rulers built a succession of capital cities, initially Fujiwara but most
famously Nara and Heian, in the Kinai Basin, meaning the watershed of
the Yamato and Yodo rivers and their tributaries. Based on Map #7 of
Nihon Rekishi, 1961.

In Japan the Yamato ruling elite had clustered near lovely rolling
foothills in the southeast corner of the Nara Basin (see Map 3-2).
Starting in the 680s its monarchs launched similar but larger building
projects, using comparable rectangular layouts. The first of these pro-

jects to achieve full fruition was that begun in 708 by the monarch Genmei (r. 708–715). By the 720s that grandiose venture had given her regime a huge capital, Nara, that sprawled over some 2,000 hectares.

Yamato monarchs were able to launch these grand projects because their regime had direct access to large populations of corvée labor, the agricultural output of extensive nearby lowlands, and timber from surrounding hill country, which could be transported to the construction site by river and ox cart. Even with these advantages the building of Nara proved an immense drain on society and ecosystem. Authoritarian will prevailed, however, and the city was built, complete with broad avenues, grand gates, sprawling palaces and aristocratic mansions, numerous temples great and small, and back streets lined with the undistinguished lodgings of diverse service personnel. Nara came to house an estimated population of 100,000, most of them minor people who looked after the needs of the several thousand members of the city's titled aristocracy.

Like governmental organization, then, the new style of capital city owed much to Chinese antecedents. Other facets of elite life and culture also reflected this external influence. Most basically these ruling elites adopted the pictographic Chinese written language for their official script, using it in government regulations, official histories and correspondence, learned discourse, and parts of their recreational writing, most notably poetry.

Both the Korean and Japanese languages are radically different from spoken Chinese in sound, syntax, and means of inflection, so the use of written Chinese dictated the use of spoken Chinese in situations that involved writing. It created an awkward bilingualism that encumbered ruling groups with burdensome linguistic tasks even as it distanced them yet further from hoi polloi. It also introduced complexity and ambiguity into elite Korean and Japanese perceptions of China, Chinese culture, and its proponents, both at home and abroad, and that complexity persisted thereafter.

Elite acceptance of the Chinese language was more complete in Korea than Japan. On the peninsula it appears to have become a lingua franca, at least for all literate activities. Not until the fifteenth century was a rational and efficient alphabet (han'gŭl) for representing spoken Korean devised, and even then the literate few chose to continue using the Chinese they had worked so hard to master and that set them apart from lesser folk. Not until the twentieth century did han'gŭl (alone or combined with pictographs) become the established writing system of Korea. In Japan the process of devising ways to represent the native language began much earlier, and it proceeded not by radical innovation but by incremental tinkering that slowly modified the spoken language even as it gave rise to a changing, hybrid writing system that combined pictographs with a syllabary (*kana*). Today a standardized form of this hybrid system constitutes the Japanese written language.[11]

Unsurprisingly, elite adoption of Chinese script was accompanied by an influx of Chinese thought. This included the philosophical systems of Confucianism, Daoism, and *yin/yang* notions of genderized phenomena, as well as Chinese literary styles, most famously of poetry and history writing. Chinese art forms, including music, dance, painting, sculpture, and architecture also were adopted, with the most important vehicle for these forms being institutional Buddhism. As with script, these new elements then began long complicated journeys of interplay with indigenous cultural practices and preferences to produce distinctive forms of oral, literary, and visual cultural expression.

In both Korea and Japan Buddhism added rich new dimensions of religious thought and sensibility to the indigenous systems of shamanism and polytheistic spiritual praxis. More importantly for our purposes, the creed also brought major material and institutional changes as grand temples and pagodas, myriad statues, religious paintings, and other ritual devices were produced, and as landed assets and their producers were assigned to support the proliferating monasteries and their populations of monks and support personnel.[12]

C. *The Broader Society*

It is tempting, of course, to view these societies in simple dyadic terms of rulers and ruled, or literate elite and illiterate mass. And in gross terms that approach has merit. In fact, however, as the formal ranking systems suggest, the societies of both Korea and Japan were much more variegated than that. In both, as noted above, the elite was elaborately differentiated, ranging from the few lavishly

---

[11] A fine collection of essays on the history, structure, and logic of *han'gŭl* is Kim-Renaud, 1997. A scholarly study of the evolution of writing in Japan, with a valuable bibliography of earlier works, is Seeley, 1991.

[12] On the rise of Buddhist institutions in Korea, see Ahn, 1991, pp. 1–6.

endowed royals and senior aristocrats to the far more numerous, much more modestly funded lesser aristocrats and regional grandees.[13]

The rest of society was predominantly agricultural households, most of them clustered loosely in hamlets whose size tended to reflect the extent of nearby arable land. For purposes of tribute extraction, as earlier noted, the rulers implemented censuses and land surveys, and they tried to organize—or at least to conceptualize—the hinterland population in systematic terms of so many households within each political district, so many persons per household, and so much land of one or another type per household member. In fact in both Silla and Nara these formulations were mainly statistical fictions used in calculating tribute obligations rather than expressions of reality. But for a century or more they served that fiscal purpose tolerably well.

The hinterland population was diverse. It included the households of local strongmen who controlled appreciable parcels of land with their resident cultivators. Far more numerous were small holders, *de facto* tenant farmers, and landless laborers, with these last being the most mobile and constituting most of the "vagrants" of the day. On the margins of the peasantry were coastal residents who fished, produced sea salt, and furnished sea transport and in mountainous areas hunter-foragers who provided pelts and diverse other goods for the lowland populace. From this mixed population the rulers assembled both the corvée labor required by their construction projects and the conscript soldiers stipulated in militia regulations.

Silla and Nara/Heian (and Koryŏ in its day) also included a varied array of artisans and traders. The elite controlled such commerce as existed, and of it the most visible part was the official inter-state trade that occurred on tribute missions. This primarily entailed exchange with Chinese regimes and their affiliated merchants. But in addition, some bilateral trade occurred in the form of official missions between Parhae, Silla, and Japan, and Koryŏ later on.[14] Mostly this official trade brought Chinese luxury goods to Korea and Japan in exchange for a mixture of raw materials and craft items.

---

[13] For a glimpse of life among the most favored few in Japan, see Piggott, 1990.

[14] The scale of maritime trade depended in part on the state of marine technology, about which much uncertainty remains. The arts of shipbuilding and seamanship are examined in Tōno, 1995, pp. 53–58, Sung S, 1977, p. 3, Farris, pending-I, and in works cited in his bibliography.

Other trade goods were carried by non-official entrepreneurs, some
going overland between Silla, Parhae, and China, others going by
sea between those areas and Japan. Chinese merchants handled much
of this trade, but some was conducted by Koreans who exploited
their central location and strong tradition of coastal shipping to
engage in maritime commerce with both China and Japan.[15] The
most celebrated example of this maritime entrepreneurship was the
professional soldier and regional grandee Chang Po-go (d. 846).
During the 830s–840s he established control over the southwestern
littoral of Korea and used his personal army and fleet to dominate
coastal shipping and the entrepreneurial trade with China and Japan.[16]

For all its visibility, this inter-state trade was of only modest scope
and dealt in little more than luxury goods for elite consumption.[17]
Domestic trade was mainly urban provisioning, and initially most of
it was managed by the officials and grandees who operated the
domestic tribute system.[18] Although it serviced a small population,
the trade was richly diverse. In the case of Heian around 900, for
example, goods included,

> food (rice, barley, salt, bean paste, a kind of vermicelli, fruits and nuts,
> seaweed, pungent bulbs, sweet gluten, etc.); many types of cloth, cloth-
> ing, and dyestuffs; tools and implements of various sorts (combs, nee-
> dles, writing brushes, charcoal ink, iron and gold implements, lacquerware,
> wooden implements, pottery); transport animals (horses and oxen); oils;
> and equestrian gear. But there were also shops specializing in less hum-
> drum goods, such as jewels (pearls and jade), weapons and armor
> (swords, bows, arrows, etc.), medicines and medicinal ingredients (herbs,
> cinnabar, etc.), and aromatics.[19]

A listing for eleventh-century Kaesŏng would likely have been similar. But because of the presence there of a substantial community
of resident Chinese and Korean traders, as well as visiting embassies
and entrepreneurial shippers from Song-dynasty China, it would have
contained more products of the import-export trade.[20]

---

[15] On the Koryŏ trade of Chinese merchants, see Sung S, 1977.

[16] Lee K-b, 1984, pp. 95–97; Reischauer, 1955, pp. 274–94.

[17] On *ritsuryō* foreign trade, see Verschuer, 1999, which will also lead readers to
earlier studies. Also Batten, 2003, esp. Ch. 7.

[18] On domestic trade in Nara-period Japan, see Farris, 1998b, which will lead
to older works.

[19] McCullough, 1999a, pp. 163–64.

[20] Sung S, 1977, pp. 9–13, mentions items in the Koryŏ-Song trade.

As time passed, irregular entrepreneurial trade became more promi-
nent, but it was largely handled through the household organizations
of aristocrats, regional strongmen, or Buddhist temples. Autonomous
merchants were essentially non-existent; even those in Kaesŏng, probably the most active commercial town of the day in either Korea
or Japan, did their best to maintain elite sponsorship. And while
attempts to deploy coinage were made, in neither Korea nor Japan
did viable monetary systems become established during these centuries. Instead, most trade remained barter, much being expedited
by the use of rice and cloth as "near-money," meaning goods of
such ubiquitous presence and use that they could be traded at fairly
consistent rates of exchange.[21]

Regarding artisans—such as scribes, accountants, food processors,
brewers, potters, masons, metal smiths, leather workers, carpenters,
and lumbermen—in both societies most were employed by the consumers of their production, meaning governments, aristocratic households, and Buddhist temples. The character of construction work is
suggested by a Heian court lady's description of a major temple project of the year 1019.[22] The daily labor levies from aristocratic estates,
she tells us, numbered "from 500 or 600 to 1,000 men," and "every-
one [at court] was immensely heartened by the availability of so
many hands." She continues,

> Near the top of the building 200 or 300 carpenters were at work,
> shouting "*Esa! Masa!*" in unison, as they raised massive beams attached
> to thick cables.

Hundreds of other artisans and laborers worked at other parts of
the project.

> On the avenues, shouting laborers pulled immense tree trunks roped
> to work carts; on the Kamo River, raftsmen sang cheerful, lusty songs
> as they poled their loads of lumber upstream. . . . Crews tugged at
> fragile rafts, which somehow managed to keep afloat under the weight
> of mighty rocks as big as cliffs.

---

[21] Coinage in *ritsuryō* Japan has been studied extensively; see, for example,
Sakaehara, 1980. On the utility of "near money," see, for example, Goodwin, 2000,
with a bibliographical guide to earlier works on the topic.
[22] Quotations from McCullough, 1980, pp. 500–01; also reproduced in McCullough,
1999a, pp. 178–79.

Doubtless the work looked somewhat less lightsome to the laborers themselves. But surely, then as now, being employed was generally preferable to the alternative, even though the work entailed some form and degree of servitude, ranging from simple economic dependency to formal slavery.

Slavery—meaning state-sanctioned buying and selling of humans—requires comment. A substantial literature speaks of slaves in both Silla and Koryŏ—modest numbers in the former; much larger ones in the latter.[23] On the other hand, one finds very little mention of them in Japan even though *ritsuryō* regulations clearly defined slave categories and even though slave traders were able to buy and sell desperate people at least as late as the thirteenth century, doing so despite repeated government prohibitions.[24]

Probably the most important truth is that in both societies, the economic tenuousness of life commonly left the less fortunate utterly dependent on those above, and whether this dependency was expressed as slavery, servile labor, or tenantry, the similarities of condition generally outweighed the differences. Nonetheless, formal slave status retained its social legitimacy in Silla and Koryŏ, and slaves were formally treated as chattel that could be bought and sold. Why the status survived longer in Korea than Japan is unclear. To some extent it may reflect the presence there of more ethnic diversity due to migratory interaction with adjacent northeast Asian areas. Also, Korea may well have had a larger and periodically rejuvenated supply of slaves in the prisoner-of-war population produced by the recurrent warfare of these centuries.

Whatever the dynamics, during Koryŏ slaves seem to have become more consequential elements in the power of regional strongmen and central aristocrats than were low-status people in *ritsuryō* Japan.[25] As a result some among the more gifted or fortunate slaves were able to acquire substantial influence as estate managers or as lieutenants and advisors to their masters. In times of social disorder, and especially in Koryŏ, hard-pressed or resentful aristocrats would complain

---

[23] On slavery in Korea, see Kim C-s, 1974; Hong, 1981; Salem, 1976; Salem, 1979.

[24] On slavery in *ritsuryō* rules, see Torao, 1993, pp. 425–26. Souyri, 2001, pp. 88–89 and *passim*, discusses slavery briefly.

[25] Salem, 1976, examines the exchange value, in terms of cloth and domestic animals, of slaves in Koryŏ.

about slaves rising above their station, using that charge as a basis for demanding legal or forceful punishment and remediation.

This tension over uppity slaves in Korea surely reflected a more basic characteristic of both societies. On one hand the population of elite consumers grew as decades passed, thanks to the branching of high-ranking patrilineages, the growth in lesser officialdom and regional grandees, the multiplication of Buddhist establishments with their resident monks and nuns, and the associated proliferation of menial attendants for all of these groups. On the other hand, production appears to have increased very modestly, which fostered more and more intense competition for what was produced.

To elaborate, as time passed, tillers in both Korea and Japan reclaimed more and more land, a process expedited by their utilization of horse- and ox-drawn plows. They put more of their arable into paddy tillage and gradually enlarged total output. But they engaged in little technological and agronomic innovation, and as a consequence output per capita and per hectare of land seems to have changed very little.[26] As the availability of undeveloped land diminished, the pressures of a "steady-state" situation intensified, finding expression in heightened political factionalism, greater competition to control the yield, and worsened hardship among producers, who were being squeezed more vigorously by tribute takers.

This steady-state character of basic production surely was abetted by the land-control systems of the day. Their earlier-noted complexities and variety notwithstanding, all were designed to maximize elite income by maximizing the portion of harvest that went to tribute takers. In consequence, producers had little incentive to increase their production and, when pressed too hard, considerable incentive to abandon their productive work and seek other means of survival. Non-growth in production seems also to have been fostered by patterns of epidemic disease.[27] The impact of disease in Korea is still unclear, as we note below, but in Japan smallpox and measles struck repeatedly during *ritsuryō* centuries and were particularly devastating, decimating village populations, idling arable, and thus undercutting

---

[26] The ox and plow were used in Korea before 700 CE and came to be used more extensively in Japan as *ritsuryō* centuries passed. On Japan, see Morris, 1999.

[27] On disease in Japan during these centuries, see the pioneering study by Farris, 1985.

the upward flow of tribute even as it limited the subsistence base of the general populace.

Given the elegant and enduring wants of the ruling elite, in the absence of socio-economic expansion, influence accrued to those best equipped to employ the coercive measures that could extract tribute from what was produced and regulate its distribution among the favored few. From the beginnings of aristocratic bureaucracy, needless to say, instances of both state-sanctioned coercion and "outlaw" uses of military force had occurred in both Korea and Japan, and their frequency and intensity grew as generations passed. Nevertheless, until the later twelfth century the violence had mostly been sporadic, and in the end it had always been contained within a civil-centered political order. However, around 1170, as noted earlier, military cliques seized much fuller and more consolidated control in both places, and for the rest of this period, military figures and factors remained central to political affairs, doing so in the case of Japan until after 1600.

This indigenous disorder was supplemented, especially in Korea, by periodic incursions of foreign invaders seeking to expand their areas of control and their level of tribute extraction. Of these invaders the most influential were the Mongols, who, as we note below, exercised a harsh hegemonial role on the peninsula for more than a century after the 1230s and whose attempts to invade Japan in the 1270s–1280s added further burdens to the tottering remnants of the *ritsuryō* regime.

D. *Environmental Issues*

The extent of human demand on an ecosystem is determined, as noted in Chapter 2, by the size of population and the level and content of demand per capita. In Korea and Japan the development of agriculture and metallurgy had spurred demographic growth and heightened elite demand for a millennium or more prior to 700 CE. The rise of aristocratic bureaucracies with their urban centers and tribute-taking systems intensified this elite demand during the following centuries. In both temporal and geographic terms, however, the effects of these developments played out unevenly. And as with all matters ecological, sorting out the variables in complexly synergistic processes is difficult. However, the topics of demography, urbanization, and landscape seem to merit attention.

Demography. Nearly as much uncertainty surrounds the size and condition of the Korean and Japanese populations during these centuries as in pre-700 times. Migration into and out of the two countries does not appear to have been a significant demographic factor, so domestic birth and death rates were the key determinants of population size.

In the case of *ritsuryō* Japan, demographers combine the few surviving local census figures with scattered records of agricultural output to estimate the archipelago's overall population as of 700 CE at about 5,000,000. For the next three centuries or so the number seems to have fluctuated in the five to six million range and then gradually risen to perhaps seven million by 1150. This sustained demographic stability appears to reflect the effects of epidemic disease, harvest irregularity, and harsh tribute-taking, as they played out in sporadically high death rates, bouts of hunger and poor nutrition, and low fecundity.[28] One suspects that the extent of vagrancy among the poor, as well as the established marital pattern—in which adult women commonly remained as workers in their natal households long after they were married—also helped hold down birth rates.[29]

For Korea there seem to be no data on which to base even rough estimates such as these. However, the similarities between the Silla/Koryŏ and *ritsuryō* systems of land control, food production, and tribute-taking would suggest basically similar demographic experiences. Also, insofar as malaria—the "three-day fever" as it was known in Korea—undercut fecundity or boosted mortality rates, both societies utilized the paddy culture that sustained healthy anopheline mosquito populations, enabling them to transmit the malaria pathogen (*Plasmodium* spp.) to humans.[30] Moreover, it is plausible that smallpox epidemics, which repeatedly ravaged *ritsuryō* society, particularly in more urbanized regions, had a comparable effect in Korea. Smallpox had been introduced from India to China before 500 CE, from whence it was carried to Korea and Japan by the 550s or so.[31] For both societies records of the next few centuries suggest that smallpox

---

[28] Farris, 1985, explores this topic.
[29] Tonomura, 1994, pp. 135–38.
[30] Kiple, 1993, pp. 379–80, 388, 391, 395.
[31] Magner, 1993, p. 390.

was a recurrent plague, at least among the favored few, until it evolved by the twelfth century or so into an endemic disease of childhood that was of substantially less demographic consequence.

Still, there were differences. Although records from Korea do report epidemics hitting the peninsula during these centuries, their frequency seems substantially less than in Japan.[32] And their demographic and socio-economic impacts are unknown. One suspects that the communicable diseases other than smallpox may not have affected Korea to the same extent as Japan because general immunities had become established there generations earlier thanks to the more sustained contact with continental neighbors.

On the other hand, the interplay of deforestation, land clearance, and climate fluctuation could well have had a more severe demographic impact on the peninsula because of Korea's more sharply seasonal rhythms of precipitation, because cultivation had been pursued for more centuries, and because the peninsula's relatively more accessible upland forest areas could have been more extensively cut off, with destructive downstream consequences. Finally, the more chronic problem of warfare could have depressed birth rates even as it raised death rates, so the Silla/Koryŏ population likely held within the range of two to four million.[33]

Regarding trends in per-capita demand on the ecosystem, the essential point for both Korea and Japan seems straightforward. During these centuries the population of elite consumers—top aristocrats, monastery and nunnery residents, local grandees, military men, and their families, followers, and menial attendents—grew, diversified, and competed more and more forcefully for tribute yield. As individuals, they may have lived little if any better than had earlier generations of tribute recipients. As a group, however, they consumed more, and as a consequence, the mass of producers may have derived little if any per-capita benefit from the increase in their total output. Indeed, they may even have experienced net losses.

The condition of the laboring poor was captured with particular poignancy by this account from a Korean source. Although proba-

---

[32] Farris, 1985, Appendix B, pp. 156–161, which covers the centuries 698–898.
[33] McEvedy and Jones, 1978, p. 177, propose for all of Korea 2 million for 800 rising to 4 million by 1200. Silla—and Koryŏ even more so—controlled the most densely populated regions of the country. Ch'oe Y-h, 1987, p. 105, suggests at least 3.4 million at the end of Koryŏ.

bly apocryphal, it suggests what people of the time would have found credible and reveals images they found compelling. A corvée laborer, unable to provide his own necessities as work rules required, had relied on his comrades for food, much to his own and his wife's chagrin.

> One day his wife came with food and said, "Please ask your friends to come and eat." The worker said, "Our family is poor. How did you provide food? Did you have relations with another man to get it, or did you steal it?" His wife replied, "My face is ugly, with whom could I be intimate? I am stupid, how could I steal? I simply cut my hair and sold it." Then she showed her head. The worker sobbed and could not eat. Those who heard this were very sad."[34]

In Japan the regulations for corvée labor and military conscripts were similar, as were the sufferings. Indeed, the rate at which the poor fled to escape obligatory duty was a source of continuing dismay to their betters.

One of the primary uses those betters had for corvée labor was to construct capital cities and the buildings therein, and as suggested by the Heian court lady's description of temple construction in 1019, labor shortages sometimes complicated such enterprises.

Urbanization. It was through these construction projects, most notably the building of capital cities, that the ruling elites of aristocratic bureaucracy achieved their greatest environmental impact. Initial construction, subsequent maintenance and repair, and replacement after fire or other misfortune sustained an unprecedented level of demand for timber, fuelwood, and other forest products, for the foodstuffs and other necessities of workmen and dray animals, for the metals, clay, and other resources that the projects utilized, and for the sheer space consumed by structures and the processes of their construction and maintenance.

A major factor that made this surge in construction so environmentally costly was its use of new architectural techniques.[35] The earlier Korean and Japanese "thatch-roof-and-post-hole" method of building had produced modest buildings framed with wooden posts set in the ground, walled with wattle, thatch, or mud, and roofed

[34] Quoted in Shultz, 2000, p. 39.
[35] See Totman, 1989, pp. 12–16, and endnotes that identify further reading.

with thatch or bark laid over pole rafters, the whole being fastened
together with vine or other binding material. The new "mortise-and-
tenon" construction style, which was central to both Buddhist monastic architecture and Chinese-style governmental construction, placed
heavy pillars atop stone foundations, and used sturdy framing tim-
bers to hold them in place. It walled the structures with boards or
re-enforced plaster, and roofed them with tile laid over heavy-duty
rafters and boarding, with the whole fastened by solid joinery and
wooden pegs (see Plate 11). Whereas the older style had made do
with modest quantities of materials derived from smallish trees and
other growth, the new monumental style required large trees and
great quantities of construction timber, fuel for tile-making, and labor-
intensive stone masonry.

Once the great urban projects had been launched, moreover, they
produced large, long-lasting concentrations of consumers, dispropor-
tionately privileged, who placed heavy and sustained demand on the
surrounding ecosystem, primarily for foodstuffs, fuel, and textiles.
Because of the severe constraints that topography and technological
limitations imposed on transport, the burdens were particularly onerous in the immediate environs of the cities.

In Silla, as noted earlier, a moderately sized but vibrant capital
was established at Kyŏngju, and branch headquarters were erected
at sites to the west and north. Although evidence in the matter seems
to be lacking, one suspects that Kyŏngju placed a severe burden on
the Hyŏngsan River valley and adjoining areas, eventuating in excessive deforestation, hillside erosion, and downstream complications.[36]

Nor are the circumstances of Koryŏ's capital, Kaesŏng, much
clearer. Because it was situated in the region that earlier had sustained Chinese commandery headquarters for centuries, it may not
be amiss to suspect that the vegetation on nearby terrain had already
been substantially depleted and that assemblage of the Koryŏ elite
only exacerbated the problem. If, as one scholar estimates, the walled
city and its immediate environs were home to some 500,000 people, it could only have placed immensely onerous burdens on the

---

[36] Photographs of denuded hills and valley in Lee S-y, 1960, p. 19, reveal the
devastated condition of the Hyŏngsan River valley in the 1950s. The chronology
eventuating in that situation is not reported, though surely the Korean War of
1950–53, which created a huge refugee population in the Pusan vicinity, magnified
earlier pressure on surviving woodland.

surrounding ecosystem.[37] Even if the urban population was much smaller than that, as seems likely, the city's environmental impact would still have been substantial.

Indeed, changes in Koryŏ land-control regulations suggest that the urban elite was overloading the accessible forest cover around the city. At least, whereas senior officials had initially been awarded substantial acreage of woodland to accompany the arable from which they extracted tribute, and lesser officials received much lesser amounts, the modified rules of 998 and 1076 slashed senior awards of woodland by more than half and totally eliminated the awards to lesser officials.[38] This change may simply have reflected growth in the elite population, but one suspects that it also reflected continuing conversion of hillside to arable or scrub, which prompted the monarchy to retain what timber stands it could for its own use. Surely the loss of high forest during Koryŏ was also fostered by the spread of Buddhist temple construction beyond urban centers into hinterland locations as deemed socially beneficent by geomantic reasoning.[39]

The woodland situation is somewhat clearer in Japan.[40] There, ambitious construction projects in the Nara Basin dated from the mid-seventh century, culminating during the 710s in Genmei's creation of her great capital city at Nara. Even then the construction binge did not stop, however, because rulers continued erecting lesser palaces and headquarters at one site after another and in 784 launched another full-scale city project at Nagaoka, shifting it to Heian in 794 (see Map 3-2). Smaller-scaled rectangular headquarters towns were supposed to be erected in provinces throughout the realm, and several of them did in fact get built. Even more demanding were major projects that created splendid Buddhist monasteries, mainly in the Kinai region.

As the eighth century advanced, the environmental consequences of this Kinai-centered building boom played themselves out. Although the costs of timber processing led to habitual recycling of material, loggers still cut off the accessible forests. Timber scarcities led builders to draw timber from ever farther afield and precipitated scrambles

---

[37] Park Y-w, 1998, pp. 100–01.
[38] Duncan, 2000, pp. 47, 89.
[39] Kamata, 1996.
[40] I have treated this topic in Totman, 1989, pp. 9–33 and more concisely in Totman, 2000, pp. 67–71, 84–86. See also Breen and Teeuwen, 2000, pp. 38–39.

among the elite to secure control of surviving stands. Logged-off hill-sides eroded, clogging rivers, complicating lowland agriculture, damaging crops, and adding to public hardship. Deforested areas regrew to brushwood and undergrowth that periodically erupted in destructive and terrifying forest fires, only gradually re-establishing patches of well-stocked high forest.

Confronted by the many-faceted evidence that excessive logging was hurtful, the government periodically tried to control logging as a way to preserve valued stands and reduce downstream damage. And temples and shrines invoked religious sanction in their attempts to protect their woodland sites and stands. But the wants of elite builders, both sacred and profane, generally prevailed as long as they had the wealth and power needed to persevere.

During the ninth century, however, the construction boom petered out. The great city of Heian was never completed, and most of the other sites were abandoned. Construction projects of later years created new headquarters towns at other locations about the realm, notably Kamakura and Hiraizumi, and from time to time new projects graced the Kinai region with a few handsome monuments.[41] But the original grandeur of Nara and Heian was never replicated. So they came to be celebrated in nostalgia and recollection, images evoked to limn the splendor of what was, much as Kyŏngju became emblematic of Silla's glory in the Korea of a later day.

In short, *ritsuryō* urbanization extracted a heavy price from the surrounding ecosystem, and one suspects that a similar price was paid by the environments around Silla/Koryŏ capitals.

Landscape. Around the cities, then, the creation and maintenance of aristocatic bureaucracy appears to have achieved considerable environmental damage. For Korea and Japan more broadly, however, the story was more ambiguous.

The deforesting of lowlands, which had begun centuries earlier, as noted in Chapter 2, proceeded apace, facilitated by the slowly growing availability of iron axes, hoes, spades, and plows. By 1150, most—but certainly not all—of the reasonably accessible terrain within the jurisdiction of the Koryŏ and Heian regimes had been cleared of forest canopy (see Plate 12). Centuries of woodcutting and land

---

[41] On Hiraizumi, see Yiengpruksawan, 1998; also Hudson, 1999, pp. 204–5, 219–21.

opening by the corvée, slave, and hired laborers of governments, monasteries, aristocratic landholders, local grandees, and estate managers, as well as by innumerable ordinary peasants, had opened valley floors, plains, and gentler hillsides to sunlight, converting them to arable acreage and "wasteland." The former grew dry grains, rice, and diverse other crops (see Plate 13). The latter, much of which was purposely lying fallow, but some of which was simply logged-off sites or abandoned arable, sported various wild grasses, forbs, shrubs, and other low growth and the fauna that thrived therein.

Vast sweeps of terrain that had once been nearly uninterrupted woodland had been transformed into intricately patterned vistas of hillside forest intermingled with lowland fields and, here and there, the scattered huts and homesteads of cultivators and their social betters. As centuries passed, more and more of the land was utilized as paddy fields, which during the months of cropping would sparkle brightly as sunshine reflected off the water's placid surface.

Besides the stunning visual transformation that land clearance accomplished, it also had substantial environmental consequences. These relate, more uncertainly than one would like, to biota, soils, and weather.

Land clearance of this magnitude clearly would have changed the biotic composition of both Korea and Japan. Humans, their collaborating flora and fauna—rice, barley, millet, other grains, other edible plants, decorative flora, chestnut and mulberry trees, silk worms, horses, oxen, dogs, chickens and so forth—and opportunistic "parasites" (such as mosquitoes, house mice, and various microbes) clearly expanded their presence. Diverse trees and those understory species that preferred lowland forest canopy clearly lost, being confined to residual sites or less favored terrain.

On the other hand, because land clearance created uncountable miles of forest edge, with its combination of sunlight and nearby shade and shelter, it in fact produced a lot of terrain that could support richly diversified and vigorous flora and fauna. Also, as noted above, paddy culture created expanses of relatively warm, shallow water that sustained not only rice plants and mosquitoes but numerous other forms of life, of which frogs may have been the most noisy but stately herons and other migratory water birds are the most well known. In some localities, and especially around cities, clearance of lowland and adjacent hillside surely reduced species diversity. On balance, however, one suspects (evidence one way or the other being too thin to settle the matter) that the landscape changes as a whole yielded a net gain in biodiversity and total biomass production even as it tilted the balance against a number of creatures.

Evidence on soils is also minimal. In both Korea and Japan the original lowland forest soils were mostly products of erosion and sedimentation, and they ranged from coarse gravels to fine silts. Japan also contained, as noted in Chapter One, areas covered by thick layers of volcanic ash that had matured into nicely friable loam. Most lowland areas of both realms had been stable since the final Pleistocene meltoff, which had given their soils time enough to mature, acquiring clearcut soil horizons and well distributed nutrient loads. Tillers could make the soil nutrients available to their field crops by spading and plowing. And in swampy areas subsoil horizons of watertight clay pan facilitated the formation and use of paddy fields.

As noted earlier, use of the animal-drawn plow spread during these centuries. Moreover the simple stick plow gradually gave way to the plow-with-moldboard. And while it didn't cut a deep furrow, it enabled plowmen to turn the soil in a more uniform manner than they could with either spade or stick plow, thus spreading soil nutrients more evenly and achieving more consistent crop growth. By converting lowland into level paddy fields, moreover, tillers also provided *de facto* overflow areas that helped to capture snowmelt and accommodate sudden torrents of rainfall, thereby mitigating the effects of deforestation and climatic irregularity.

Cropping did, of course, remove nutrients from the soil, and within a few years after an area was reclaimed, the soil's accumulated nutrient load would be depleted. That depletion had two effects. It would cripple the soil's crop-growing capacity by denying plants the nutrients they needed to flourish, and it reduced the soil's capacity to hold water in suspension, hence exacerbating any drought conditions that might develop.

In Japan, and probably in Korea, farmers coped with this situation mainly by a strategy of fallowing: leaving depleted fields idle for a few years, then burning and mulching the natural growth that had sprung up, re-using the fields for a time, and subsequently re-idling them. The slowly growing number of farmers who used draft animals did have manure to apply, but in the case of Japan, at least, they appear to have fed the animals with fodder removed from the harvested fields or taken from fallow and wasteland, and whether the complete energy transaction of such animal use resulted in a higher crop yield per hectare or per capita is unclear.[42]

Finally, these landscape changes may well have interplayed with exogenous climate variables to have an impact on weather and hence on the harvest and society. Particularly in Japan, evidence suggests that drought, crop failure, and resulting food shortages became more common during these centuries than they were earlier or later.

To explain, the extensive land clearance and deforestation in and around lowland areas of both countries could have fostered higher ambient temperatures, lower precipitation, more rapid runoff and leaching, and consequent drought and harvest shortfalls. Cyclical weather patterns, notably the El Niñõ-La Niñã Southern Oscillation, which can have a substantial effect on levels and rhythms of precipitation in northeast Asia, could have heightened the impact. And any longer-swing cycle of global warming would have had a more sustained impact.[43] In combination these factors could well have negated much of the gain in production that resulted from increased land clearance and plow usage. And insofar as tribute takers based their levies on more or less fixed assumptions about the yield to be expected from different types of land, such crop shortfalls would largely have been borne by the producers.

E. *A Summation to 1150*

By 1150, then, aristocratic bureaucracy had flourished and faded in both Korea and Japan. During its heyday, however, it had accumulated a substantial legacy. Its creators established control over realms of unprecedented size. They articulated complex systems of social and political organization and employed sophisticated construction

---

[42] Morris,1999, pp. 183–94, discusses plow usage in Japan. Two main issues are imbedded in this conundrum. One is human labor yield; the other, the value of the animal utilization. Regarding human labor yield, how does one best measure "per capita" output: should it be by work hour, work year, lifetime, or other criteria? Regarding animal power, the issue is energy cycling. Only a portion of a draft animal's nutrient intake gets translated into work output and usable excreta. Would the same nutrients, processed by microbes into plant food, have yielded more foodstuffs for humans if utilized as mulch?

[43] Farris has reconnoitered the climate issue for *ritsuryō* Japan in Farris, pending-II, a paper presented at a conference in Spring 2002.

techniques to erect grand capital cities and secondary centers. These they linked together via durable systems of transportation and communication and anchored firmly in the supportive capacity of the hinterland and its producer population. Finally, they fostered cultural accomplishments, in terms of arts and letters, that can still, a millennium later, excite and delight our aesthetic and philosophical sensibilities.

By 1150, however, the glory was badly tarnished, and the beneficiaries of aristocratic bureaucracy were at one another's throats as never before. The basic reason was pedestrian and familiar: these ruling elites never figured out how to live within the limits of the productive system that supported them but were unable to compensate for that failure by conquering and exploiting other lands and people. The builders of these regimes erected their grand structures atop the existing agricultural systems and had only modest success in making those systems more productive or in managing the rivalries for what they produced. They did enlarge total output by promoting land clearance so as to bring more acreage into "useful" production. But as they approached the limits set by the topography and water supplies of Korea and Japan, they had little luck at increasing the output of land already in production.

In Japan at least, they seem to have presided over a considerable increase in the use of animal power and moldboard plows, and that change certainly expedited the opening of more land to tillage. As noted above, however, whether it achieved an increase in nutrient output per capita or per hectare, however those be calculated, is unclear. And one sees little evidence in either Korea or Japan of the other types of agronomic and technological change that in later centuries would substantially enhance the productivity of both labor and land.

Similarly, one does see signs of transport and trade activity, but it was mostly limited to the conveyance of tribute from producer to consumer and the exchange of luxuries among the favored few. Commercial activity seems to have achieved little in terms of promoting broader efficiencies of production or distribution, and it was insufficient to establish systems of coinage whose fungibility would permit gains in efficiency of exchange.

Instead, the rulers labored to steer as much production as possible to their own use, doing so with enough success to sustain elite standards of living as a whole even while their numbers rose. As decades passed, the favored few also acquired substantial numbers of retainers, menials, and other hangers-on who recognized that such connections afforded the best access to life's necessities. In the process, of course, substantial interest groups took shape—most notably royal and aristocratic patrilineages, the households of regional grandees and military men, and Buddhist clerical establishments—and competition among them intensified as their total consumption pressed more and more firmly on the broader society's productive capacity. As that occurred, fracture lines appeared, lines that reflected, as noted earlier, the elite power structures of these polities. Nevertheless, these ruling systems were well enough organized and their lines of contact to the hinterland sufficiently sturdy, so that for centuries their leaders coped with the tensions and sustained their regimes.

That accomplishment reflects the success those rulers had in commandeering, by one means or another, practically all the output that villagers did not require for survival—and sometimes some of that, too. Due in part to this situation, the lives of producers, marginal in any case, seem, in Japan at least, to have become more vulnerable to vicissitudes of harvest and visitations of microbes, which slowed and at times reversed the growth of both population and production and may well have undercut individual productivity. As generations passed, defiance and defections by producers, contests between them and consumers, and rivalries among elite groups became more pronounced, leading to modifications in tribute-system procedures. Those moves contributed, in turn, to changes in elite composition and structure, to a redistribution of power, and in the outcome to a shift of power downward from central elites to regional grandees, tax farmers, estate managers, and military men. And when push came to shove in the decades after 1150, the most skillful and advantaged practitioners of violence prevailed.

Finally, these centuries of human endeavor had a number of environmental effects. In the broadest sense they carried well toward completion the visual transformation of landscape that began millennia earlier when the first patch of woodland was cleared for cultivation. That transformation modified the floral and faunal composition of Korea and Japan in favor of the human-centered biological community, but it may also have yielded a net gain in biological diversity and biomass production compared to the earlier era of fully-forested landscape. The major forms of environmental damage were associated with the densely settled capital cities, whose construction and use led to serious deforestation, soil erosion, hillside denuding, and downstream damage in nearby areas. Even that injury, however, was on a sufficiently modest scale so that it provoked little purposeful meliorative response. And it would have been remediable within a few human generations had sites been sheltered from sustained exploitation.

Disorder and Disintegration (1150–1350)

The two centuries dating from around 1150 were difficult ones in Korea and Japan for both the operatives of aristocratic bureaucracy and the populace more broadly. The operatives appear to have fared more poorly in Japan; the general populace, in Korea. For Japan the problems were largely self-inflicted; for Korea, they were a combination of domestic and foreign-spawned tribulations.

Regarding the operatives, the established patrilineages of the Koryŏ regime seem as a group to have preserved their position largely intact despite aristocratic insurgency, military coup, commoner revolt, Mongol invasion, and piratical attack. They retained or accumulated substantial estate holdings and the assemblages of slaves, tenant farmers, and others whose labors sustained them. As a result, particular vicissitudes notwithstanding, the Koryŏ elite as a whole was able to continue playing its key role in Korea's political life despite the turmoil of the times and even the eventual displacement of Koryŏ with the Chosŏn (Yi) Dynasty in 1392.[44]

In Japan, on the other hand, the old aristocratic elite, their affiliated monastic establishments, and many of the most esteemed military lineages fared poorly, ceding more and more control of landed wealth to warriors of lesser pedigree and to other upstart locals. In consequence, by the 1390s nearly the entire *ritsuryō* elite had been marginalized or displaced. In a political melee that dragged on for another two centuries, new monastic groups and new lineages of military men, almost all sprung from people of obscure ancestry, struggled to construct a stable new order. As we note in Chapter 4, the victors in that process finally did so around the year 1600.

At lower social levels, meanwhile, living conditions in Korea seem

---

[44] Duncan, 2000, p. 99.

to have remained—or become even more—harsh due to the combination of intensified elite rivalry for advantage and the exactions
and depredations of outsiders, most notably Mongol invaders from
inner Asia and pirate squadrons operating out of southwestern Japan.
Japanese commoners were spared most of those outside injuries
despite two Mongol invasions and occasional raids by piratical bands
from Korea or nearby areas.[45] They also found that deterioration in
the *ritsuryō* elite's control of land reduced, or at least redirected, their
tribute obligations even as it gave more and more of them opportunity and incentive to exercise more control over local affairs and
utilize the more productive agronomic techniques that began spreading across the islands during these centuries. By the fourteenth century these agronomic changes were translating into greater productivity
per capita and per arable land unit as well as growth in general
population, primary production, and commerce.

The broader environmental ramifications of these trends are well
hidden due to paucity of both data and retrospective inquiry. In
terms of human demography, whereas Korea seems to have experienced a period of overall stability and showed only the first signs
of sustained population growth during the mid-1300s, Japan appears
to have begun a period of expansion during the 1100s that was to
continue—surely with ill-recorded ups and downs—into the early
eighteenth century. For the biosystem more broadly, the pattern
and trends of landscape and biota that characterized early centuries
of aristocratic bureaucracy appear to have continued, although in
Japan the decline in fallowing would gradually have consolidated the
hegemonial role in lowland areas of the human-centered biological
community.

A. *Political Process*

In both Korea and Japan the aristocratic bureaucratic order gradually lost cohesiveness as elite groups competed for income and jockeyed for advantage, in the process undermining monarchial authority
and achieving a disorderly diffusion of power and privilege among
new and diverse claimants. Around 1170 the process culminated in

---

[45] On pirate attacks on southwest Japan, see McCullough, 1999b, pp. 80, 89–90,
94–95.

the seizure of power by military factions. However, the coups played out dissimilarly in the two places.

Korea. In Korea the initial coup of 1170 was followed by rivalry among the victors and a rash of revolts by discontented groups that included Buddhist monks, villagers, and common soldiers.[46] The persistent disorder led in 1196 to a second military coup in which Ch'oe Ch'ung-hŏn (1149–1219) seized—and retained—such firm personal control of the regime that during his years of domination he put four kings on the throne and ousted two. The *Koryŏsa* (History of Koryŏ), an official history completed in 1451, described Ch'oe's relationship to King Sinjong (r. 1197–1204), the first of the four, this way:

> Sinjong was put upon the throne by Ch'oe Ch'ung-hŏn, and all matters of life and death, decisions to accept or reject, were in Ch'oe's hands. Sinjong stood above his subjects holding only empty authority. Alas, he was nothing but a puppet.[47]

Ch'oe suppressed insurgencies by lesser groups, weakened the monasteries, eased the burdens of some among the lowborn, and enhanced the estates and armed forces of his own household, effectively displacing government troops as the main keepers of the peace.

Beginning, however, with an invasion of northern Korea in 1218, Mongol armies repeatedly endangered Ch'oe rule.[48] The Mongols had recently descended from the steppes of central Asia onto the tribute-rich agricultural plains fronting the Yellow Sea, including those of Korea, where they made continual demands for tribute goods and services. In Korea these demands provoked resistance that led to further invasions, pillage, and slaughter, and in 1232 to retreat by the Ch'oe-controlled Koryŏ court onto the large (approximately 350 km²), defensible island of Kanghwa, offshore from Kaesŏng (see Map 3-3). Scattered local resistance continued, however, eliciting further invasions, more plunder, and harsh general suffering.

The Mongols were unable and unwilling to mount a full-scale assault on Kanghwa for several reasons: they were fully occupied by

---

[46] Shultz, 2000, is the most thorough study of this military rule. It also contains a good bibliography.

[47] Quoted in Lee K-b, 1984, p. 142.

[48] Henthorn, 1963, provides a rich, well-illustrated, politico-military narrative of Mongol-Koryŏ relations.

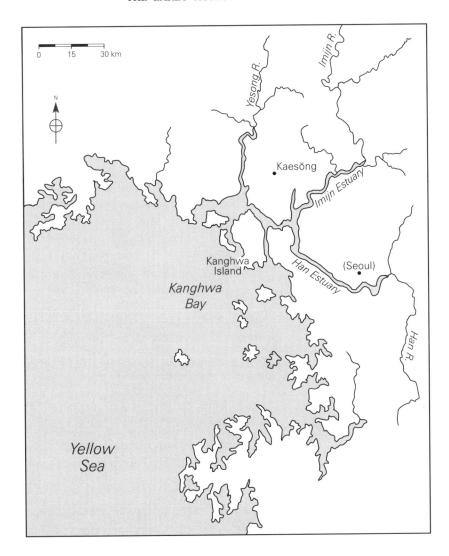

Map 3-3. *The Vicinity of Kanghwa Island.*

After the Koryŏ government relocated from Kaesŏng to Kanghwa in 1232, the Mongols proved unable to mount a successful invasion and subdue them. Although separated from the mainland only by narrow channels, Kanghwa Island was protected by extreme variations in tide, which reversed water flows at quarter-day intervals, exposing broad mud flats at low tide and giving invaders a short "window of opportunity" to establish a beach-head. Based on MSTS, *Korea Japan.*

their advance into China, were equipped for land warfare rather than amphibious operations, and were already in control of much of Korea and its tribute potential. So the military-dominated Koryŏ regime settled in there, supported by local productive output plus such tribute as it could bring by boat from Korea's southern bread-basket. In 1258 the Ch'oe leader was assassinated, and civil author-ities tried to reach a settlement with the Mongols so they could return to Kaesŏng, but other military officials did not acquiesce until 1270, when the return finally took place.

Having accepted status as a tributary of the Yuan Dynasty (as the Mongol regime in China was known), Koryŏ leaders soon found themselves compelled to construct, equip, and man warships for Mongol use in their disastrously sanguinary but failed attempts to invade Japan in 1274 and 1281. Meanwhile, the Mongols had estab-lished commandery-style control over much of the area in north-west Korea formerly held by Koguryŏ and Parhae, while a Mongol appointee tried to exercise a viceroyship over the Koryŏ throne and its shrunken realm. Moreover the Mongols, who had plundered the peninsula widely before the Koryŏ court's submission, continued to require tribute in gold, silver, pelts, paper, silk, ramie, grain, and other goods, as well as "service hostages," mainly women to serve as personal attendants and artisans to produce valued products. The producer populace thus found itself forced to bear not only the costs of the Koryŏ ruling elite but also an onerous new set of burdens.[49]

The court's acceptance of Mongol suzerainty ended the pre-emi-nence of military leaders, and until the faltering Mongols were forced out of Korea in 1356, that situation created new opportunities for well-placed civil officials to enhance their careers and family fortunes by facilitating Koryŏ-Yuan relations. In reward they accumulated "vast estates and hundreds of slaves."[50] So, by the time the Mongols left, the Koryŏ regime had come to consist primarily of a cluster of powerful aristocratic households and a royal house that relied on its own estate holdings more than its official government tribute lands for self-preservation.

King Kongmin (r. 1351–74), who ousted the Mongols, strove to restore monarchial power by reclaiming land for the crown and

---

[49] Henthorn, 1963, pp. 211–15; Lee K-b, 1984, p. 157.
[50] Lee K-b, 1984, p. 158.

building a supporting officialdom recruited from lower-ranking officials and local functionaries. In so doing he began revitalizing the ideals of Confucian governance that had flourished in early Koryŏ even as he rebalanced the venerable roles of monarchy and aristocracy in a manner more akin to the halcyon days of Silla and pre-Ch'oe Koryŏ. In the end, however, problems of the day overwhelmed him and his successors, and in 1392 the regime fell to another military insurrection.

Japan. In Japan, meanwhile, aristocratic bureaucracy fared even less well. There, during the 1150s, competing senior aristocrats hired the leaders of groups of swordsmen to protect and promote their interests through threats and acts of violence. These leaders were men who mostly held one or another military title in the *ritsuryō* hierarchy and who claimed—with apparent validity in the better known cases, at least—descent from cadet lines of the royal family.

The process of utilizing such men placed more and more power in their hands, even as it pitted them against one another in the nominal service of higher authority. During the 1180s a military clique from eastern Japan, commanded by Minamoto no Yoritomo (1147–99) and purporting to act on behalf of the royal household, launched a series of deployments and battles that had by 1190 routed its rivals, secured high ranks and honors for its leaders, and ensconced them in a royally sanctioned "shogunal" headquarters (*bakufu*) at Kamakura. The victors were charged with keeping the peace and sustaining the tribute system on behalf of the monarchy and its civil aristocratic and monastic allies, and they were authorized to deploy men to provincial posts where they could implement those tasks.

Within a generation Yoritomo's patriline was extinct, but a forceful vassal family sustained Kamakura's role as sole protector of the courtly few. As decades passed, however, lesser warriors—both those who had been bested in earlier fighting and those whom Kamakura had deployed about the country to maintain the peace and tribute flow—settled down, acquired landed income and followers, and evolved into hereditary local interest groups. In the process they found themselves more and more divorced from, or even at loggerheads with, their superiors in Kamakura. Their alienation was heightened during the 1270s–1280s when many of them served valiantly in repelling the Mongol invaders and then received little or no reward for their efforts. By the early fourteenth century many had become, in effect, local swords for hire.

During the 1320s Go-Daigo (1288–1339), an uncommonly ambitious
scion of the monarchial line, began maneuvering to seize power and
re-establish royal control of the polity. In soliciting support from
those "swords for hire" and other ambitious or disgruntled figures,
he fared well enough to mount a successful military assault on leaders
of the Kamakura regime. He proclaimed a new era of monarchial
governance and in 1333 launched an energetic program of political
reform.[51] His apparent triumph had depended, however, on the
collaboration of military men, and unlike Yoritomo 150 years earlier, they were not willing to play the role of obedient servant to
the throne. Instead, the most powerful of them, Ashikaga Takauji
(1305–58), defied Go-Daigo and established his own shogunate in
1338, regarding it as the successor to Kamakura.

However, whereas Minamoto no Yoritomo had suppressed rivals
during the 1180s and compelled the *ritsuryō* court to recognize his
role as its protector, and whereas Ch'oe Ch'ung-hŏn had succeeded
in establishing control over Koryŏ and entrenching his family's position during the 1190s, Takauji found himself during the 1330s atop
a much larger body politic, one whose local units were more
autonomous and more able to maneuver among higher-ranking rivals
to local advantage. Most famously, Go-Daigo fled Kyoto and established the "southern court," a rival regime headquartered in mountains south of the city. In doing so he provided a rallying point and
legitimizing symbol for diverse aristocrats, warriors, and others who
hoped to advance their interests by challenging Ashikaga primacy.
Decades of sporadic warfare were to pass before Ashikaga leaders
achieved during the 1390s an equilibrium of sorts with various landed
interests, thereby depriving the southern court of its base of support
and ending its challenge.[52]

---

[51] A recent iteration of this celebrated story is Goble, 1996. Its bibliography will
lead one to earlier works. Aspects of fourteenth-century Japan are treated in the
fifteen essays in Mass, 1997. Most valuable for this study is Troost, 1997.

[52] One is tempted to liken Go-Daigo's "southern court" and its role vis à vis the
Ashikaga to Koryŏ leaders on Kanghwa Island and their role vis-à-vis the Mongols
a century earlier in that both were intransigent holdouts against the "new order."
Much as Mongol and Koryŏ leaders had reached an agreement that enabled the
latter to return to Kaesŏng in 1270, so the Ashikaga and southerners negotiated
the latter's return to Kyoto in 1392. Whereas Koryŏ survived as a tributary of
Yuan, however, and subsequently managed to outlive it, Go-Daigo's successors were
quietly sent into oblivion, their few supporters unable to mount more than sporadic, feeble protests.

Subsequently, to foreshadow Chapter 4, whereas the 1390s ushered in the Chosŏn Dynasty in Korea, which endured with unprecedented success until about 1900, the Ashikaga were faltering by the 1430s as Japan slipped into a season of turmoil that was to persist for generations. That turmoil, as we note in the next chapter, ravaged the remnants of the *ritsuryō* order, most of the Buddhist monasteries that had flourished during earlier centuries, and many of the warrior lineages that had claimed descent from royal ancestors. In short, although the violence and suffering associated with military rule and foreign invaders was surely much harsher in Korea than in Japan, it ended much sooner there, doing so by 1400, whereas in Japan it dragged on until nearly 1600.

B. *Elite Culture*

In both Korea and Japan a major theme in the higher cultural history of aristocratic bureaucracy during its later centuries was the diffusion of arts and letters outward beyond the capital cities and downward from the urban elite to intermediate strata. These latter included the households of regional grandees, provincial officialdom, estate managers, lesser warriors, uppity slaves, and Buddhist monks of undistinguished ancestry.

However, much as the story of political process suggests that aristocratic bureaucracy was proving more durable in Korea than Japan, so the record of higher culture suggests—on very slim evidence—that the Korean elite was retaining a tighter grip on the production and enjoyment of cultural amenities than were their fellows to the east. The thinness of evidence from Korea reflects the political disorder of the day. Cultural output surely slowed as lives were disrupted by warfare, flight, hardship, and insecurity. And much of what was produced—scholarly and literary works, paintings, sculpture, and architecture—was lost to fire and pillage.

The Korean sense of cultural loss was reflected in celebratory and nostalgic tales of founding heroes. And the associated resolve to salvage what one could was epitomized by the famous story of the *Koryŏ Tripitaka*, the immense Buddhist scriptural canon. During the tenth century Korean monks had gradually produced a carved-woodblock edition of the Chinese-language version, an undertaking that took over fifty years to complete. The great stack of blocks was stored at a temple in Taegu, where it was destroyed during one of the

Mongol invasions. Appalled at the loss, monks living in exile on Kanghwa Island commenced producing a new edition, and during the decade 1237–47 they completed the task, carving the text into 81,258 blocks of wood.[53]

Creation of the *Koryŏ Tripitaka* also reflected the vitality of Buddhism during these centuries of difficulty. Important philosophical treatises appeared; older sectarian movements were reinvigorated; and new ones were introduced. Besides religious works, the times witnessed production of prose tales and narrative poems by lesser figures among the elite, works addressed to the growing population of literate, lower-ranking and provincial officialdom and smaller-scale land holders; i.e., the sorts of people whom King Kongmin recruited to office in the 1350s–1360s during his attempt to weaken the most powerful aristocratic households.

In Japan, where the surviving evidence is more voluminous, one sees similar trends—the diffusion of arts and letters to more people in more of the realm, modifications of genre and theme to fit more diverse interests, evidence of aristocratic nostalgia for a lost past, attempts to recover the past, and the vitalization of Buddhist institutions and spread of Buddhist religiosity to a wider public.[54]

In terms of historiography, for example, whereas the histories of the early *ritsuryō* era dwelt on the affairs of the monarch and his or her chief officials, by the eleventh century they dwelt at much greater length on the lives of court ladies and others in courtly circles, and by the thirteenth their focus had shifted outward to warriors, both the elegant and less esteemed. Other works of history or social commentary lamented lost virtue or celebrated divine founders. Prose tales, which in early *ritsuryō* times meant didactic Buddhist anecdotes, developed into lengthy narratives both didactic and entertaining, religious or not, and they spoke to and about a broad range of peoples, male and female. As for Buddhism, whereas that of Nara/Heian had involved elegant doctrine aimed at the favored few in the capital city, by 1200 the clerical community was much more varied and scattered. And it was disseminating a much more eclectic and doc-

---

[53] Lancaster, 1996, pp. 182, 187–88. He identifies the wood as birch (*Betula schmidtii Regel*).

[54] Souyri, 2001, treats these themes in chapter 5. Totman, 2000, pp. 113–38, 172–98, also treats them, and his notes and bibliography identify some of the many splendid earlier, specialized works of scholarship.

trinally simple form of religion to a much more numerous and diverse faithful who were spread widely about the realm.

In short, the cultural distancing of elite from hoi polloi that had accompanied the rise of states had begun to reverse course. After 1350, as we note in Chapter 4, that process accelerated in both Korea and Japan, elite efforts to the contrary notwithstanding.

C. *The Broader Society*

This diffusion of elite culture outward and downward reflected socio-economic changes that were making the general society more diverse, more complex, more richly organized, and better equipped to cultivate recreational, philosophical, and aesthetic sensibilities. These trends are more visible in Japan than in Korea, partly due to the scarcity of surviving Korean evidence, but mainly, it appears, because of the greater success that Koryŏ's established elites had in retaining control of productive resources and because of Korea's more onerous experience in foreign relations, especially with Mongol invaders and overlords.

Japan. As earlier noted, the changing pattern of elite control during later Heian had shifted peace-keeping and tribute-collecting power downward into the hands of officials at the provincial and district levels, and to armed enforcers and estate managers of various sorts. The entrenching of military authority from the 1150s onward consolidated those trends, but even then the power of regional and local figures was hardly unconditional. They were still obligated to provide stipulated goods and services to their betters, although the petering out of city construction, changes in the military system, and other trends of the day probably reduced the demand for corvée labor. Furthermore, they had to provide the goods and services from the resources under their control, and if they squeezed their work force too hard, they were always at risk of losing people to other overseers. Consequently they had an interest in promoting the productivity and hence the output of the land and labor within their jurisdiction, thereby satisfying their superiors and meeting their own wants, while leaving their producers sufficiently well off to stay put.

To that end the local elite promoted land clearance and pressured their farmers to convert more acreage to paddy culture. They cajoled and coerced them to settle in villages and encouraged them to collaborate in managing irrigation systems and other communal resources.

And they urged them to manage their lands so as to maintain a level of fertility that would allow cropping year after year in lieu of the fallow-till-fallow cycle of earlier centuries.

Push and pull factors—the push of higher authority and the desire to survive; the pull of better living circumstances that one could hope for thanks to the increased capacity to maneuver among one's betters—prodded villagers as well as their superiors to pursue policies that would increase agricultural output, particularly of dry-field crops, which were easier to grow than rice and which tribute takers tended to ignore.[55] Then, as warfare, piracy, and banditry became more common, the further incentive of village self-defense reinforced the trend toward self-managed, self-sustaining village communities.

This combination of forces seems to have spurred the development and gradual diffusion of improved forms of agronomy, initially in central Japan, later in western and eastern regions. These changes, which we examine in more detail in Chapter 4 because they became widespread from the fourteenth century onward, helped sustain those more self-reliant villages and gave them yet more reason to organize and manage their own affairs.

By then, moreover, the increase in agricultural output that sustained a growing, diversifying society was also helping to spur trade and commerce. Continental trade expanded substantially during the twelfth century, leading to the proliferation of Chinese coins in Japan. By the thirteenth, the coins were being used in domestic as well as foreign trade. Meanwhile, as *ritsuryō* leaders lost control of affairs, more and more of the domestic trade came into the hands of organized guilds (*za*) of merchant-artisans who came to handle most of the provisioning for both central and hinterland elites. In the process they became a widespread population of entrepreneurs, their *za* often linked to particular shrines, temples, or regional magnates. They handled such diverse goods as, "reed mats, cloth, sewing needles, malt, lamp oil, charcoal, firewood, and lumber."[56] By 1350, Japan had developed into an appreciably more populous, structurally more complex, and economically more productive and dynamic society than it had been during the heyday of aristocratic bureaucracy. That tra-

---

[55] Souyri, 2001, pp. 90–91, emphasizes dry-field cropping. Troost, 1997, explains these village developments.
[56] Totman, 2000, p. 109.

jectory, however, was still in its early stages and would not reach its apogee for another three centuries.

Korea. Across the straits to the west, one sees fewer hints of new agronomic trends. During late Koryŏ fallowing evidently continued to be the standard method for revitalizing soils, although government decrees tried to end the practice by advocating the application of fertilizer materials to those fields claimed as royal tribute land. Around 1320 Koryŏ authorities prepared a Korean edition of a Chinese agronomic treatise on dry-field farming. A few years later they urged closer study of Chinese paddy culture and the use of water wheels. With lowland fields largely opened, however, most new land clearance during later Koryŏ was on hillsides, where workers laboriously leveled slopes to form terraces for dry-field grain and vegetable cropping. Well into the 1400s, dry fields continued to be more extensive than paddy land, by one estimate covering some 70% of the tilled acreage.[57]

Domestic political trends militated against village-initiated agronomic change insofar as military households and others of the elite were successful in accumulating estates and extracting tribute from them. And surely civil conflict and the continuing mobilization of corvée and other servile labor for diverse purposes interfered with any efforts to increase village output.

Foreign-spawned suffering, most notably that inflicted by the Mongols, added to Korea's woe. Facing the obdurate Ch'oe and other military men and encountering scattered resistance from local leaders, Mongol commanders appear to have engaged in considerable mayhem: plundering, killing holdouts, burning areas, and taking substantial numbers of captives for various uses. And, as noted earlier, even after a modus vivendi was worked out between Koryŏ and Yuan in 1270, the Mongols continued to impose onerous tribute burdens on the realm.

In coastal areas, meanwhile, *waegu* (*wakō* in Japanese) pirate squadrons operating out of southwestern Japan had become a modest menace from about 1220 onward. In 1226, for example, a Japanese court diarist reported that pirates had attacked Koryŏ, where they looted a walled town and some nearby villages.

---

[57] Yi T-j, 1983, pp. 34, 40–42.

> A gang of Chinzei [Kyushu] outlaws and others called the Matsura
> Gang in several tens of warships went and fought on outlying islands
> of that country, destroying people and houses and looting valuables.
> It is said that almost half of them [the outlaws] were killed or wounded,
> and the remaining looted and returned with silver articles and other
> things.[58]

Assaults on this scale continued until 1260 or so, as in this Korean
report of a pirate attack that year. Near today's Pusan a Japanese
vessel,

> came to Multo within the boundaries of the tax-ships anchored off
> that island and carried away 120 *sŏk* of grain and rice and forty-three
> *p'il* [bolts] of pongee. Also they entered Yŏndo [modern Kadŏto] and
> carried away all the food, clothing and articles essential for livelihood.[59]

In following years, as Mongol forces consolidated their grip on Korea,
waegu activity declined. After 1350, however, with Japan rent by civil
strife, *waegu* proliferated.[60] And with Koryŏ newly freed from the
Mongols but still lacking its own strong army, they were able to
plunder and devastate large areas of the peninsula's southern and
western lowlands, aided by the ease with which their shallow-draft
vessels could move among the thousands of islets and ascend the
estuaries of larger rivers.

In northwest Korea, moreover, armed Manchurian brigands plundered the countryside, adding to the sum of rural hardship.[61] By the
1390s, however, Korea's armies were revitalized, Japan more orderly,
and the new Ming Dynasty in firmer control of China. Over the
next few decades the Chosŏn Dynasty established itself, and the
pirates and brigands were largely suppressed.[62] By then they had ravaged many of Korea's most productive lowlands, however, and recovery came only slowly and with much effort.

The difficulties of these centuries hurt the powerful as well as the
weak, which prompted them to secure their interests as best they
could. Korean travelers of the day observed the hardship that so
many people were experiencing, as in this 1351 entry in one liter-

---

[58] Quoted in Hazard, 1967, p. 262.
[59] Quoted in Hazard, 1967, p. 275.
[60] Hazard, 1973 and 1976 focus on the late Koryŏ suppression of *waegu*. Souyri,
pp. 126–28, treats this piracy briefly.
[61] Duncan, 2000, pp. 183–84.
[62] Robinson, 1992, is an excellent study of this topic.

ate traveler's diary, which suggests how the struggle for survival could play out:

> On the fifteenth day [of the eighth month] I left Pangsan and arrived at Yanggu Prefecture, where I found the houses of both the *hyangni* [local functionaries] and the peasants falling down and their cooking hearths cold. When I asked passersby what had happened, they said, "This country has been administered by the officials at Yangch'ŏn. It has always had limited land and the soil is poor, so there have been few people and products. Recently powerful families have seized the fields and cause distress for the peasants. Rents and taxes are great, but there is no room to work even an additional button's worth of land. Every winter the rent collectors come in large numbers. If the peasants cannot pay, they are hung up by their hands and feet and caned to the bone. The residents, unable to endure this, have fled."[63]

Absconding, which had been a preferred mode of escape in early *ritsuryō* Japan but difficult by the thirteenth century, evidently was still feasible in Korea, although perhaps only under dire circumstances.

D. *Environmental Issues*

Perhaps the most notable points regarding environmental matters in Korea and Japan during these two centuries are the paucity of data and the ambiguous implications of what seems plausible.

Population trends and their determinants are obscure. In the case of Koryŏ, it appears that the turmoil of the times restrained increase, perhaps depressing overall numbers during the Mongol century, holding them well under four million. Within aristocratic households, however, or at least those that continued to flourish, better medical practice began to improve life chances, as suggested by this Chinese report:

> According to the old custom of Korea, when people fall ill, they never take medicine, they only worship ghosts and deities to curse and loathe the illness. [However, Chinese doctors were sent to Koryŏ to give medical instruction in the decades around 1100, and now] many people are well versed in medicine.[64]

By 1250 Korean medical specialists were compiling their own tracts on medicine, devoting attention to obstetrics and pediatrics, and starting,

---

[63] Quoted in Duncan, 2000, p. 186.
[64] Quoted in Sung S, 1977, p. 13.

it appears, to reduce infant mortality, leading to growth in aristocratic household membership.[65]

In Japan the demographic story is somewhat different. There the
depressive effects of recurrent epidemics declined as smallpox and
measles evolved into endemic, usually non-fatal diseases of the young.
A few major crop failures and famines slowed population growth,
but by the fourteenth century an upward trajectory seemed well in
place, as evidenced in the above-noted growth of village society. By
1350 the total population probably exceeded eight million, and perhaps was in the vicinity of ten.

As for the landscape, the decay, decline, and abandonment of capital cities surely reduced pressures on the ecosystem of central Japan
and may have had similar effects in the vicinities of Kyŏngju and
Kaesŏng, allowing some forest recovery and soil rejuvenation thereabouts. Warfare, for all its cruelty to people, was of a non-polluting,
pre-industrial type, and it may well have eased burdens on biota in
some locations by reducing or displacing human populations while
intensifying it in areas subjected to war-caused wildfire or to scav-
enging by refugees and the victims of plunder.

In broader terms the trajectory of earlier centuries probably continued in both Korea and Japan, with further expansion of land
committed to both dry-field and paddy culture, more deforesting of
accessible hillsides, and more downstream silting. Warfare, piracy,
and political turmoil temporarily disrupted life in many places, creating abandoned villages and arable, which would return to the wild
until resettled and reclaimed some years later.

In Japan the decline in fallowing, as noted earlier, reduced still
further the habitat for undomesticated lowland biota. Concurrently
the growth in village population combined with political turmoil to
spur more dry-field cropping and more swidden ("slash-and-burn")
culture—the intermittent clearance of upland areas to grow crops,
preferably without the tribute collector's knowledge. Also, the increased
use of fertilizer materials entailed some transfer of leaffall and other
mulch materials from wasteland and hillside to tilled land. Together

---

[65] Yi T-j, 1997, addresses this issue to argue for rapid society-wide population
growth in later Koryŏ. Duncan, 2000, p. 192, sees the inferred change as restricted
to the elite, who are the source of Yi's data. The most notable compilation of the
day was the *Hyangyak kugŭppang* (of 1236 or 1243), a broad-ranging compendium of
information on health problems and remedies. See also Magner, 1993, pp. 390–92.

these two practices probably accelerated erosion on hillsides, with downstream complications of silting and heightened flooding. All in all, however, in both Korea and Japan the decline of aristocratic bureaucracy, whether accompanied by social stasis or growth, seems to have had only modest environmental consequences, regardless the trauma it posed for the elite few or society at large.

Recapitulation

In neither Korea nor Japan did developments of the centuries 700–1350 have transformational effects comparable to those earlier achieved by the adoption of agriculture and metallurgy. Rather, the centuries witnessed continuations and elaborations of trends that trace back to earlier times—trends shaping the character and organization of ruling elites, the structure and operation of society as a whole, and the environmental impacts thereof.

In summing up developments to 1150, we earlier noted that these ruling elites built and occupied grand capital cities, developed elaborate aristocratic bureaucracies that enabled them to control and exploit the producer population, and on that basis sustained elegant urban cultures of and for the favored few. We noted that there were few signs of enhanced well-being among the general populace or of expanded agricultural output per capita or per hectare. There were, however, increases in the area under cultivation, with accompanying changes in lowland landscape and biotic composition. In the vicinity of capital cities, excessive exploitation achieved substantial environmental damage, but beyond there the centuries seem to have produced no noteworthy declines in biodiversity or biomass productivity.

One sees considerable evidence that by 1150 the elite's aristocratic bureaucratic order was functioning poorly, that power was diffusing among more and more rival claimants, and that in consequence disorder was spreading. In both Korea and Japan these trends eventuated late in the twelfth century in seizures of power by military men. In Korea that outcome was undone around 1350, after which civil leaders reaffirmed older practices of aristocratic bureaucracy, whereas in Japan, as we shall note in Chapter 4, an analogous outcome was not realized until after 1600.

The diffusion of power that eventuated in military triumph after 1150 was accompanied by diffusion of higher culture among intermediate social strata. These strata were emerging as the old power structure decayed, as commerce expanded, and, in Japan at least, as agronomic change began to increase farm productivity and underwrite broader social growth. These trends foreshadowed sustained socio-economc changes and broader environmental changes that later became more pronounced in both Korea and Japan, as we shall note at greater length in following pages.

CHAPTER FOUR

THE LATER AGRICULTURAL ORDER (1350–1870 CE)

Much as the centuries 700–1350 encompassed a long period (700–1150) of relative order followed by a shorter one (1150–1350) of intensifying disorder, so the centuries 1350–1870 seem to have embraced a long period of socio-economic growth (1350–1700) followed by a shorter one (1700–1870) of social stasis and environmental stress. Both the story of socio-economic growth and that of environmental overload are more clearly visible in Japan than in Korea. But it seems possible to argue that in both places the trajectory of growth continued through the seventeenth century, until the counter-pressures of an over-burdened ecosystem began to stymie the growth, moving both societies into a difficult period of demographic stability and socio-economic churning that continued into the years around 1870.

As the above phrasing suggests, it was elite politics—the flourishing and failure of aristocratic bureaucracy—that framed the history down to 1350 or so. During the centuries after that date, however, it was a broader, more basic socio-economic story—the acceleration and playing out of the types of growth trends that had begun appearing in Japan before that year—that constituted the central story of Korea and Japan's history.

The elite political history that unfolded within this broader context was basically a story of initial stability that gave way to disorder which, in turn, yielded to new order until nineteenth-century problems overwhelmed the regimes of both peninsula and archipelago. In the Korean case the stability of early Chosŏn was disrupted by invading armies from the 1590s through the 1630s, to be restored thereafter by a newly envigorated Chosŏn leadership. In Japan the brief stability of the Ashikaga regime dissolved during the 1460s, and restabilization did not occur until the decades around 1600, when rulers imposed an unprecedented level of control on the realm.

In both societies the socio-economic growth that continued, however erratically, down to 1700 or so, entailed the widespread adoption of more productive agricultural techniques and a corresponding increase in output—total, per arable hectare, and possibly per work-year. It also encompassed, more extensively in Japan than Korea, the expansion of fishing, mining, and other primary production, monetization of an expanding and diversifying commerce, enlargement and proliferation of villages and towns, accompanying change in social relationships and growth in the elaborateness of society, and the spread of higher cultural attainments more widely among middling strata of society.

In the broader terms of environmental history, these centuries of dynamic growth had the inevitable consequence of bearing ever more heavily on the ecosystem. By 1700 little more usable land was available for reclamation in either country, spurring intensified efforts by producers to maximize income from the land they did have. The lack of reclaimable land also heightened competition to control the usufruct, as evidenced by heightened disputes over water rights, spreading tenantry, and escalating protests over rent, taxes, and other perceived inequities. And in the rest of the realm, the three quarters or more that were not being cultivated, excessive deforestation was producing, in Japan at least, disputes over woodland use rights and shortages of forest products as well as downstream injuries and burdens.

In both countries the earlier surge of population growth was petering out by 1700 amidst heightened social hardship, malnutrition, disease, and, in Japan, intensifying regimens of birth control. In the face of myriad difficulties, moreover, a broad array of reformist and transformist ideas and movements began to appear. Then, from about 1790 onward, the powerful exogenous forces of European imperialism introduced new problems and possibilities that, by the 1870s, began propelling both societies into the uncharted world of industrialization, a world that western Europe itself had started blundering into only a few decades earlier.

A Political Narrative, 1350–1870

Although the "framing story" of these centuries may be socio-economic rather than political, the latter merits attention for a couple of reasons. First, as in earlier centuries, elite political history remained the most richly documented portion of the Korean and Japanese experience and the portion most fully examined by historians. Given the paucity of usable data in general, such a relatively complete source cannot be ignored. Second, as major exploiters of human labor and natural resources during the eras of both growth and stasis, the elite remained significant participants in the wider history despite their diminishing capacity to control it.

To explain that last phrase, as the two societies became larger and more complex during these centuries, ruling elites periodically devised more elaborate structures of control and exploitation, and these adaptations sufficed for a time to preserve their positions, at least in attenuated form. Despite those measures, however, as generations passed, the rulers found themselves less and less able to control the larger history—that of the fisc, the economy more broadly, literate culture, popular recreation, or even human movement, not to mention use (and misuse) of the land and its creatures. Rather, they were buffeted more and more, not just by rival elites, whether domestic or foreign, but also by socio-economic processes and non-elite groups that increasingly lay beyond their control. Indeed, one could argue that reversing that trend was a major objective of political reform in both Korea and Japan during the decades from around 1870 onward.

A. Korea

King Kongmin (r. 1351–74), as we noted in Chapter 3, attempted to revitalize the post-Mongol Koryŏ monarchy, but he encountered immense difficulties. His maneuvers antagonized powerful landed families, and his government was further weakened by the incursions of marauding bands from Manchuria. Worse yet was a surge in the plundering activity by Japanese pirates (*waegu*), whose armadas of small boats terrorized coastal villages and penetrated Korea's agricultural heartland by moving up estuaries of the Naktong, Kŭm, Han, Imjin, Taedong, and other rivers. Then during the 1380s leaders of the recently established Ming Dynasty in China proposed to pacify their northeastern border region by establishing a new commandery whose jurisdiction would cover the northern part of Korea.

These developments served to energize Korean military leaders, spurring rivalries, conflicts, and the rise to power of the army commander Yi Sŏng-gye. He overwhelmed his rivals, ended the turmoil of late Koryŏ, and founded a new regime, the Chosŏn (or Yi) Dynasty, which he headed under the reign name T'aejo (r. 1392–98) and controlled with the collaboration of his political allies. He moved his headquarters southward from the Koryŏ capital of Kaesŏng to today's Seoul, which lies in the heart of Korea's agricultural lowlands and close by the Han River, Korea's most central waterway.

T'aejo rewarded his allies with substantial estates, creating thereby a new landed ruling elite.[1] He did so in conjunction with a countrywide cadastral survey that enabled his government to tax arable land more effectively and also to abolish the estate rights of numerous other entrenched landholders. He and his successors reorganized and envigorated the monarchy's central and regional governing structures, both civil and military. They brought the last of the Japanese pirates to heel, replacing them with regularized trading activity in the Pusan vicinity.[2] And they outmaneuvered the Ming, thwarting plans for a commandery and extending their own control northeastward to the Tumen River despite the resistance of local peoples. In doing so they secured control of all the area we know today as Korea.[3]

This Chosŏn ruling elite, like its predecessors, was largely hered-

---

[1] On T'aejo's land awards, see Clark, 1982.

[2] On early Chosŏn's political relations with Japan, see Robinson, 1992 and 2000.

[3] Wagner, 1977, notes the gains made by people from Korea's northern provinces in acquiring *yangban* status during the Chosŏn centuries. One suspects that economic development of the north, particularly the newly secured northeast, may have been at the base of their gain in socio-political stature.

itary, being known as *yangban*, or members of the "two orders" of civil and military officialdom.[4] To preserve the advantages that good connections and genealogy first brought their way, *yangban* devoted their energies to securing government office and acquiring income-producing land. As generations passed, their numbers grew, intensifying the competition for access to both office and land. By the year 1500 factional lines were forming, and in following decades these hardened, becoming hereditary.[5] Faction members cast their differences in rigid Confucian terms, which they learned in private academies that factional leaders utilized to train successive generations of offspring for government service.

The competition for advantage that underlay this factional feuding had broader ramifications because it meant that estate holders and tax collectors squeezed producers more vigorously. Doing so, however, created rural hardship and revived the peasantry's practice of absconding to escape tribute levies, which served only to stunt growth in agricultural output and the level of rent and taxes it could sustain.[6] By the later 1500s these problems of factionalism, fiscal stress, and an overburdened peasantry were producing harsh political infighting and social unrest, prompting scholars to advocate reforms of diverse sorts. Before the turmoil got out of hand or any substantial reform measures were enacted, however, the realm was convulsed by an unprecedented assault from the east.

By 1592 a Japanese military commander, Toyotomi Hideyoshi (1536–98), had overwhelmed his rivals to become the master of Japan, thereby ending generations of warfare. For reasons that continue to perplex historians, he decided to conquer China, and when the king of Chosŏn declined to grant his armies free passage up the peninsula, he resolved to traverse it forcibly.[7] The Koreans resisted; Chinese armies assisted them; and after an initial advance northward to the peninsula's upper end, the invading armies were driven back to an enclave in southeastern Korea. Advance units remained there until

---

[4] The character of the early Chosŏn ruling elite has generated a great deal of discussion. A recent treatment of the debate is Palais, 1996, pp. 32–47.

[5] The classic study of this factionalism is Wagner, 1974.

[6] Lee K-b, 1984, pp. 202–204.

[7] Regarding Hideyoshi's continental policy, solid works that will lead to other sources are Elisonas, 1991, and Berry, 1982. On the war in Korea, see Palais, 1996, pp. 75–91. On Hideyoshi's geographical understanding and misunderstanding, see Kamiya, 1994, and Walker, 2001b.

after Hideyoshi's death in 1598, when Japan's leaders abandoned the whole disastrous enterprise.

By then, however, the years of brutal fighting and occupation had ravaged the Chosŏn regime and subjected the population, especially in southern regions, to years of hardship. The invading army sustained itself primarily through plunder and appropriation, which weighed harshly on the general populace. Battle casualties were high. Records of all sorts were lost or destroyed, confounding local and regional governments. The Seoul regime itself, as well as many of its operatives, was impoverished and its governing routines thoroughly ruptured.

Coming atop decades of oppressive rule, the added hardship provoked popular upheavals, and after the invaders departed, Korea's rulers felt compelled to develop new systems of administration and taxation. Reforms of the early seventeenth century served to break up some of the large estates, redistributed control of the land, restored more of it to government tax roles, and apparently achieved more equitable and less harsh taxation. Even as the rulers labored to reconstruct their base of power, however, they found new dangers appearing from a more traditional direction, the northwest.

There Nurhachi (1559–1626), a local leader in the Liaodong region of Manchuria, had begun extending his control over neighboring groups even before Hideyoshi's invasion. During the 1590s Ming rulers, who needed a cooperative Manchuria while they helped Chosŏn to contain Hideyoshi's army, recognized him as a regional chieftain. In following years his armies swelled, along with the area of Manchuria under his control. Collisions with Ming forces occurred, and by the 1620s Chosŏn's leaders found themselves under pressure to ally with one side or the other. These pressures became entangled in domestic factional conflicts, leading in 1627 to a Manchu invasion of Korea and to Chosŏn's acceptance of "younger brother" status. Renewed Korean resistance to Manchu demands in 1636 led to a second invasion, another defeat, punishment, and resentful submission to the Ch'ing Dynasty, as Manchu leaders styled their nascent regime. In following decades the Manchus completed their conquest of China, and within the context of a re-stabilized East Asia, the Chosŏn regime continued to govern Korea, sanctioned by its tributary relationship to the Ch'ing.

During the eighteenth century, as earlier, the monarchy was controlled by factions, but by then their number had proliferated, and more and more of them found their members excluded from office and influence. During the nineteenth century relatives of the king's wife came to dominate the regime in Seoul, and *yangban* in most other lineages found themselves reduced to the role of outsider or bribe-paying subordinate.

Under these circumstances more and more *yangban* members chose to give up the quest for office, settling instead in villages and towns on their small hereditary landholdings. There they devoted their energies to operating family academies and practicing the literate arts deemed appropriate to a modestly stipended gentry-intelligentsia. These arts included poetry writing and the crafting of essays that criticized the regime, spelled out reform policies, formulated philosophical bases for reform and righteous governance, or explored less political agendas of a religious, philosophical, or other scholarly sort.

Commonly, moreover, these men remained figures of consequence in their village or locality, and their alienation from Seoul fostered the diversion of tax proceeds into local pockets, which eroded government income and heightened the squeeze on those producers whom the regime still could control.[8] This trend only compounded public discontent with the rulers. As the nineteenth century advanced, that discontent manifested itself in denunciatory placarding, brigandage, the rise of millennialist movements, and local uprisings that the regime sometimes found difficult to suppress. By the 1870s, even as a new surge of foreign complications was gaining momentum, the regime already had its hands full coping with domestic disaffection.

B. *Japan*

The shared larger rhythm of Korean and Japanese political history during the centuries 1350–1870—from stability to disorder to renewed stability and eventual nineteenth-century disarray—cannot conceal dissimilarities of the two experiences in all three phases. At the same time, as we note below, some apparent differences should not obscure underlying similarities.

Perhaps the most striking dissimilarity lay in the performance of the Ashikaga and early Chosŏn regimes. The founders of Chosŏn, as mentioned above, were able to topple Koryŏ, displace their rivals,

---

[8] On the local role of resident *yangban*, see Kawashima, 1979 and 1988.

entrench themselves in power during the 1390s, and sustain their regime thereafter, even through the turmoil of the 1590s–1630s. In sharp contrast, founders of the Ashikaga regime were unable to reverse the growth of local power that had emerged in Japan during preceding centuries. Instead, as they jousted with the "southern court" during the decades after 1338, they had to settle for a coalition regime that acknowledged a high level of *de facto* local control in return for nominal subordination by—and mutually beneficial cooperation with—regional barons (*daimyō* or "great names"). The readiness of those daimyo to collaborate was a measure, in turn, of their own weakness vis à vis lesser local figures.

The Ashikaga-Chosŏn dissimilarity had several aspects. Whereas Chosŏn leaders awarded estates to their henchmen and denied them to others, the Ashikaga had to recognize most of the land-holding arrangements that already existed. And whereas the Chosŏn regime was able to extract tribute from producers throughout the realm, the Ashikaga received tribute from only a small part of Japan, relying instead on various other forms of income. Finally, and symbolically, whereas Chosŏn leaders had displaced Koryŏ kings, secured the monarchial title for themselves, and established their own capital at Seoul, Ashikaga leaders left the Japanese royal household intact and settled for the title of shogun, with its implication of appointment by and subordination to the monarch. And they situated their headquarters not far from the royal palace in Kyoto, as Heian came to be called.

Weak from the outset, Ashikaga leaders only gradually extended their influence into Kyushu during the 1370s–1380s. Within a generation thereafter they lost control of northeasten Japan. By the 1440s they faced insurrection in central Japan, and after the 1460s they lost control of almost all areas outside of Kyoto itself. In their place, generations of local lords, ambitious underlings, regional religious leaders, and mobilized groups of villagers and townsmen battled and maneuvered for advantage, using or abusing nominal shogun as seemed advantageous.[9]

During the sixteenth century, however, local lords gradually developed more effective systems for organizing, controlling, and exploiting their lands and people. They learned how to maximize their

---

[9] Souyri, 2001, chapters 7, 8, 10, 11 elaborate these themes.

control, how to minimize the threat of rebellion among their followers, and how to use these more secure power bases to extend
their sway over adjoining areas, thereby becoming regional barons.
By 1580 the last powerless Ashikaga shogun had been driven into
exile and the realm was controlled by a handful of these barons, the
daimyo.

During the 1580s Hideyoshi succeeded in battling and bargaining
the other daimyo into submission, giving himself a *de facto* dictator-
ial position before launching his ruinous attempt to conquer China.
That failure and Hideyoshi's death in 1598 set the stage for renewed
struggle among the daimyo. As matters worked out, however, a cluster of battles during the summer of 1600 proved decisive, and a
coalition under the firm control of Tokugawa Ieyasu (1542–1616)
emerged supreme.

Like Minamoto leaders of the 1180s (and like successive Korean
dynasts) Ieyasu established his own capital, choosing to remain at
Edo (today's Tokyo), his baronial headquarters in eastern Japan. Like
the Minamoto and Ashikaga, however, he left the surviving royal
household in place and took the title of shogun with its symbolic
suggestion of subordination. More importantly, rather than trying to
extend his own system of administration and tribute-collecting into
the domains of daimyo, he, like the Ashikaga founders, recognized
most of their land-holding and local governing arrangements in return
for nominal oaths of allegiance. He thereby created a sort of "fed-
eral" or "feudal" system of governance, in contrast to the centralized regime of Chŏson.

Whereas this set of choices had produced a weak Ashikaga regime,
however, this time it produced a strong regime. It did so for a number of reasons. First, Ieyasu's own autonomous power base was far
stronger than that of the Ashikaga founders. Secondly, the daimyo
who became his henchmen, whether willingly or *faute de mieux*, had
much better control of their own areas, including local clerics, officials,
and warriors, as well as their own followers and the producer populace. They were, as a consequence, under much less pressure than
earlier generations of daimyo to expand their power as a means of
protecting their interests vis-à-vis these locals. When no longer threat-
ened from above, therefore, they found it prudent to accept Tokugawa
suzerainty and to work on behalf of their mutual well-being by collaborating with Edo to keep subordinate people in their "proper"
place, thereby preserving the peace.

Most important to keeping the peace was controlling the vast military force that two centuries of warfare had created. In part this was achieved by a countrywide demobilization that returned hundreds of thousands of fighting men to other jobs, mostly as farmers. The remaining 400,000 or so experienced warriors, most of whom were in the service of daimyo, were designated *samurai*, given specified ranks, stipends, and duties, and mostly required to live in the headquarters towns of their lords. The ranking system was elaborate, ranging from a few richly endowed, high status samurai—the shogun, daimyo, and their senior advisors—down through middling layers of administrators to lower *samurai*, the bulk of this hereditary warrior class. These minor figures were paid very modestly and given petty police, guard, attendant, and administrative tasks in the highly structured governmental organizations of their hereditary lords. In essence, that is to say, an elaborate new form of aristocratic bureaucracy had been created.

For a century this highly structured Tokugawa regime flourished, but by 1700 both shogun and daimyo found themselves slipping into dire fiscal straits. Thereafter financial problems and schemes for their remediation dominated political life, supplemented during the 1800s by intensified unrest among the rural populace, by other manifestations of public discontent similar to those found in Korea, and then by the escalating demands of foreigners. The troubles culminated in 1868 in collapse of the shogunal regime and formation of the Meiji monarchial government.

C. *Korea and Japan: Similarities*

During the years 1350–1600, as noted above, the dissimilarities of the Korean and Japanese political experiences seemed particularly striking.[10] After 1600, as well, one important political dissimilarity persisted; indeed, it gradually became more pronounced. With time's passage, as mentioned earlier, swelling numbers of *yangban* settled in

---

[10] Indeed the dissimilarities of the Ashikaga and early Chosŏn regimes are so striking that one is tempted to liken Ashikaga rule in Japan to that of the Mongols in Korea a century earlier. The latter were outsiders and conquerors, it is true, and also stronger and more ruthless, but both regimes ruled primarily by way of weak coalitions, compromise, and indirect control through unreliable collaborators of convenience. On this theme, see also footnote 50 in Chapter 3.

villages throughout the realm but mainly in the vicinity of Seoul or other larger towns (see Plate 14). In the process they became a countrywide local elite, sustained primarily by land rents and other local income. In Japan, however, *samurai* lived, with some exceptions, in the headquarters towns of their lords (see Plates 15, 16), where they were readily available for service and subject to relatively easy control. Indeed, they were so thoroughly urbanized that when penurious daimyo periodically tried to resettle them in the countryside, few agreed to go.

In consequence of this dissimilarity in residential arrangements, whereas large numbers of *yangban* lived in sustained proximity of commoner neighbors, sometimes able to exploit them, and with their own advantages and pretensions evident on a daily basis, minor *samurai* mostly lived out of sight, so to say. Sequestered in the headquarters towns and cities of their lords, they were effectively ghettoized, ill-placed to exploit commoners, and thus less susceptible to public scrutiny and resentment.[11] During the nineteenth century, therefore, as social conditions worsened, *yangban* as a group were well placed to bear the brunt of popular discontent whereas in Japan the discontent was directed more sharply at the ruling elites and their mercantile collaborators.

This difference in residential patterns and its consequences notwithstanding, from 1600 onward the similarities between Korean and Japanese political arrangements seem the more noteworthy consideration. To begin with, although the formalities of administrative organization were dissimilar—in Korea a structurally centralized alliance of land-holding aristocrats who staffed an officialdom that administered a unitary realm on behalf of their leader, the king vs. a structurally decentralized coalition of daimyo under their senior member who, as shogun, was expected to keep the peace on behalf of the Japanese monarch—the Tokugawa settlement of 1600 in fact secured a cluster of shared elite interests much as Yi Sŏng-gye's settlement had done during the 1390s and his successors' reforms in the aftermath of Hideyoshi.

In another way, as well, a central difference between the Chôson and Tokugawa regimes concealed a similarity. In Korea the ruling

---

[11] A delightful autobiography-of-sorts that shows how much difficulty even a middle-ranking *samurai* had in exploiting commoners is Katsu, 1988.

elite were *yangban*, people who saw themselves as Confucian gentle-
men in a world where civil governance and cultural pursuits were
held in much higher esteem than mastery of the martial arts. In
Japan the ruling elite were *samurai*, self-professed military men who
purportedly had supplemented their skill in the martial arts with
mastery of the arts of the Confucian gentleman. Hence they were
qualified to handle civil as well as military aspects of governance. In
fact, however, both *yangban* and *samurai* were members of a highly
stratified, hereditary elite, sustained by land-based, household income
that was augmented by office-related stipends when they handled
government tasks. Most of those tasks were of a civil bureaucratic
sort, ranging from a few high administrative posts to a plethora of
menial positions, which men generally held in accord with their family rank.

The similarities of *yangban* and *samurai* status and function were
reinforced by a shared ideology that was transmitted through formal
schooling. In earlier centuries elite thought in both Korea and Japan
had contained diverse elements, Buddhist and Confucian most promi-
nently. During the centuries after 1350, well disciplined Confucian
thought came to prevail, doing so in Korea sooner than Japan. In
both places more recent Song-dynasty formulations, particularly that
known as Neo-Confucianism (or Ch'eng-Zhu thought), enjoyed dominance during the seventeenth century. It conveyed an image of
society as a multi-layer status hierarchy that reached downward from
the ruling elite, whether *yangban* or *samurai*, through these successively
lower layers (which we examine below). *Yangban* and *samurai* were
expected to master the arts of good governance, set an example of
virtue for all society, and rule accordingly.

During the eighteenth and nineteenth centuries, as the two societies encountered more difficulties and as status realities diverged
ever more sharply from Neo-Confucian prescriptions, alternative formulations enjoyed more and more favor. Initially these were relatively conservative reformist and meliorist ideas, often alternative or
modified Confucian formulations advanced by *yangban* and *samurai*
scholars. As the eighteenth century aged, however, and especially
during the nineteenth, political thought in both Korea and Japan
acquired more radical arguments. More and more of the opinions
were being articulated by scholars of lesser status, position, or privilege, and more of them spoke to aggrieved urban and rural commoner populations. And in their writings proponents advanced more

basic ideas on rectification, some of which included millenarian propo-
sitions that sought a fundamental reordering of society and radical
redistribution of privilege.[12]

In political trajectory, as well as political structure and thought,
Korea and Japan had much in common after 1600. Most basically,
perhaps, by the late 1600s both regimes were pushing the limits of
their tax bases, and for most of the next two centuries fiscal issues
remained their dominant political concern.

On both sides of the straits fiscal shortfalls beggered governments
and created financial hardships for the ruling elites, most severely
for lesser *yangban* and *samurai*. In Chosŏn, where membership in the
yangban class kept growing, factional division provided a mechanism
for allocating the fiscal yield, gradually moving more and more members of lesser *yangban* households into the countryside, as earlier mentioned, where they survived as local men of influence or cultural
distinction and petty, often impoverished, landlords or farmers. In
Japan, with its more rigid system of elite categorization and roles, a
major response to fiscal constraint was to limit firmly the size of the
samurai class by allowing no proliferation of branch households. In
both societies ways were found, such as marriage, adoption, sale of
perquisites, and pursuit of gainful employment, to funnel commoner
wealth into elite hands. However, these mechanisms also contributed
to a blurring of status lines, as we note below. Nevertheless, the solutions gave both Chosŏn and Tokugawa ruling elites funding sufficient
to quel domestic unrest and perpetuate their dominance until late
in the nineteenth century.

The Age of Growth (1350–1700)

These centuries of political vicissitude were also centuries of broad-
ranging socio-economic growth down to 1700 or so, and of more
complex change thereafter. The several aspects of growth were all
interconnected, needless to say, but for purposes of examination we
can disaggregate them into the categories of agriculture, commerce,
demographics, society, and environment. Again, the evidence in the

---

[12] Eckert, 1990, Chs. 11–12, and Totman, 1993, Chs. 16, 19, develop these
themes.

Japanese case is more extensive than in the Korean, and it suggests that changes there were more substantial. Also, there was considerable variation in timing and particulars both between Korea and Japan and among regions within each country. Still, the basic trends and dynamics of change seem similar on both sides of the straits.

A. *Agriculture*

The changes that were to characterize Korean and Japanese agriculture during these centuries first became evident in central Japan during the two centuries or so before 1350, as mentioned briefly in Chapter 3. A core characteristic of these changes was labor intensification: they required cultivators to invest more hours of time per hectare of arable, doing so for longer portions of the year and on a more regular basis. As *quid pro quo* they increased the harvest per hectare, enabling more and more people to survive on a given amount of arable.

Labor intensification—working harder at their farming in plain English—required both opportunity and incentive. In Japan farmers were able and willing to work harder thanks initially to the earlier-noted decay of the *ritsuryō* corvée labor and conscript military systems and later due to the inability of central rulers to control hinterland activities and the need of local elites to keep their producer population from absconding by restraining their own impulse to exploit. In Korea periodic political disruptions during these centuries may similarly have given locals more control of their own life routines and hence incentive to invest more effort in crop production.

In both countries the developing horticultural regimen compelled villagers to collaborate ever more fully with one another, so that the more intricate work routines could be implemented in a timely manner and so that disputes over the use of shared resources—labor, water, fertilizer-fodder-fuel materials, or other valued goods—could be avoided or resolved without the involvement of higher authority. That requirement, in turn, necessitated better local organization, meaning arrangements that were both more disciplined and more able to elicit willing cooperation from the members of a village or locality.

Neither top-down authoritarian control nor any ideology of laissez faire fitted this emerging rural order. Rather, it seemed to require a self- and community-disciplined sense of group interest that tolerated enough individual diversity to be acceptable to its members while proscribing conduct deemed hurtful to the community as a whole. In central Japan such communal village arrangements (most commonly called *sō*) were present by 1350, their use spreading across the realm in following centuries; in Korea an analogous arrangement (the *kye*) appeared from around 1500 onward.[13]

There were several agronomic and technological aspects to this emergent community-centered system of production, and cumulatively they expanded both "private" and "public" production, meaning on the one hand output for household consumption and, on the other, output for the tax or rent collector or the market. Villagers increased private output by utilizing more patches of soil close by their house and sheds to grow vegetables, fruit trees, or other crops and to house pigs, chickens, horses, cattle or other domesticated creatures (see Plates 17, 18). They also went into the hills more often to open patches of swidden that could produce usable crops.

Public output increased with the expansion of both dry-field and paddy cropping.[14] Dry-field cropping remained more extensive than paddy culture in both Korea and Japan, but probably because governments were primarily interested in rice cropping, dry-field developments are not well recorded.[15] Also, the practice entailed much less engineering than paddy tillage and therefore left less evidence on the ground. Nevertheless, it appears that in both countries substantially more land was opened to dry-field production during these years, and its output per hectare also grew as better agronomic practices were adopted.[16] Specifically, more intensive fertilizing gradually replaced fallowing, and crop diversification led to a better fit between crop and field. Also, furrow seeding of dry grains replaced broadcast seeding (see Plate 19), which improved germination rates and facilitated later weeding, fertilizing, and harvest.[17]

---

[13] On *sō*, see Troost, 1997, Tonomura, 1992. On *kye*, see Ko S-j, 1986, and Chung, 1974.

[14] Souyri, 2001, p. 91 and *passim*, stresses dry-field cropping in Japan and argues, correctly I suspect, that the importance of rice cropping "has no doubt been over-estimated."

[15] On Korea, see Yi T-j, 1983, p. 40. For Japan, see Saito, 2002, p. 225, who writes: "During medieval times, there were comparatively more dry-fields than wet paddies in Japan."

[16] Changes in Korean agriculture are touched briefly in Mitchell, 1979–80, p. 82; Park, S-r, 1992, p. 85; and Shin, 1978, p. 193.

[17] Agricultural "productivity" is commonly thought of in terms of input-output

One noteworthy cropping development of the era was the introduction of cotton culture. Hitherto the predominant cloth for daily
use had been woven from the coarse, stiff fiber of the plant ramie.
Cotton production was introduced to Korea in the final years of
Koryŏ, and the cloth it yielded was so much more comfortable than
ramie that demand rapidly rose. Korean farmers not only produced
cotton for domestic use but from the 1420s onward exported it to
Japan in place of earlier exports of ramie and hemp. A few decades
thereafter Japanese farmers in Kyushu obtained seed from Korea
and started growing their own cotton, but until the late 1500s cotton
exports from Korea to Japan continued to flourish. The Hideyoshi-
Manchu intrusions of 1592–1636 disrupted cotton production on the
peninsula, and during the seventeenth century Japan finally became
self-sufficient in its growth and manufacture.[18] Loss of that export
market, together with government efforts to tax cotton production
and to reserve fertile lowlands for food production, evidently discouraged further expansion of cotton output in Korea, but in both
countries it remained a major crop thereafter.[19]

More richly recorded than changes in dry-field cropping was the
increase in paddy culture. In Japan numerous groups—villagers
throughout these centuries, regional barons mostly from the sixteenth
century onward, and the ruling Tokugawa coalition that emerged
during the seventeenth—all labored to increase arable acreage, build
more and better irrigation systems, and get more rice and other produce to the consumer.[20] Most visibly, perhaps, baronial governments
were sufficiently powerful in the decades around 1600 so they could
mobilize corvée labor gangs large enough to clear lowlands near
major rivers, erect massive flood control dykes, and develop complex irrigation systems, thereby bringing large acreages of fertile land
into paddy tillage.[21] Less visibly, with the end of warfare villagers
opened up innumerable small parcels of land to cultivation, putting

---

ratios of land or labor. Where both labor and land are ample, however, the question may be couched in terms of "seed-yield ratio," as noted below in footnote 25.
See Palais, 1996, pp. 363–64, and Farris, forthcoming, for discussions respectively
of grain seed yields in Korea and Japan.

[18] Koh, S-j, 1975.
[19] Palais, 1996, pp. 111–12.
[20] Troost, 1997, adumbrates "medieval" agronomic developments. The classic
English-language study of "early modern" agricultural developments is Smith, 1959.
[21] See Yamamura, 1981.

yet more land into crop production. By 1700 Japan's arable acreage was roughly triple what it had been before 1350, and an appreciable part of that increase was in large-scale lowland paddy fields.

Even as more land was opened and more elaborate irrigation systems developed, the use of water wheels became increasingly common in both Korea and Japan. Ponds that trapped and held water for regulated release through the growing season also proliferated. Water so trapped had the added virtue of being warmed by its sustained exposure to sunlight, with the consequence that it—like water in the paddy fields proper—heated the soil, raised nighttime temperatures of the ambient atmosphere, and thus lengthened the growing season by reducing the risk of nocturnal frost in both spring and fall.

Farmers used fertilizer—ashes initially, mulch and such manure as domesticated animals produced in later years—much more widely and more regularly, which enabled them to double- and even triple-crop fields (see Plate 20). A strategy that became common in southerly regions of the archipelago was to grow a summer crop of wet rice, harvest it, heap up the paddy field soil to make ridges or raised beds for dry cropping, smooth and firm the heaped soil and plant the beds to one or another grain or vegetable crop, harvest it in the spring, and re-level the field for a new rice crop. The massive increase in hand labor required by this practice was facilitated by the continuing spread of iron tools. In Japan iron use accelerated during the fourteenth century as better smelting techniques cut costs, enabling even smallholders to possess "iron grub hoes, sickles, axes, and hatchets."[22]

In 1420 a Korean visitor to central Japan described the multiple-cropping regimen when he reported that farmers near present-day Osaka sowed winter crops of barley and wheat,

> which they harvest in the early summer of the following year. After that they plant rice seedlings. In the beginning of the fall they cut their rice ... and plant buckwheat, which they cut in early winter [prior to planting the barley and wheat]. They can plant seeds three times in one year on one paddy field because they can make it into paddy by damming the river and letting water in and then make it into a dry field by removing the dam on the river and letting the water out.[23]

---

[22] Troost, 1997, p. 97.
[23] Troost, 1990, p. 75; reproduced in Totman, 2000, pp. 147–48. On Korea, see Palais, 1996, pp. 109–10, 366–67, 855.

In following centuries this sort of multiple-cropping came to be widely employed, mainly in the warmer, southern parts of Korea and Japan, where the growing season was sufficiently long.

Southwestern Japan also was the region that benefited most from the introduction of a type of "long grain" (*indica*) rice known as Champa or *akamai* ("red rice"). Although fitted to a warmer, south-east Asian climate (Champa is southern Vietnam; see Map 2-1), *akamai* coped better than existing *japonica* varieties with drought or fertilizer scarcity and so was more reliable in the face of climatic irregularity.[24] Later, when irrigation systems became more dependable, its use appears to have declined, but during these early centuries of agricultural intensification, it proved a boon in warmer areas, contributing, no doubt, to the demographic and socio-economic growth of southwestern Japan.

Gradually Korean and Japanese farmers also adopted the use of seed beds in their rice cropping (see Plate 21). Instead of spading or plowing their paddy fields, flooding and smoothing them, and then sowing the rice seed, they first broadcast the seed on small, pre-watered, pre-warmed parcels. During the next few weeks, as those seeds were sprouting, they harvested any winter crops that were maturing on their paddy fields and then leveled, fertilized, and spaded or plowed the land for its summer crop. This strategy thus lengthened the growing season and improved the efficiency of the work schedule.

At the opportune moment farmers then transplanted the seedlings into paddy fields, spacing them in rows. That strategy enabled them to replace failed seedlings as needed and later to fertilize the growing crop. It also reduced the need for weeding by giving the rice seedlings a head start that helped them shade out such weeds as did grow. The cumulative result of this highly disciplined and labor-intensive system of tillage was a substantially increased harvest per arable hectare and per household work-year. And the improved germination rates, the fertilizing, and the better weed control led to commensurate gains in seed-yield ratios.[25]

---

[24] Saito, 2002, p. 226.

[25] "Seed-yield ratio" refers to how many consumable seeds each planted seed will produce: hence the volume of rice (or other) seed necessary to grow a given volume of harvest. In situations where seed, rather than land, water, labor, tools, or other factors of production, is the factor in shortest supply, seed-yield ratio is a significant measure of productivity.

B. *Commerce*

Before examining secondary manufacturing and trade, primary production requires a few more words. Apart from agriculture, the record
in that area—mainly fisheries, forestry, and mining—is spotty during the centuries 1350–1700. One suspects that fishery output rose
in both Korea and Japan as urban growth created a larger consumer public.[26] Thus, by the late 1600s, people in Seoul were consuming marine products brought from the south and east coasts of
Korea.[27] As for Japan, seafood had long been valued in Kyoto, and
it is said that after Edo arose during the seventeenth century,

> Fish from nearby Tokyo, Sagami, and Suruga bays, as well as the
> coastal areas of Chiba and Ibaraki, were sent by ship from the fishing
> villages to riverside fish markets, and they were then sold at four mar-
> kets in Edo.[28]

Regarding forestry, the consumption of timber, fuel wood, and charcoal, as well as mulch and fodder, grew substantially as cities and
towns expanded and agriculture intensified. In Korea the creation
and later growth of Seoul required much timber (see Plate 22), mainly
from the T'aebaek Range, enough to produce illegal entrepreneurial lumber marketing by 1700 or so.[29] The rise of towns elsewhere
on the peninsula added to the demand for timber and fuel. In Japan
the proliferation of baronial headquarters and subsequent formation
of the Tokugawa ruling order were accompanied by an immense
rise in timber use that lasted into the 1630s (see Plate 23).

Metal mining was maintained throughout these centuries, with
more and more pits being opened or deepened as miners consumed
placer deposits and easily accessible veins. In Korea, 66 iron mines
and 17 smelters reportedly existed by 1430, mainly as government-
regulated enterprises whose operation was restricted to the agricultural off-season.[30] Copper and bullion mining faced more difficulties,

---

[26] Whether improvements in ship construction during these centuries affected
the fishing industry is unclear. On Japan, see Souryi, pp. 148–51, and Farris, pending-I.

[27] Baek, 1999, pp. 167–69.

[28] Nakai, 1991, p. 566. Souyri, 2001, pp. 92–95, 157–58, mentions medieval
fisheries in Japan.

[29] Palais, 1996, p. 980.

[30] Palais, 1996, p. 30.

becoming entangled in political and diplomatic issues that led to periodic government suppression and, by the sixteenth century, to the importing of gold and copper from Japan in exchange for cotton and other exports.[31]

In Japan iron mining expanded to provide more and more weapons for mushrooming baronial armies and tools for farmers and other producers. Especially during the violent decades around 1550–90, daimyo promoted mining to secure the metal they needed, deepening pits, improving ventilation and drainage systems, and employing Chinese smelting techniques to give themselves the needed quantity and quality of metal. And during the early seventeenth century, as trade blossomed and coinage came into widespread use, mining of gold, silver, and copper boomed.

As that last comment suggests, one of the striking aspects of these centuries was the general expansion of commerce. The transfer of goods and services had a long history in both Korea and Japan, as earlier chapters have indicated, but little of it was monetized. Rather, from the time regimes first arose, most was handled as tribute that sustained ruling elites, their subordinates, and collaborators. Transactional relationships (other than the peace-for-pay exchange that is basic to all ruling and religious systems) and the monetary devices to facilitate them remained of little importance in both the peninsula and archipelago.

During the centuries after 1350, on the other hand, Korea and Japan experienced a broad-ranging expansion of commercial activity, mainly domestic but also foreign.[32] The two facets were intertwined, each fostering the other and both linked to monetization. Despite their interconnectedness, however, foreign commerce proved the more erratic because it remained a more purely luxury trade and was more vulnerable to the vagaries of political life. By comparison, domestic trade showed a robust and sustained growth and elaboration, moreso, it appears, in Japan than Korea.

Korea. To look at Korea first, during the centuries before 1350, much of the peninsula's domestic trade had been conducted as barter at local markets and by "packmen," itinerant traders who carried

---

[31] Koh S-j, 1975, pp. 7–8.
[32] Commerce in Korea is treated in Lee K-b, 1984, pp. 186–87, 224–32. Also in Nahm, 1988, pp. 102–107. On Japan, see Totman, 2000, pp. 152–58, 233–36, 247–50.

small quantities of cloth, utensils, medicines, salt, foodstuffs, and other portable items for exchange at periodic markets.[33] At times a few large-scale entrepreneurs with official connections engaged in foreign trade, and at Kaesŏng, capital of Koryŏ, a population of tax-farming official merchants developed to collect and process tax income on behalf of the rulers while conducting supplemental trade on their own. They did so in conjunction with a resident population of Chinese merchants who, as noted in Chapter 3, facilitated the official tribute exchange with China and the unofficial trade that accompanied it.

When Yi Sŏng-gye established Seoul as the capital of Chosŏn in the 1390s, he left the tax-farming merchants of Kaesŏng in place. In following centuries they continued to be active in the tribute-transfer business, gradually expanding their own entrepreneurial activity as well, and in the process they helped sustain the town as a vital regional center. It appears that the expatriate Chinese merchant community also remained there, perhaps because Kaesŏng was nearer the border than Seoul, its urban facilities already in place, and its residents less exposed to the dangers of political factionalism.[34]

Seoul itself, being a new government town, initially had little commercial activity. The government designated market sites there in 1410, and by 1414 it had established nearly a hundred shops to service the city populace.[35] In 1419 it authorized a small group of merchants, the "Six Licensed Stores" as they came to be known, to handle official provisioning—of cloth, paper, and fish products most notably—and one suspects that commercial activity expanded thereafter. At least, within a few decades Seoul had grown into a large city, sprawling beyond its city gates and walls as fingers of plebian settlement followed roads out into the hinterland and down to Han River landings.

By the mid-fifteenth century Seoul's population had come to exceed 100,000, mainly *yangban* office holders and seekers and their families and subordinates. In addition to these groups, some 2,800 artisans and their families worked as government employees and after-hours entrepreneurs. They engaged in smelting and metallurgy and produced a wide array of goods, including,

---

[33] Lee H-y, 1975, is a brief treatment.
[34] Peterson, 1979, looks briefly at Kaesŏng merchants, mainly in terms of their access to the examination system and *yangban* status.
[35] Palais, 1996, pp. 30–31.

specialized ramie and silk textiles, shoes, furniture and cabinets, kitchen
utensils, leather goods, tiles, paper, lacquerware, pottery, weapons, and
armor.[36]

Following these early decades of expansion, the city's growth slowed
until after the disruptions of the 1590s–1630s, when the city's mercantile class displayed a period of really striking growth, doing so as
part of a nationwide blossoming of commercial activity.[37]

This blossoming was spurred by post-1600 changes in land-tax
policy, which introduced flexibility into the payment system, encouraging the use of "near-money" substitutes, notably cotton cloth, in
lieu of rice or labor service. The changes permitted producers to use
their time more fruitfully and to fit crops to field conditions, thereby
enhancing output. And they allowed entrepreneurial tax farmers to
engage in trade-offs that enabled them to accumulate capital, which
they could then use in further mercantile ventures.

The use of true money was slower to develop. From time to time
the government promoted minting of coins, but, as in so many places,
it usually did so as an income-producing venture. The quest for
profits fostered erratic minting, hoarding, severe instability in the
value of the coinage, and a consequent reluctance of people to use
it as a medium of exchange. Indeed, true money did not come into
common use until after 1678, when copper coins began coming into
more regular production and goods moved about more freely.[38] By
1700, coins were in use throughout the realm, but "near money'
continued to be used in many transactions.

The population of Seoul approached the 200,000 mark during the
late 1600s, and city merchants proliferated accordingly. Their presence rendered the city's old licensed-store system obsolete, and in
1791 it was finally abolished. Outside the city, down along the banks
of the Han, wholesale grain merchants established themselves, engag-
ing in shipbuilding, operating fleets of vessels that hauled grain and
other goods all along Korea's coasts and estuaries, maintaining warehouses, handling the bustling grain trade between river wharf and
city, and arranging other city provisioning, such as that in salt, fish,
lumber, firewood, and ice in winter.[39]

---

[36] Palais, 1996, p. 29.
[37] On Seoul after 1600, see Kim D-u, 1994. Also Yi T-j, 1995.
[38] Palais, 1996, pp. 30, 50–56, 855–75, 924–57, 973, 987–89, 996.
[39] On the Han River merchants, see Kang M-g, 1979, who mentions the dubious
trade practices for which they gained notoriety.

The merchants of Kaesŏng proved equally vigorous, establishing branches widely about the realm and becoming major purveyors of ginseng for both domestic and foreign consumption. Their influence in affairs was sufficiently great that they came to be regarded by the cultural elite with a mix of admiration for their mercantile skills and disdain for their "cliquish and miserly" qualities, a set of Confucian stereotypes that was also used to characterize their Japanese contemporaries, the merchants of Osaka.[40]

Elsewhere, the towns of P'yŏngyang, Taegu, and Kyŏngju flourished as regional tribute-processing and market centers.[41] On the northern border some cross-river trade occurred with groups in Manchuria and the Maritime Provinces. And to the south, the Pusan vicinity, as the main entrepôt for trade with Japan, bustled after *waegu* piracy was brought under control during the years around 1400. The cross-straits trade was diverse, consisting primarily of,

> imports of Japanese silver, copper, tin, sulphur, swords, sandalwood, alum, sugar, pepper, water buffalo horns, Sappan wood (for medicinal use), licorice root, and elephant tusks in return for Korean cotton cloth, rice, hemp, ramie, ginseng, floral-design pillows, sealskins, and books.[42]

Hideyoshi's invasion disrupted the trade temporarily, but diplomatic arrangements of 1609 led to its resumption. By 1700 several hundred resident Japanese employees worked at authorized warehouses in Pusan, handling the freight carried in and out by some fifty Japanese vessels that called each year.[43]

Deeper in the Korean hinterland, trade expansion produced greater numbers of peddlers and, during the years of Manchu troubles, the formation of peddler guilds with their regulations and government sanction. Periodic market sites proliferated, their number coming to exceed 1,000 during the eighteenth century. Local artisans who worked as entrepreneurs—rather than as employees of the elite—also multipled. They and their goods ("linen, cotton, grains, meats,

---

[40] Peterson, 1979, p. 12. On Osaka merchants, see McClain and Wakita, 1999.

[41] On towns, see Lee H-t, 1977.

[42] Palais, 1996, p. 32. Clearly some of the imported goods were transshipped from elsewhere. See Kang E. H-j, 1997, for an extended examination of the diplomatic and rhetorical arrangements that facilitated and regulated Korean-Japanese trade throughout these centuries.

[43] On post-Hideyoshi trade at Pusan, see Yi C-h, 1985.

fruits, marine products, salt, and various handmade products") became
the heart of the periodic markets.[44]

Gradually more towns gained population, and one by one their
periodic markets opened more frequently, stayed open more days in
succession, and finally evolved into permanent ones that could meet
the burgeoning consumer demand of a growing "middle class" of
lesser *yangban*, landed commoners, artisans, and merchants. Most
notably, perhaps, as decades passed, these fragments of commercial
activity were increasingly knitted together into the beginnings of a
national market place. During the seventeenth century maritime transportation networks began forming within the major estuarine watersheds—the Naktong in the south, the Kŭm, Han-Imjin, and more
northerly estuaries of the west—with vessels moving grains, cloth,
salt, and other goods within and between watersheds.[45]

In sum, by 1700 Korea was a much larger, more complex, and
commercially more dynamic society than it had been when Yi Sŏng-
gye founded his regime three centuries earlier.

Japan. Across the straits, meanwhile, the overall trend in Japan's
commercial development was similar, except that it began sooner
and appears to have developed more vigorously. Initially, as suggested in Chapter 3, mercantile development, like agronomic change,
reflected the decay of the centralized *ritsuryō* political order. That
dynamic continued after 1350 when Ashikaga rulers, in contrast to
those of early Chosŏn, failed to re-establish firm central control of
taxable resources. Rather, elite provisioning remained a chaotic scramble that created broad opportunity for entrepreneurial maneuver.

Domestic trade grew apace as diverse entrepreneurs—itinerant
merchants using back packs and pack horses, merchants and craftsmen affiliated with Buddhist temples, and artisans working in Kyoto,
headquarters towns of daimyo, and a few entrepôt towns—produced
and traded a wide variety of goods.[46] This commerce developed most
richly in central Japan, but exchange occurred throughout the realm.
At first merchants supplemented the "near-money" of cloth and rice
with coinage imported from China, but gradually domestic coins

[44] Market items quoted from Baek, 1999, p. 157.
[45] Baek, 1999, pp. 163–69.
[46] A fine recent study that will guide one to earlier works on Japan's Ashikaga-
period economy is Gay, 2001. On the role of women in this trade, see Tabata,
1999.

appeared.[47] Foreign trade, mainly with Korea and China but marginally with Europeans after 1550 or so, also flourished, doing so into the eighteenth century.[48]

During the 1500s, as daimyo consolidated their positions, they found it convenient to rely on cooperative merchants. After the Tokugawa triumphed in 1600, their leaders continued that practice. And they gave a substantial boost to commerce by moving aggressively to establish a stable, reliable coinage. In following decades its use became ubiquitous.

Inadvertently, and contrary to its intent, elite ideology may well have abetted this commercial growth. As apologists for Tokugawa rule elaborated Neo-Confucian notions of a properly hierarchical society, they affirmed that matters mercenary were below the dignity of a *samurai* and his institutions, being properly handled by members of the lowly merchant class. Thus given an exclusive right to handle commerce, the latter had by 1700 established themselves throughout the realm as operators of large shipping, wholesaling, money-lending, and retailing operations. They had become the key intermediaries between primary producers—of foodstuffs, forest products, mine output, cloth, paper, and myriad other goods—and consumers of all sorts, from overlord to outcaste.

As in Korea, even moreso in Japan, this growth in commerce was associated with urbanization. Until 1600 Kyoto remained the central metropolis, while a large number of baronial towns and a few entrepôt settlements appeared about the countryside. After peace was restored that year, Edo began a century of stunning growth that transformed it into the world's greatest city, numbering about a million residents by 1700, approximately half of them in *samurai* households and half lower-status people of diverse sorts. Kyoto, as the residual royal capital, and Osaka, as a major entrepôt, contained some three to five hundred thousand apiece. And scores of baronial towns about the realm numbered thousands apiece, a fact reflecting the polity's decentralized nature.

In the countryside, meanwhile, socio-economic change of the centuries after 1350 was placing control of more and more land in the

---

[47] A pioneering study of medieval coinage in Japan is Brown, 1951.
[48] A recent treatment of Tokugawa foreign trade that will guide one to valuable earlier works is Lee J, 1999. On trade via Hokkaido, see Walker, 2001b. An excellent bibliography of works on Tokugawa foreign relations is Walker, 2002.

hands of local strongmen who relied primarily on kinsmen and quasi-kin dependents to work their arable acreage or handle such other activities as the family pursued. Rather like the rural *yangban* population in Korea, this hinterland population of relatively well-to-do villagers developed into a substantial consumer populace that added countrywide richness to the commercial economy even as its members became participants in the diffusing higher culture of the day.[49]

C. *Demographics and Society*

In both Korea and Japan this growth in commerce and urban settlement was accompanied by overall population increase and social elaboration. For neither society are solidly reliable statistics available, but for both we have usable official census figures from about the same period: Korea from about 1680 onward and Japan from about 1720. Because the figures in both cases include some people and disregard others, demographers have to modify them to arrive at reasoned estimates, and these vary somewhat from scholar to scholar. For Korea official figures of about 5.2 million may represent a real population of about ten to twelve million in the year 1678, whereas in Japan an official figure of 26 million for 1721 may represent a real population of about 30 or 31 million.[50]

In Chapter 3 we mentioned, for the decades before 1350, figures of 3–4 million for Korea and 8–10 million for Japan. Insofar as these numbers are reasonable approximations, they suggest that during the 350-plus years to 1700, both societies roughly tripled in size. The absence of satisfactory figures for the intervening years leaves it unclear whether this increase occurred rather steadily, or whether it was more marked during one or another part of the period.[51] But the magnitude of gain surely means that it was proceeding in a generally sustained fashion, despite periodic setbacks due to famine, disease, and war.[52] And enhanced efficiencies in primary production

---

[49] A recent look at Japan's rural elite, with guide to earlier studies, is Platt, 2000.

[50] On Korea see Baker, 1988, and Mitchell, 1979–80. On Japan, demographic studies of the Tokugawa period are extensive. A splendid recent bibliographical review and listing of titles is Kurosu, 2002.

[51] Ch'oe Y-h, 1987, p. 105, reports an estimate of "4 to 5 million" for late 1400s Korea.

[52] The difficulty of determining the role of famine and disease in shaping population trends is, for Japan, nicely evidenced by Saito, 2002. Farris is also addressing this conundrum in a work now in progress.

were basic to that outcome, underwriting the commercialization, urbanization, and diversification in material goods that characterized the age.

Equally noteworthy were changes in society's composition.[53] In Korea, the intelligentsia formally characterized their society in 4-caste Neo-Confucian terms of a hereditary ruling caste (*yangban*) and below it, in descending socio-ethical order, peasants, artisans, and merchants. From the outset that formulation fitted poorly, failing to account for important groups—notably priests, entertainers, outcastes, and slaves. Then it was steadily undermined by socio-economic change that heightened disparities within the *yangban* and peasant castes and obfuscated distinctions between all four formal categories.

To look at the process of obfuscation, during the 200 years to 1590, as earlier noted, *yangban* multiplied and factionalized. In part the growth in numbers was due to natural increase, which doubt-less was abetted by improvements in medicine and natal care.[54] However, a growing part of the increase was accomplished by lesser folk—technical experts, advantaged peasants, or merchants—who acquired *yangban* status by purchasing it, passing the requisite exam-inations, or fabricating ancestral lines that justified a claim to it.[55]

Below the elite, society gradually changed as new agronomic prac-tices became established, population grew, and urban-centered com-merce expanded. Thus, from about 1500 onward, as noted above, more and more villages set up communal associations (*kye*) to handle tasks, such as management of irrigation water or communal prop-erty, that required cooperation among their members. Then the dis-ruptions of the 1590s–1630s interregnum and the post-1600 changes in land-tax policy accelerated this trend. In villages all across the realm, moreover, those developments spurred the emergence of a more wealthy landlord class and the spread of tenantry, which height-ened disparities between the village privileged and the proliferating

---

[53] The issues of Chosŏn society's structure and changes therein have generated much disagreement. See Palais, 1996, 32–41 and *passim*. Other works in English include Yoo, 1988, and a set of three essays by Hahn Young-woo, Kim Young-mo, and Park Yŏng-sin in *Social Science Journal* 6 (1979): 90–147.

[54] Yi t-j, 1997, pp. 9–11; see also Duncan, 2000, p. 192, and Magner, 1993, pp. 392–93.

[55] See Ro J-y, 1983, on commoner-*yangban* mingling. On commoners in the exam-ination system, see Ch'oe Y-h, 1974, and Yi S-m, 1981.

tenants and landless laborers, both slave and non-slave. To be a "peasant" could thus mean many things.

Meanwhile, communal and interest-group organizations were appearing more widely through society. Some scholars promoted "community compacts" as a means of strengthening social discipline and virtue.[56] More influential, it appears, were organizations of local clerks, gentry, slave groups, or others, which enabled their members to evade tribute obligations or otherwise protect their interests. And artisans and merchants devised mechanisms, such as the above-noted peddler associations and Kaesŏng and Han River merchant organizations, to safeguard and handle their growing businesses. By the eighteenth century, as we note more fully below, socio-economic change was starting to transform society from top to bottom, rendering the 4-caste Neo-Confucian vision utterly obsolete.

In Japan a similar story unfolded in a somewhat dissimilar manner. Because Ashikaga leaders failed to establish firm top-down control, they were unable to impose even a rhetoric of order on society. During the two centuries to 1590 a handful of scholars propounded Neo-Confucian concepts, but they were nearly irrelevant. With political control highly fragmented and unstable, merchants and artisans were able to maneuver with considerable success, turning their skills to advantage as opportunistic purveyors to their social superiors. In addition religious leaders organized and mobilized their followers, and more and more villages managed their own affairs and defended their interests against the raiders and ravages of recurrent warfare.

Not until the early seventeenth century was the Neo-Confucian notion of a four-caste system adopted as the official ideal of the newly consolidated Tokugawa ruling elite. As in Korea, the schema missed notable groups—aristocrats in Kyoto, priests, entertainers, and outcastes—but for much of that century it did represent credibly well the basic structure of an urban ruling elite, a rural producer populace, and an intermediate, largely urban population of artisans and merchants who serviced the ruling *samurai*. However, from the eighteenth century onward, as we note below, the inadequacy of the 4-caste notion became too apparent to ignore, spurring new social formulations.

---

[56] On "community compacts," see Ch. 19 of Palais, 1996.

D. *Environmental Issues*

Environmental issues continued to be ill recorded for most of the period down to 1700, which suggests the modesty of their perceived impact on the literate few. The role of contagious disease as an irregular and undiscriminating killer seems to have persisted with little change, although illnesses associated with urban crowding and heightened spatial mobility may well have become more prevalent, along with malaria.[57] The effects of climatic perturbations—whether short-term swings associated with the El Niño southern oscillation or long-term swings of the "little ice age" type—are unclear.[58] But they surely pale in comparison to the effects of human activity.

In both Korea and Japan the key variables shaping environmental trends during these centuries were population growth, urbanization, and the agricultural expansion and intensification that made them both possible. Although documentation is slender, especially for Korea, these variables could only have accelerated several trends. *In toto* they furthered the shift of lowland biota in favor of the human-centered community of people, domesticates, and their parasites. More extensive logging and fuelwood collecting to build and sustain cities, towns, and structures for the elite converted more high-canopy forest to scrubland, which would have heightened the instability of microclimates.[59] Intensified removal of litter and scrub growth for mulch, fodder, and fuel led to more soil erosion, deteriorating fertility on some hillsides (see Plate 24), severe dessication on others, and thence to more erratic streamflow, heightened episodes of lowland flooding and drought, and accompanying crop losses.

In Korea one would expect the environmental ramifications of sustained social growth to have been most pronounced in the vicinity of urban centers, such as Pusan, Kyŏngju, and Kaesŏng, and especially around Seoul, where the greatest concentration of people and structures was found. Most of the broad, highly indented western slopes of the T'aebaek Range were accessible from Seoul via

---

[57] Kiple, 1993, pp. 382–89, 392–400, treats these centuries.

[58] On the difficulty of assessing climatic variables, besides Saito, 2002, see Atwell, 1986, 1990, and 2001.

[59] The logic here is simple: forest canopy slows the skyward radiation of ground heat and reduces air movement, thereby holding warm daytime air through the night, and thus modifying the cooling effect of nighttime (and the warming effect of daytime) in adjacent areas.

tributaries of the Han and Imjin rivers (Imjin traffic reaches Seoul by way of the Han estuary), and these waterways enabled the city to secure the timber and other forest products its population required. Other mountainous regions supplied other towns. And throughout Korea less remote hillsides and wasteland provided most of the mulch, fodder, and fuel that society required.

In Japan the earlier centuries of woodland exploitation that created and sustained *ritsuryō* capitals had long since removed most good timber stands from the Kinai region. During the centuries after 1350 more uplands in the region evolved into scrubland and thence became barren and dessicated. Builders relied more and more on timber brought from more distant sites, and because of difficult transport and prohibitive costs, they gradually adopted more modest and timber-efficient styles of architecture. Elsewhere the construction activity of daimyo consumed some forest, and widespread warfare damaged more. Then, as a hard-earned peace came to the realm from the 1580s onward, an unprecedented, nationwide construction boom toppled trees from one end of the archipelago to the other. By the 1630s accessible timber was becoming costly and hard to find. By the 1660s downstream destruction due to deforestation and other overuse was spurring attempts at remedial legislation.[60]

It was urban growth and the construction of temples, shrines, mansions, palaces, and other monuments to triumphant rulers that consumed most of the high-forest timber. However, in terms of total wood consumption, the volume of construction timber was vastly exceeded by that of fuelwood and charcoal. Simply cooking and heating for the growing population was a major demand. But in addition, the widespread adoption of tile roofing, increased ceramic production, and great expansion in metallurgy to provide tools, weapons, coins, and myriad other items for this populace added fuel needs that made further inroads on forest growth (see Plates 25, 26).

In Japan, and probably in Korea, upland deterioration and lowland damage were also fostered after 1350 by increased slash-and-burn cultivation. With reclaimable land growing scarce and rural population swelling, one survival strategy of hard-pressed villagers was to clear patches of hillside, grow unreported and untaxed crops on them for a couple of years, and then abandon them after soil

---

[60] See Totman, 1989.

nutrients had given out. The practice altered forest composition, damaged soil, and produced considerable erosion and downhill trouble. And the fires that villagers commonly employed to clear their patches sometimes broke free to become destructive wildfires.

Probably the most widely destructive practice, however, was a direct byproduct of intensified fertilizer use. As farmers abandoned fallowing, employing in its stead fertilizer materials that would sustain regular annual cropping and multiple-cropping, they gathered more and more leaffall and litter from nearby hillsides and wasteland (see Plate 27). As centuries passed, ever more hillsides were raked clean of all debris, new growth became sparse, and desperate villagers took to removing lower branches of trees and digging up roots to obtain the necessary mulch, fuel, or other material. In the process, however, they made the hillsides more and more vulnerable to erosion, thereby contributing to downstream sedimentation, flooding, and destruction. The process of creating barren hillsides, which had first become evident in the Kinai Basin during early *ritsuryō* days, had by 1700 spread throughout central Japan, most severely in the region between Nagoya and Hiroshima.

Although this process is better documented in Japan, one suspects that by the eighteenth century, it was at least as advanced among the lower, more accessible hillsides of Korea, particularly its more densely settled western half and southern coastal littoral. Perhaps the best indication of such widespread hillside deterioration was the development in both countries of extensive scrub pine growth. Because the pine grows slowly, it cannot compete with several other indigenous tree species, but it can survive where others fail on barren, dessicated soils. Given the temperate climate and rich forest biota native to Korea and Japan, the widespread presence of scrub pine betrayed an "unnatural" absence of competitive growth and the existence of soil conditions in which it almost alone among woody-stemmed plants could survive.

* * *

In several ways, then, structural, technological, and cultural changes in Korea and Japan during the centuries ca 1350–1700 had equipped the two societies to expand greatly their capacity to exploit their natural environments, thereby enabling them to achieve the socio-economic growth discussed above. As the seventeenth century advanced, however, the exploitative potential of their intensive agricultural order was largely realized. Gradually, place by place and in one function after another, the two societies reached or were reaching the limits of their "niche," as evidenced by the loss of reclaimable land, full use of water supplies, denuding of accessible forest regions, depletion of exploitable mines, and erosion, stream silting, and heightened frequency and severity of flood and drought. These environmental trends, in turn, begat secondary social consequences and further environmental ramifications that played themselves out with increasing visibility during the centuries ca. 1700–1870.

The Age of Stasis (1700–1870)

In the Introduction to this study we noted the awkwardness of the year 1350 as a "break point" in history. The date 1700 presents similar but less extreme difficulties. Most obviously, the shift from growth to stabilization had no tidy starting point in either Korea or Japan; less obviously, it was not evident in all social trends. Also, the dating and character of change is even less clear in Korea than in Japan.

The date 1700 does, however, have some virtues. One, apart from its "round number" quality, is that it falls midway between the first reasonably usable census figures for Korea (1678) and Japan (1721). More substantively, it does seem to fall near the center of things. We earlier noted the growing difficulties faced by ruling elites from around 1700. In broader terms of economy, society, and environment, some aspects of the shift to stasis were becoming clearly visible by the 1660s, while others were not well established until the 1750s of so.

A. Agriculture

Agriculture remained the economic heart of Korea and Japan during this period, but in both places the expansion in food production appears largely to have ceased by the eighteenth century. Moreover, because tillage practice had become so finely tuned, it was more vulnerable to vagaries of weather, resulting sporadically in more severe crop failures, hunger, and hardship.

Another problem, one that is inherent in large-scale, even-aged monoculture cropping (i.e., the nurturing of a single plant or animal species, with members all of the same age, in a large contiguous area), also became more evident, the problem of insect infestation. In all likelihood local infestations of one sort or another had reduced harvests erratically over preceding centuries, but during 1732, large parts of southwestern Japan lost much of their rice harvest to the leaf hopper.[61] Farmers employed diverse measures to control both insect and microbial outbreaks, but their reliance on monoculture cropping assured that the problem would persist. Nevertheless, the record on such matters appears to be too sparse to reveal how strongly they shaped the larger history of either Korea or Japan.

In any case, in Korea, and in Japan south of Hokkaido (most of which still lay beyond the pale), nearly all of the reclaimable land was being cultivated by 1700 (see Plates 28, 29, 30).[62] Increases in arable acreage and expansion of paddy tillage had almost ceased by then, and farmers were focusing their energies on expanding output per hectare and producing the most profitable crop. Those criteria encouraged the growing of more non-foodstuffs, notably tobacco, cloth materials, and ginseng in Korea, and cotton, tobacco, and mulberry for feeding silkworms in Japan, all of which governments taxed less efficiently than rice and which had large and durable markets that assured a good return per hectare. Also, lacking access to more arable, people used more completely the productive land they did have. Most notably, perhaps, they grew sweet potatoes, doing so in the warmer regions of Japan from around 1700 and in Korea from the 1760s onward. The plants would flourish in odd corners of space and produce nutritious tubers below ground, safe from blight, boar, insects, or most other harm, thereby providing a reliable substitute for food crops that were not grown, had failed, or been lost to the tribute taker.[63]

The entrepreneurial calculus of market cropping was evident in these early nineteenth-century comments by the celebrated Korean scholar of "Practical Learning" (*sirhak; jitsugaku* in Japanese) Chŏng Yag-yong (Tasan; 1762–1836):

---

[61] The leaf hopper is *unka*, or *Cicadula sexnotata*. Totman, 1993, pp. 236–37.

[62] Kang C-c, 1975, p. 80, reports arable acreage figures for Korea.

[63] In the cooler, drier parts of Korea, however, the sweet potato proved less valuable than the white potato, which was grown from the 1840s onward. On potatoes in Korea see Park S-r, 1992, pp. 85–86, and Eckert, 1990, p. 185; for Japan, see Sippel, 1972.

Around the capital and in larger towns, ten *mu* of land [growing] gar-
lic, cabbage, cucumber or onions is considered to be worth hundreds
of *yang* in cash. The tobacco fields in the western provinces, the hemp
fields in the northern provinces, the ramie fields of Hansan, the ginger
fields of Chŏnju, the sweet potato fields of Kangjin and the herb fields
of Hwangju are all ten times as profitable as the highest grade rice
fields. In recent years the field cultivation of ginseng has also begun,
and this is incomparably more profitable than ordinary grains. Various
medicinal plants, as well as cotton, are twice as profitable as grain.[64]

This crop diversification and specialization required a more attentive agronomy and diverse technical improvements, and in both
Korea and Japan commentators such as Tasan began producing
essays and farm manuals that discussed agricultural problems and,
in varying degrees of detail, spelled out remedies. Such writings proliferated during the eighteenth century. In Korea they were largely
the work of *yangban* scholars of the Practical Learning school and in
Japan the work of diverse people, including officials, gentry-intellec-
tuals, village heads, and successful farmers, most of whom were
influenced by the same Practical Learning.[65]

Particularly in Japan, where the farm manuals oftimes were based
on direct observation, trial and error, and the testimonial of practicing farmers, many of the works acquired a highly functional quality. Thus, one observer, when writing a general essay on cotton
cropping in the early nineteenth century, gave this advice on how
to select the best cotton seed:

> In choosing cotton seed, pick a bush of medium height with luxuri-
> ant shrubbery and no dead branches, and take cotton bolls in full
> bloom with heavy fibers from a branch three or four branches from
> the bottom. This should be done when half the bolls on the tree have
> opened. . . . In buying seed from other districts, examine it in the palm
> of the hand. Good seeds have a slightly black look, bad ones a red-
> dish hue. Also knead the seed with the fingers. Round seeds generally
> are poor; pointed seeds generally are good. For storage, remove the

---

[64] Kim Y-s, 1986, p. 551, quoting the *Kyŏngse yup'yo* (Design for Good Governance)
by Chŏng Yag-yong.

[65] Given the processes that were rapidly swelling *yangban* ranks, these Korean
scholars may in social fact have been a more diverse group than the term implies.
It should also be noted, as Kalton, 1975, pointed out for Korea, that "Practical
Learning" was not a distinct, philosophically integrated "school" of thought but
rather more like a critical perspective on affairs that sought to identify and rem-
edy problems of the day.

seed from the surrounding cotton and dry it in the sun. Then take it out from time to time to expose it to the sun in order to keep it absolutely free of moisture.[66]

Sometimes the specifics in such advice were erroneous, and surely the care with which it was followed differed from farm to farm. But the high price of failure tended to elicit careful husbandry, and by 1870, Japanese agriculture had become one of the world's most intensive in terms of both labor inputs and yield per arable hectare. In Korea, meanwhile, it appears that a lesser level of output per hectare of paddy land had been achieved, perhaps because climate was less favorable and because cultivators were less able to obtain or afford the fertilizer material necessary to high yields.[67]

Of the many measures advocated by writers and adopted by tillers, perhaps the key one was intensified fertilizing, which was made all the more essential by the cultivation of cotton and tobacco, whose nutrient requirements are notoriously high. In both Korea and Japan mulch continued to be gathered by hand from woodland and waste, along with fodder and fuel (see Plate 31). However, the centuries of gathering had denuded more and more nearby hillsides, and as the trek for mulch became longer, more arduous, and more costly, tillers increasingly sought substitutes.

A number of substitutes were found. Double cropping provided one, with a winter crop, preferably a legume such as soya or Chinese milk vetch, being grown and plowed under for its nutrient value.[68] In both Korea and Japan, farmers supplemented their mulch, whether grown or gathered, with night soil, industrial waste, and more and more fish meal (see Plates 32, 33). In the vicinity of Japan's larger cities, these commercial fertilizers nearly supplanted the older materials. By the nineteenth century the cost of fertilizer had become the single greatest business expense facing most farmers in some localities,

---

[66] Smith, 1970, pp. 139–40. The writer, Ōkura Nagatsune (1768–1856?) was the son of a successful cotton-growing and processing landholder.

[67] Palais, 1996, p. 366, referring to yield per arable acre, claims that "the average productivity of the rice crop in Korea in 1910 was significantly less than Japan or China."

[68] Soya is *Glycine soya* or *G. max*; Chinese milk vetch is *Astradagus sinicus*. Another valuable legume was Korean lespedeza (*Lespedeza stipulacea*). Legumes produce nitrogen-fixing nodules on their roots, which release their nutrient load into the soil as they decay.

and their cropping and by-employment choices were heavily influenced by the need to generate cash to pay for it.

B. *Commerce*

Turning to other areas of primary production, insofar as mining and forest industries have been studied, they seem to tell the same story as agriculture. In Japan the previously noted, early seventeenth-century boom in gold, silver, and (somewhat later) copper production faded as accessible ore was removed and pits abandoned. By late in the century this trend was creating scarcity of coinage, changes in monetary policy, and contraction of foreign trade. Iron mining continued, but output remained sufficiently restricted that scrap iron was always highly valued, which prompted people to scavenge through burned buildings to save every nail or other bit of iron they could find. During the nineteenth century, when governments attempted to revive copper production because they wished more cannon for coastal defense, the efforts encountered resistance from downstream villagers who objected to the water pollution that mine operations caused.[69]

These problems in Japanese mining had effects that reached deep into Korea. There, as previously noted, the early Chosŏn government had actively discouraged bullion mining, preferring to import the metal from Japan. Loss of that source of supply during the eighteenth century created monetary difficulties that prompted more and more scholars and officials to advocate renewed mining. Finally in the 1780s the government re-authorized copper mining, but not until the 1820s did it actively promote it as a means to obtain bullion for coinage.[70] In following years some twenty seven copper mines were activated, but output remained modest because of the mining techniques: namely, placer mining of surface deposits and "crushing," which meant heating the veins of ore *in situ* by burning packed wood at the excavated site and then pulverizing the fractured rock to loosen the metal for extraction.[71] In the end substantial increases in Korean

---

[69] Sippel, 2002, a paper delivered at the 2002 Meeting of the Association for Asian Studies.

[70] Palais, 1996, pp. 988–89.

[71] Hamilton, 1904, p. 219, describes Korean mining technique. Lee H-k, 1936, pp. 190–91, and Kang M-g, 1985, pp. 20–23, also discuss mining.

and Japanese mine output occurred only after 1870 with the introduction of technologies developed in Europe.

Forest production, like mining, also boomed in Japan during the
early seventeenth century, as noted earlier.[72] By mid-century, however, it was falling off sharply, and it remained at a lower level thereafter. With most of the accessible woodland south of Hokkaido
stripped of old-growth construction timber, fuel production for both
home use and sale became the major component of the woodland
harvest. In Korea the maintenance of Seoul appears to have sustained wood cutting in the T'aebaek Mountains, and doubtless other
towns had a similar impact on their hinterlands. By the eighteenth
century little valuable timber seems to have survived on accessible
sites across peninsular Korea, and many of the lower hillsides seem
to have been severely denuded (see Plate 34).

In contrast to mine and forest depletion, fisheries seem to show
a different face. In Korea fishery work had a long history, and it
appears to have continued, and perhaps expanded appreciably, through
the eighteenth and nineteenth centuries, remaining a major form of
employment for many coastal villagers and providing market goods
for the earlier-noted expanding trade networks.[73] As one visitor noted
during the 1870s,

> Enormous quantities of herrings are caught on the west and south-
> east coast, also of sardines, with which all the markets of the main-
> land are supplied, and the surplus is used as manure.[74]

And all along the mountain-girt east coast, fishing was the mainstay
of many coastal villages.

In Japan the rise in fertilizer prices made fishmeal production
profitable, and during the eighteenth century fishermen responded
by expanding their catches of herring and other marine life that
could be dried and bagged for sale. They employed larger nets and
extended their activity northward, up along the herring-rich coasts
of Hokkaido.[75] In places expansion of the catch depleted fish stock,

---

[72] On the lumber industry, see Totman, 1995; on forest depletion, Totman, 1989.
[73] Baek, 1999, pp. 157, 168. Bishop, 1897, p. 158. Writing under her maiden
name of Isabella Bird, she earlier wrote a delightful 2-volume report (Bird, 1881)
of her observations in Japan.
[74] Oppert, 1880, p. 170.
[75] Howell, 1995.

and local mechanisms to regulate fishing became established.[76] But in overall terms it appears that the fleet remained sufficiently small and its technology modest in scale so that it did not overfish coastal seas as a whole and was able to sustain growth in the fishing industry. Not until after 1870 and the adoption of new maritime technology did widespread overfishing become a pressing issue in Northeast Asia.

With food output and most other primary production stabilized by 1700 or thereabouts, the growth in secondary production also slowed appreciably, although changes in product content and patterns of production and distribution continued. In Japan, market farming that had initially developed in western and central regions gradually spread more widely across the realm. During the eighteenth century, for example, villagers in the hilly region north of Edo began to grow such diverse crops as "hemp, tobacco, rape, and gourds." And their locally grown and woven silk and cotton goods developed into regional commercial products that replaced cloth from western Japan in the Edo marketplace, thereby generating cash income that enabled them to buy such items as "sugar, salt, soy sauce, dried-sardine fertilizer, and clothing."[77]

Perhaps the most noteworthy changes in distribution occurred in Korea where the signs of an emerging national marketplace became visible a century or so later than in Japan. The profitability of regional market farming, which Tasan noted, as well as the vitality of Korea's fisheries and the expansion in bullion mining, reflected the continuing development of this national marketplace. Spurred initially during the early seventeenth century by fiscal reforms that enabled tax-farming entrepreneurs to occupy the middle ground between tribute producers and consumers, long-range transactions were later expedited by the increase in coinage and the extension of marine shipping beyond estuarine watersheds to form stronger transport links between Seoul and other regions. Shippers, for example, hauled fisheries produce from the Pusan vicinity around the peninsula and up to landings near Seoul. Then highway improvements during the eighteenth century facilitated inland transit, such as between the Seoul-Kaesŏng vicinity and the northeast coastal region around Wŏnsan.[78] It appears

---

[76] Kalland, 1995, is a meticulous study of a coastal fishery in northwest Kyushu.
[77] Sippel, 1998, pp. 201, 203.
[78] Baek, 1999, pp. 163–69.

that entrepreneurial middlemen were en route to displacing the tribute-collection mechanism as primary vehicle for movement of goods throughout the realm.

In both countries the particulars of material culture continued to change, as higher cultural production reveals most clearly. Much of the change entailed substitution and displacement rather than growth, however, a trend reflected in the emergence of attempts at rationing.

These rationing measures, which are particularly visible in Japan, were essentially an institutional effort to compensate for broader processes of social change that were producing, as we note below, a general redistribution of social and material benefits among individuals and groups. The most notable efforts were regulations that purposefully tried to restrict who in Japan could enjoy what types of housing, clothing, food, and innumerable other goods and services. These regulations proliferated from the late 1600s onward, becoming a vast body of rules and admonitions whose very abundance surely reveals the modesty of their effectiveness.

C. *Demographics and Society*

The population estimates for this period, which seem uncommonly credible, are instructive. Korea's population, which roughly tripled during the period 1350–1700, appears to have fluctuated erratically in the 10–14 million range during the 170 years to 1870, after which it surged to some 50 million during the next century.[79] That of Japan, which also roughly tripled during the same period to 1700, appears to have fluctuated thereafter in the 28–33 million range, and then during the century after 1870 to have grown about as rapidly as Korea's to nearly 110 million.[80]

The overall demographic stability prior to 1870 was reflected in stabilization of urban numbers. In both societies urban growth had petered out by about 1700. Thereafter Seoul held steady in the 200,000 range and Edo at over a million, while Osaka and Kyoto lost about a quarter of their residents. Elsewhere in Japan, and likely

---

[79] Mitchell, 1979–80, pp. 68–73, examines Yi Dynasty population. Kwon T-h, 1975, p. 2, charts Korea's reported rates of population growth during the years 1678–1877. Rand McNally, 1982, p. 163, reports 1981 census figures for North and South Korea (56,585,000 combined) and Japan (117,360,000).

[80] Hanley, 1997, pp. 132–33, presents the official Tokugawa census figures.

in Korea, smaller towns largely stopped growing or even declined, in part because the tax base of ruling elites ceased expanding and in part because more and more artisanal output, such as cloth manufacture, migrated into the hinterland, closer to raw materials and lower-cost land and labor.

This is not to say that geographic mobility ceased; it did not. To the contrary, it probably intensified.[81] Changes in agronomic practice and rural social organization created new needs and possibilities that spurred movement in pursuit of work. One destination was the cities because, in Japan at least, and probably in Korea, life there presented enough exposure to disease and other difficulties that the lower-class resident population was not self-sustaining.[82] Instead, a continuing influx of hinterland people was required to sustain city size, even as changes in the locus of artisanal production lured other travelers to non-urban workplaces.

More noteworthy than increases in geographical mobility were increases in social mobility as class and status patterns modified in conjunction with economic change. Already noticeable before 1700, as earlier mentioned, the trend accelerated thereafter, doing so on both sides of the straits.

Korea. During the eighteenth and nineteenth centuries the situation of many *yangban* worsened. The earlier-noted trends of factional exclusion from office and advantage and of lesser folk acquiring *yangban* status grew more pronounced, increasing appreciably the number of impoverished *yangban* families living in the countryside. Within the peasantry, meanwhile, disparities in agricultural success exacerbated tensions between those who were lucky, utilized the new agronomic techniques successfully, and therefore did well, and the larger numbers of unfortunate or less skillful who lost their land, becoming tenants and wage laborers.

More extreme were the changes affecting slaves. From the middle or later eighteenth century onward, their numbers dropped sharply, although the dynamics producing that trend are not fully clear.[83] Early in the dynasty, it is estimated, slaves constituted nearly a third of the total population.[84] The numbers subsequently dropped, how-

---

[81] On travel in Tokugawa Japan, see Vaporis, 1994.
[82] Hayami, 2001, pp. 52–54.
[83] In Ch. 6, Palais, 1996, examines the slave issue at length.
[84] Kwon Y-u, 1988, p. 263, estimates "from one fourth to one half of the pop-

ever, even as the overall population grew. The 350,000 government slaves of the late fifteenth century fell to fewer than 200,000 by the mid-seventeenth, and the decline continued thereafter, leading the Seoul government in 1801 to release nearly all of its 66,000 remaining slaves, although local governments could retain theirs.[85] The larger number of private slaves, probably a million or more in early Chosŏn, also declined, a trend that accelerated sharply during the later eighteenth and nineteenth centuries. Thus, one study indicates that in the Taegu vicinity, where some 40% of the population had been slaves in 1690, only 1.7% were in 1858.[86]

A major way that slaves secured release during and after the crisis years of Hideyoshi's invasion was by serving in the military in lieu of commoners, in return for which they could obtain eventual manumission. Some slaves were able to buy their release. Others fled their masters, evidently believing they could fare better elsewhere, perhaps in town. Indeed, running away may have been "the most important route to freedom."[87] However, it appears that many private slaves simply were discharged by their masters. As long as overall population was swelling, masters presumably would do so because they could find other, less burdensome labor available to work any additional land they might open to tillage. Then, around 1700, as population ceased to grow and reclaimable land became scarce, farmers had to get by on the parcels they had. As a way to minimize their labor costs, they could "release" a slave from his formal bondage, restyling him a tenant or employee. The master would thereby retain the person's service while freeing himself from obligation to care for the slave and his family, should doing so become burdensome.

In the outcome, then, at all levels of society, from *yangban* to slave, social positions and jobs that had been substantially compartmentalized by status group were opened up to unprecedented competition. Within the context of a straitened ecosystem, that trend created opportunity for some but risk for many others, and that outcome

---

ulation." Palais, 1996, pp. 15, 41, says "approximately 30 percent" and "over 30 percent" during Koryŏ. Ch'oe Y-h, 1987, p. 105, reports an estimate of "1.5 million or one third" in the late 1400s.

[85] Eckert, 1990, pp. 182–83.

[86] Mitchell, 1979–80, p. 86. Palais, 1996, pp. 251–52, reports other figures that also show the trend of decline.

[87] Palais, 1996, p. 250.

heightened anxiety and social tension, which manifested itself during the nineteenth century in the escalating unrest and political disorder that we noted earlier.

Japan. In the archipelago, meanwhile, a similar pattern was playing out. At the top of society, as elite income ceased expanding, castles and other government facilities deteriorated. Moreover, collaboration among daimyo and between daimyo and shogun became more difficult, feeding mutual suspicion and ill-will. Fiscal stress also deepened the hardship of low-ranking *samurai*, who found their lords trimming their stipends in various ways, which prompted more and more of them to pursue by-employments, to trim household expenses as best they could, which included the dismissal of servants, and to limit the size of their families by birth control and out-placement of children.

Unsurprisingly, these circumstances fostered widespread *samurai* demoralization and discontent. The discontent was mainly directed against senior officaldom above, but uppity merchants also became objects of criticism. Those merchants not only lived more elegant and comfortable lives than many *samurai* but were able to acquire quasi-*samurai* status by providing funds and fiscal expertise to baronial governments. They were able to arrange marital ties to financially needy *samurai* households and as money lenders were in a position to make their borrowers' lives more or less difficult as circumstance and personality dictated. Reflecting this change in relative fortune, from about 1700 onward the rhetoric of *samurai* intellectuals became more assertively defensive of *samurai* status rights and denunciatory of alleged merchant greed and social unworthiness. And fairly enough, intellectuals associated with the merchant community responded with a rhetoric equally assertive of merchant virtue and social value.[88]

Meanwhile, lesser urban commoners, particularly the unskilled, experienced hardship as elite income ceased growing, foreign trade declined, and domestic manufacture moved into the hinterland, cumulatively squeezing the urban job market.[89] The resulting hardship was manifested during the eighteenth and nineteenth centuries in episodes of urban rioting, the appearance of government work houses to con-

---

[88] Two studies of these urban commoner values are Sawada, 1993, and Takemura, 1997. Their bibliographies will lead readers to the fine earlier works, including the careful study by Najita, 1987.

[89] A rich study of the Edo lower classes is Leupp, 1992.

trol and aid the destitute, and the emergence and spread of millenarian movements promoted by and aimed at commoners.

In the countryside more complex changes were working themselves out. During the pre-1700 centuries, extended family arrangements had assured generations of local landholders a labor supply sufficient to work large holdings and such additional land as they reclaimed. Gradually, however, with land clearance petering out, tillage practices becoming more intensive, and wage labor more available, those arrangements disappeared, doing so in central Japan by 1600 or thereabouts and elsewhere later. That happened, it appears, because landholders found it more advantageous to recruit labor as needed, rather than to sustain relatives through good times and bad. To reduce their social obligations, they gave small parcels of arable to kinsmen and set them up as nominally self-supporting cultivators whom they would then employ only as needed.[90]

This trend, much like the reduction of farm-labor slavery in Korea, freed favored rural households from burdensome social obligations, enabling them to maximize their advantages and enjoy more comfortable material standards of living (see Plate 35).[91] For less fortunate small holders, tenants, and landless laborers, the increase in self reliance often translated into more hardship and more vulnerability to the vicissitudes of harvest and employment opportunities. And on society's lower margin, much as slaves in Korea were merging into the commoner and outcaste populations, in the process becoming competitors in the job market, so in Japan a swelling population of outcastes was coming into sharper competition for jobs with commoner wage-laborers.[92]

In Japan, then, as in Korea, it appears that by 1870 socio-economic change had seriously undercut the old system of compartmentalized life paths, introducing in its stead the elements of an entrepreneurial "free market." To an unprecedented extent this trend threw people into competition with one another. And occurring within the

[90] Smith, 1959, is the classic study of this trend. A dated but comprehensive review of earlier scholarship on the peasantry in "early modern" Japan is Totman, 1986.

[91] A recent and detailed study of this later-Tokugawa rural elite is Pratt, 1999. The changing material comforts of advantaged sectors of Tokugawa society are nicely explored in Hanley, 1997, as, for example, on p. 17.

[92] On outcastes in Japan, see Chapter 5 of Ooms, 1996, and Groemer, 2001a and 2001b.

context of an ecosystem that seems to have been fully burdened, the
trend gave rise, not surprisingly, to severe hardship. The hardship
translated, it appears, into one or another combination of reduced
fecundity and heightened mortality rates, and thence the aforementioned demographic stabilization.[93] The trend also exacerbated social
tension and political unrest. In both Korea and Japan the unrest
was manifested in larger and more frequent incidents of civil protest
or violence, in millenarian movements that won vigorous support,
and in the appearance of new bodies of reformist and transformist
rhetoric and advocacy.

D. *Environmental Issues*

Several remarks in preceding pages—about demographic stabilization, difficulty in maintaining urban populations, decay of status
perquisites, devices that rationed scarce goods, denuding of hillsides,
disputes over mine effluent, dearth of productive arable, and disci-
plining of agriculture—seemed to reflect an overloading of the human
niche in these two intensive agricultural societies. Indeed, several of
these factors combined, in Japan at least and perhaps in Korea as
well, to foster the abandonment of economically marginal fields and
farms. Increasingly during the eighteenth century, parcels of land
that had become too vulnerable to flooding or drought, too costly
or difficult to work, or too dependent on heavy fertilizing for maintenance of poor or exhausted soil were abandoned by marginal cultivators, to the disadvantage of tax collectors or of neighbors who
had to make good the village's communal tax obligation.[94]

In terms of space and other resource utilization, the human niche
seemed full, given the technology of the day. To say this does not
mean, however, that the biosystems of Korea and Japan were being
devastated. To the contrary, because of the highly mountainous character of the two and the technological limitations of their social
orders, vast reaches of high country continued to flourish as wild
realms, sustaining indigenous flora and fauna almost as richly as in
prior millennia. Indeed, as noted in Chapter 2, insofar as reclamation

---

[93] On Korea, see Kwan T-h, 1975, and Mitchell, 1979–80. On Japan, see works
cited in Kurosu, 2002.
[94] An insightful study of this issue is Sippel, 1998.

work had increased the mileage of forest edge, it may well have enhanced more than it injured biodiversity and biomass accumulation.

The redoubtable British journalist, Isabella (Bird) Bishop, wrote of the 1890s faunal repertoire in Korea:

> The fauna of Korea is considerable, and includes tigers and leopards in great numbers, bears, antelopes, at least seven species of deer, foxes, beavers, otters, badgers, tiger-cats, pigs, several species of marten, a sable . . . and striped squirrels. Among birds there are black eagles, found even near Seoul, harriers, peregrines (largely used for hawking), pheasants, swans, geese, spectacled and common teal, mallards, mandarin ducks, turkey buzzards (very shy), white and pink ibis, sparrowhawks, kestrels, imperial cranes, egrets, herons, curlews [and 23 other named, mostly smaller birds].[95]

Then, after noting the extensively denuded hillsides found widely about the country and the good forests of the northern interior and higher T'aebaek regions, she went on to list trees and shrubs in a grand jumble of Latin binomials and common English names,

> [two species of spruce, two pines], three species of oak, the lime, ash, birch, five species of maple, the *Acanthopanax ricinifolia, Rhus semipinnata, Elæagnus*, juniper, mountain ash, hazel, *Thuja Orientalis* (?), willow, *Sophora Japonica* (?), hornbeam, plum, peach, *Euonymus alatus*, etc.[96]

She listed some smaller understory species as well, nicely conveying a sense of lush vegetation. As mentioned in Chapter 1, the grand richness of Korea's surviving floral community has been confirmed by more recent and more exhaustive surveys.

In Japan, where mountain regions were even more extensive and less penetrable, indigenous biota remained comparably diverse and vigorous into the post-1870 decades. On the other hand, on the lowlands, interior valleys, and lower hillsides of both Korea and Japan the human-centered biological community had made substantial inroads by 1700, in the process modifying biosystems and intensifying conflict between humans and wildlife.

In Korea the most storied expression of the human-faunal collision was the widespread fear of tigers. Bishop and other visitors comment

---

[95] Bishop, 1897, pp. 16–17.
[96] Bishop, 1897, p. 17. The genus *Acanthopanax* seems to have no English equivalent; *Rhus* is a sumac; *Elæagnus* is oleaster; *Thuja* is an arbor vitae; *Sophora Japonica* is the Japanese Pagoda Tree; *Euonymous alatus* is the spindle tree.

frequently on the degree of caution travelers and locals alike took lest they be attacked. Whether the problem was longstanding is unclear, but one suspects that the spread of human settlement into deeper valleys, the increased spatial mobility of the age—and perhaps the more frequent occurrences of crop failure, famine, and epidemic disease, which could have made human corpses a familiar food source for tigers or other carnivores—heightened the frequency of attack.[97]

In Japan less fearsome but perhaps more damaging expressions of human-faunal collision appeared. There, too, more and more opportunity for such collision arose as people penetrated mountain valleys, hacked out more swidden acreage, and opened more fields hard by forest edge. In consequence, as Brett Walker has noted, "Peasants constantly struggled against wild boar, deer, and monkeys in the Tokugawa period."[98] The competition for space and its yield could become fierce. Around 1870 a British naval surveyor of coastlines recorded that in the mountainous Kii vicinity in central Japan,

> wild boar and deer abound. At night they descend into the valleys, and not withstanding the fields are fenced in, and traps, rattles, and watchers are there also, they do a great deal of damage amongst the rice and sweet-potato crops.

Elsewhere he noted that to keep boar away, people

> fire off guns, keep rattles going, and sing and call out all night long from these watch huts which they put up all over their cultivation. Still, boar appear to get used to anything.

The character and consequence of this increased contact between wildlife and humans in Japan was most dramatically and tragically expressed in the collision of man and wolf. An apparent increase, from about 1700 onward, in frequency of wolf attacks on people and their domesticates had the effect of transforming the wolf from an esteemed creature of sacred character long appreciated for its role

---

[97] In what may be a related issue, Dutch sailors reported the presence of alligators (or crocodiles) in seventeenth-century Korea, but they appear to have been gone by the late nineteenth. Ledyard, 1971, p. 207.

[98] Walker, 2001a, p. 330. The two quotations come from his pp. 344–45, quoting Captain H. C. St. John, *Notes and Sketches from the Wild Coasts of Nipon* (Edinburgh: David Douglas, 1880).

in keeping deer and boar under control into a feared and despised predator that was then hunted to extinction by 1905 or so.[99]

This wolf-human confrontation also highlighted another aspect of ecological history, of which we today are particularly conscious—the inter-species transfer of disease organisms, notably that from other creatures to humans, as in the recent cases of Human Immunovirus (HIV), Hanta and Ebola viruses, and (it appears) the etiological agent of Severe Acute Respiratory Syndrome (SARS).[100] During these centuries Japan's wolf population experienced a rabies plague, and a few diseased, disoriented animals bit humans, infecting them, provoking local panics, and adding to the image of the wolf as a mad canine that should be exterminated.[101]

Human pressure on the ecosystem was manifested in other ways as well. In both Korea and Japan, as noted earlier, the intensive logging and fuel gathering stripped much of the technologically accessible high forest and severely denuded the lower hillsides nearer urban centers. In Korea, during a train ride from the Yalu to Pusan, an observant traveler noted around 1900 that in the region north of Seoul, "Scattering young pine, seldom more than ten to twenty-five feet high, occupied the slopes, and as we came nearer, the hills were seen to be clothed with many small oak, the sprouts clearly not more than one or two years old." Further south he noted extensive erosion and found that, "generally the hills are well rounded and covered with a low growth of shrubs and herbaceous plants."[102]

---

[99] See Walker's forthcoming "Creating and Killing the Wolves of Japan," a wonderfully rich and insightful examination of wolf-human relations in Japan down through the ages.

[100] As of this writing the etiology of SARS is unclear.

[101] Walker treats this issue very well in his forthcoming study of wolves. One suspects that other pathogens may have been transmitted between humans and other animals at other times in Korean or Japanese history, but so far the Anglophone scholarship has not, to my knowledge, highlighted that matter. The Hanta virus, incidentally, is named for the Hanta Valley in central Korea. The virus was still unidentified during the Korean War of 1950–53, and at the time the nearly always fatal illness it conferred was known to United States army medical personnel as Hemorrhagic Fever.

[102] King, 1911, pp. 368, 372. The "many small oak" to which King refers most likely were coppice growth, meaning shoots sent out by the oak stumps and stubble that were left after harvesters had cut and removed earlier coppice growth.

Another traveler, the aforementioned Isabella Bishop, noted during the 1890s the "very considerable forests" of high mountain areas and northern interior Korea but also "the brown, bare hills of Pusan." She observed that

> The denudation of the hills in the neighborhood of Seoul, the coasts, the treaty ports, and the main roads, is impressive, and helps to give a very unfavorable idea of the country.[103]

The problem was destined to persist well into the twentieth century (see Plates 36, 37).

The scarcity of construction timber due to deforestation forced builders in both Korea and Japan to make do with smaller sticks. It helped produce the rationing measures noted earlier, and one suspects that it underlay the heavy Korean reliance on pounded mud blocks as a basic building material (see Plate 38). In both countries, moreover, governments and villagers attempted to protect some woodland from the feller's axe. In Korea, for example, where many villagers used guilds (*kye*) to manage communal affairs, the condition of woodland was one matter of concern. One village guild included the following clauses in its bylaws:

> We plan to keep pine-trees growing in the forest in order that they may be used hereafter. Any one who cuts down a large pine tree shall be brought to the Magistrate and punished. If he cuts down from one to ten young trees he shall be given 50 blows and fined 200 *nyang*. If he cuts down large branches of pine trees he shall be given 30 blows. For cutting small branches he shall be given 15 blows. Any one who cuts down a large tree, not of the pine variety, shall be given 30 blows and fined 100 *nyang*.
>
> If any one makes an arrangement with the wood cutter he shall be punished equally with the cutter.
>
> Any one who shakes the leaves from the pine trees and collects them shall be fined 50 *nyang*.
>
> When there are pine grubs coming out in the forest the villagers must destroy them before they become abundant. One person from every house must take a part in the work of destroying the grubs for three day periods in turn. Any one who is absent at the time of destroying the grubs shall be fined 20 *nyang*. Any one who comes at that time must bring his food with him.[104]

---

[103] Bishop, 1897, pp. 17, 23.
[104] Gillet, 1913, pp. 23–24. The location of the village and date of the document are not indicated.

In Japan one sees widespread evidence of attempts by governments to cope with forest loss.[105] Most basically, whereas authorities in earlier centuries had consistently encouraged land clearance to increase arable acreage, from about 1700 onward, they began to vacillate, on most occasions still encouraging reclamation, but in others proscribing it to protect and restore forest cover. As in Korea, moreover, both governments and villagers tried to control forest use by regulation and its enforcement. In addition, during the eighteenth century writings on practical silviculture proliferated, woodland-control arrangements were gradually modified in ways that expedited policies for long-term forest recovery, and attempts to restock timber forests and re-cover eroded sites through programs of purposeful afforestation gradually spread across the realm (see Plate 39). By the 1830s, it appears, the long-term decline in timber output had begun to reverse as more and more plantation stands came of harvest age.

In both Korea and Japan the denuding of hillsides promoted scrub pine growth, and in Korea the spreading pine monoculture set the stage for devastating infestations of the larval *song choong*.[106] As suggested by the village rules quoted above, local efforts to control the problem became a perennial task, but those efforts notwithstanding, the larvae remained a chronic scourge. They managed to destroy a great deal of the residual forest cover on accessible hillsides, in the process depriving villagers of fuelwood and exacerbating soil erosion with all its ramifications. And they continued doing so well into the twentieth century.[107]

The widespread overcutting and the loss to insects contributed to fuel shortages. In both Korea and Japan that trend led to more intensive use of brush, litter, tree branches, and roots. And in Japan people began in the years around 1700 to use ground coal, initially in Kyushu and later elsewhere, particularly for operating the salt-water evaporators that produced salt for commercial sale. By the 1780s coal-mine effluent at some sites was reaching downstream paddy fields, precipitating protests that elicited government moves to

---

[105] Totman, 1989, treats Japanese forests.

[106] Lee H-k, 1936, p. 182, mentions this insect. McCune, 1980, p. 132, identifies it as *cong choong* (Gastropacha Pini L.). It may, however, be the pine defoliator, *Dendrolimus spectabilis Butler*, whose larvae can strip trees of their needles and within a few years kill them. The defoliator is mentioned in Lee S-y, 1960, p. 66.

[107] See especially text and pictures at pp. 66–69 of Lee S-y, 1960.

restrict the mining. The burning of coal also generated protests from neighbors, who found their lives being fouled by the sooty smoke. Thus during the 1830s villagers near Hiroshima protested the pollution, asserting that,

> the soot and smoke stick to the fruit and leaves of rice, wheat, soy beans, red beans, cow peas, buckwheat, tea, and everything else, smearing them with oily smoke, and causing them to wither or ripen poorly, much like a general crop failure.[108]

In Japan, as noted earlier, widespread deforestation interplayed with the rapid expansion of land reclamation to create downstream damage that was eliciting remedial action by the 1660s. During the eighteenth century the number and scale of such measures expanded greatly. Increased demand for water in the face of less stable water flow provoked local conflicts over use rights. These riparian disputes led to local and government regulation and management practices designed to keep the peace and sustain production.[109] And the intensified flooding led to greatly expanded programs of government-supervised riparian construction and repair intended to keep rivers within their banks and to reduce the destructiveness of such overflow as did occur.[110]

Finally, some problems of illness became more pronounced. In both Korea and Japan urbanization appears to have heightened some disease problems, notably measles and smallpox, but also influenza and dysentery. And during the nineteenth century cholera was introduced from Europe, reaching Korea in 1821 and Japan in 1822. The problem of epidemic disease prompted various attempts at control, most commonly by isolation of the infected person or his household. Also, during the nineteenth century attempts were made in both countries to use the recently developed European method of vaccination to inoculate the populace against smallpox, an effort that was making substantial headway in Japan by 1870.[111]

---

[108] Totman, 1993, pp. 271–72.
[109] A meticulous study is Kelly, 1982.
[110] An introductory essay is Totman, 1992.
[111] On Korea, see Baker, 1988, and Magner, 1993; on Japan, Jannetta, 1987, 1993, and 2001, and Walker, 1999.

Recapitulation

In both Korea and Japan, it appears, an age of growth came and went during the centuries from roughly 1350 to 1870. Political elites scrambled to hold their footings in this continually shifting socio-economic landscape, but their successes were mixed, as many a *yangban* or *samurai* household could attest. By the nineteenth century regimes in both countries were facing challenges of unprecedented social complexity.

The breadth and extent of socio-economic growth that the two societies experienced during these centuries was impressive. Fueled by a broad-based expansion in agricultural output, overall population achieved striking growth by 1700, with large numbers of people settling in substantial towns and major cities, while the vast majority lived in villages that dotted the landscape, mostly in larger basins and valleys, but with some hard by major rivers and others nestled deep in interior valleys. The growth in human numbers was accompanied by growth in elaborateness of social organization and of the economy that provided those people—or rather, the more fortunate among them—with a richly diverse menu of goods and services.

By 1700 or thereabouts, however, one also sees mounting evidence that growth could no longer be sustained. Information, such as it is, on population size, urban settlement, arable acreage, and output of mines and forests, as well as on tax income, elite life styles, and the proliferating expressions of public hardship and unrest all suggest that society was encountering constraints that only grew more onerous as the eighteenth and nineteenth centuries advanced.

This change in social situation is perhaps suggested by changes in methods of problem management. During the centuries of growth, in more and more places, problems of resource management were addressed locally by the formation of communal units, notably the *kye* in Korea and *sō* in Japan, which settled disputes, allocated resources for their members, and provided mechanisms for dealing with outsiders. As problems of production and distribution became more acute, however, one sees the emergence, primarily among members of the elite, of reformist policy proposals grounded in so-called Practical Learning (*sirhak, jitsugaku*). And the sort of reasoned analysis and action that they advocated found practical expression here and there in texts on agronomy, remedial forest policy, and other matters.[112]

---

[112] The term "reasoned analysis" should not confuse us. Like all "rationality"—

Even as efforts of this sort to enhance production were appearing, one also sees signs that heightened competition for goods and services was eliciting new mechanisms for managing the distribution of what was available. Most explicitly, from the later 1600s onward there appeared in Japan programs of regulation and rationing. And while these were intended primarily to protect the interests of the enforcers, in effect they focused on the management of demand and distribution, tacitly acknowledging that supplies were finite. Similarly, the emergence of techniques of birth control constituted an acknowledgment that the resources to sustain human life were limited and that family management in this manner was preferable to reliance on famine and disease to keep one's household numbers in check.

More broadly, core elements of the established social structure gradually eroded as "intra-species" competition intensified. Large portions of both the *yangban* and *samurai* status groups found their condition worsening, and changes in elite rhetoric and ideology reflected that predicament. In Japan at least, and perhaps in Korea as well, urban commoners found it more difficult to sustain themselves after 1700, and tensions between outcaste and commoner groups became more acute. At yet lower social levels extended kin and slave systems that had provided some security for life's lowborn gradually disintegrated, and more and more of the disinherited sought shelter in meliorist and millenarian movements that offered balm for life's wounds.

In the background, underlying these manifestations of the shift from growth to stasis, one sees numerous signs that, given the social and material technology these people were able to deploy in their pursuit of life, they had filled their "niche," reaching the limits of their ecosystem's carrying capacity. In one of the most visible signs, throughout much of Japan and Korea the aggressive harvesting of hillsides to obtain timber, fuel, fodder, and fertilizer material had depleted timber stands, denuded and damaged substantial hill areas, and produced widespread and chronic downstream difficulties.

Wildlife also was affected. The extension of human activity farther and farther into mountain valleys and up hillsides had for cen-

including that of our own day—Practical Learning was grounded in unexamined or unprovable premises and interest-group dynamics, and it contained within itself abundant misinformation and a full share of wishful thinking. Palais, 1996, pp. 9–10, reminds us of the limits of *sirhak* "rationality" in Korea.

turies been slowly shifting the balance of species in favor of the human-centered biological community. By the eighteenth century, however, it was also producing severe collisions between humans and creatures that no longer found avoidance the best strategy, notably the tiger in Korea and wolves, deer, and boar in Japan. One suspects that those collisions were symptomatic of a much broader process of species endangerment that was developing in both countries as more and more wildlife habitat was given over to full-time human utilization.

Turning from mountainous interior regions to coastal plains, the opening to tillage of most areas bordering large streams, together with the utilization of complex irrigation systems, left society more fully dependent than ever on costly, labor-intensive programs of riparian management and repair. By maximizing their use of available water supplies, moreover, producers left themselves more completely hostage to the vagaries of climate. And the practice of large-scale monoculture cropping made them vulnerable to insect infestation, which on occasion ravaged rice crops in one or another region of Japan, much as Korea's unintended semi-monoculture of scrub pine was ravaged by grubs.

In the end Koreans and Japanese were able to sustain their system of intensive horticulture only by finding new and different sources of fertilizer. They went beyond the natural growth of hillsides by double-cropping legumes to produce mulch, by recycling manures and commercial by-products, and finally by extending the realm into offshore waters in search of marine harvest for fishmeal.

That last phrase, "extending the realm," points to another facet of this period of stasis. On one hand the evidence of these centuries suggests that the two societies had exhausted the potential of their existing material and social technology. On the other, one sees a few signs that new technologies and strategies of resource exploitation were being found, and these discoveries foreshadowed the near future.

The most obvious of these, and the most basic, was the start of coal burning in Japan, which prefigured the core technological shift undergirding industrialization: the use of fossil fuels. Less obviously, the resort to vaccination to fight smallpox foreshadowed the use of biochemical manipulation as a mechanism for dealing with unwanted aspects of the biosystem, also a salient characteristic of industrial society.

Finally, the extension of fishing beyond inshore waters foreshadowed the rise of industrial-age pelagic fisheries. More broadly, it puts us in mind of the general process of laying claim to resources found elsewhere in the world, beyond one's own acknowledged territory. In this volume the most striking instance of that practice was the Mongol conquest of Korea. Piracy also merits note. But a far more important, although less dramatic expression of the process, was the longer-term migration of peoples, whether foragers or agriculturalists, to new regions, whether into Korea and Japan or, in later centuries, from southerly parts of those realms into their northeastern sections. In our own day, of course, we know the most recent large-scale expression of this process as imperialism. And it was that expression of the phenomenon that rang the curtain down on the age of intensive agriculture in Korea and Japan.

EPILOGUE

To 1870
Since 1870

To begin with a pristine banality, we humans, whether situated in Korea, Japan, or anywhere else, are and always have been creatures of the earthly biosystem, continuously and complexly interacting with other creatures and sharing with them an utter dependence on the resources of the encompassing ecosystem. However, the character of that interaction and dependency has changed as recent millennia have passed, and in this volume we treated those changes in terms of three stages—forager, agricultural, and industrial society—with our focus being primarily on the second.

One quality of the histories of Korea and Japan that stood out strongly in preceding pages was the degree of apparent similarity in the timing and trajectory of their development. The similarity was evident in matters of ecosystem relations, technology, social structure and its changes, cultural development, and, with some very visible exceptions, political process. Of course, given our initial formulation of a 3-stage human experience, as well as the Korean/Japanese historiographical context of recent decades, this apparent likeness is perhaps unsurprising. But it still seemed worth noting.

The basement foundation of that similarity in experience was the geographical proximity and resemblance of the two realms. The disaggregation of Pangaea and subsequent migration of its fragments around the globe propelled Korea and Japan to their present-day locations and gave them their highly mountainous topographies. As part of that same global tectonic process, the collision of Indian and Eurasian plates produced large-scale topographical changes in Central Asia that gave the Korea-Japan vicinity its summer monsoon weather of recent millennia. Those factors of location, topography, and weather, in turn, shaped the way Pleistocene climatic swings influenced the biological composition of the region, giving it the lush temperate-zone floral diversity for which it is still celebrated. And finally, they set key parameters of human development over those millennia, doing so most firmly for the agricultural stage of the region's history.

To 1870

For thousands of years the sparse forager populations of Korea and Japan waxed and waned in conjunction with climatic fluctuations, having little impact on the ecosystems that sustained them. They likely contributed to the terminal Pleistocene die-off of mega-fauna some thirteen thousand years ago and probably caused an occasional outbreak of wildfire then and later. And in their travels they surely disseminated some microbes, insects, and other small creatures. For all practical purposes, however, their influence on the ambient biome was negligible, even when they began elemental forms of crop nurturing and harvesting some four or five thousand years ago.

That situation changed, however, with the introduction of a fully-fledged horticulture some three thousand years ago. As the centuries passed thereafter, producers, assisted by the spreading use of metal tools, enlarged their capacity to maintain human life. That expanded capacity permitted a sustained demographic increase, the elaboration of complex social structures and stratification, and, by 700 CE, their rhetorical legitimation in articulate ideology. Those trends also produced a gradual change in the biotic composition of both Korea and Japan, primarily in lowlying areas. There the human-centered biological community—humans, their collaborating plant and animal species, and diverse parasites—scored major gains at the expense of other creatures as more and more acreage was shifted from mixed growth to monoculture tillage.

Especially from about the fourteenth century onward the widespread adoption of several forms of agronomic intensification—notably the use of fertilizer materials, multiple cropping, and more attentive nurturing practices—increased output per hectare and permitted striking growth in the size and complexity of society. Those same developments, however, and the regimen of paddy/dry grain double-cropping in particular, sharply reduced biodiversity in ever-larger areas. By the eighteenth century this trend was sufficiently advanced to be endangering some species, modifying the behavior and ecological role of others, and in many foothill regions reducing both biodiversity and biomass volume as over-exploitation transformed more and more lush woodland into barren, dessicated hillsides.

During the eighteenth and nineteenth centuries, as recapitulated at the end of Chapter 4, the societies of Korea and Japan showed several signs of having overburdened their respective ecosystems.

Population and material production no longer seemed to be growing; signs of social tension and conflict were proliferating, as were attempts to manage the problems of scarcity, hardship, and unrest. And evidence of environmental deterioration was becoming more diverse, pronounced, and costly to society.

Even then, however, the highly mountainous topography of Japan and, to a lesser degree, Korea still served effectively to keep much of their biosystems vibrant. The topography's capacity to do so was sustained to an important degree by one striking agronomic absence—that of sheep and goats. Because those ruminants are wonderfully resourceful, omniverous creatures, who can nibble most types of vegetation down to stubble, they can strip the vegetative cover from all sorts of terrain—and have done so in other parts of the world—in the process producing massive soil erosion and permanent denuding and dessication. Had sheep and goats been nurtured in Korea and Japan, the resulting environmental devastation surely would have been vastly greater than what did in fact transpire before 1870.

Other factors also helped meliorate the environmental impact of intensive agricultural society. Most importantly, perhaps, the absence of widespread environmental pollution spared biota. In places the byproducts of mining and smelting surely damaged specific sites, as did the very limited extraction and use of coal in Japan. However, spared the rampant chemical manipulation that characterizes industrial society, most of the waste products generated by even densely settled populations were recyclable and biodegradable, and in due course they contributed anew to the biosystem's vitality.

Doubtless some unrecorded extinctions occurred over the centuries, mainly of lowland biota, and many species survived on far less habitat than a few millennia earlier. But, on the other hand, the vast increase in mileage of forest edge that resulted from land clearance in convoluted valleys also created habitat that supported larger populations of numerous other species of flora and fauna. So, as of 1870, both societies still retained exceptionally rich biotic communities. And while many hillsides had been severely abused, most retained the capacity for restoration within a few decades if given adequate protection or, in the worst cases, remedial assistance.

Since 1870

The future, however, was destined to be less benign, and key forces driving that development were introduced from afar with the arrival of powerful naval squadrons from Europe (and its North American outlier). Why Europeans chose to venture so far at such risk to themselves—what had gone awry within their own biome that drove them to such dangerous lengths in search of more resources to exploit and that prodded beneficiaries of the process to devise such elegant systems of rhetorical legitimation for it—is a question that lies beyond the scope of our inquiry. Whatever the impetus, the process occurred, and during the nineteenth century the ruling elites of Korea and Japan, who already were burdened with a surfeit of domestic difficulties, moved to cope with this new provocation.

As matters worked out, for a few decades those elites had stunningly dissimilar levels of success in that task. The Japanese elite managed to stall the advance of the intruders during the 1860s–1870s and, from the 1890s onward, to reverse it. Doing so, however, entailed adopting and adapting the expansionist policies and rationales utilized by the "Great Powers," and because Korea was so close and strategically significant, in the years around 1900 Japan's rulers moved to establish control over the peninsula. The Anglophone Powers ratified that effort as *quid pro quo* for Japan's recognition of the British position in India and American position in the Philippines. By 1910 Japan's leaders had transferred their country from the status of incipient colony to that of imperial Power, whereas Korea had been fixed—for the moment—as colony.

That geopolitical outcome, and the decades of tormented political and social history that followed in its train, so embittered Korean-Japanese relations that to considerable extent it has concealed the basic similarities of their twentieth-century historical trajectories. In both, as noted in Chapter 4, population grew rapidly to unprecedented levels. Urbanization also proceeded apace, as did basic changes in land control, the promotion and diffusion of new agronomic and fishery technology and practice, and the implementation of more energetic forest management, rehabilitation, and harvest policies. The development of mechanized mining, rapid spread of industrial manufacturing, creation of a mechanized transportation system, formation of a massive conscript military system, radical change in social infrastructure, and new forms of social mobilization, public education, and cultural expression also marked the decades down to 1940 or thereabouts.

Unsurprisingly, these trends were accompanied, as elsewhere in the industrializing world, by a sharp upswing in environmental pollution and biohabitat degradation and loss. On both peninsula and archipelago, more species of wildlife were put under stress, while those pathogens well-suited to densely settled urban sites, such as the tubercle bacillus, flourished. Meanwhile, tensions between the beneficiaries and servants of industrialization escalated, leading to political organizing and protestation, which in turn spurred the launching of counter-measures meant to contain the tensions by a mix of repression and remediation.

During the 1940s political bungling and catastrophic warfare temporarily reversed many of these trends. But during the 1950s most elements in the earlier trajectory revived, this time with Korea again an independent polity (but divided North and South). From about 1960 onward the rate of industrial growth accelerated on both sides of the straits, with North Korea initially making noteworthy advances but later falling severely behind the burgeoning South Korea and Japan.

To elaborate their post-1950s story briefly, both erected factories, transport systems, and other infrastructure pell mell. They employed industrial methods of horticultural intensification to achieve stunning increases in output per hectare and per labor work hour. They used biochemical and other means to contain tuberculosis and counter many of the other problems associated with life in industrial cities. And by employing diverse mechanisms of redistribution, they were able to reduce the disparities of material reward that accrued to members of their societies, thereby containing social discontent sufficiently to maintain the trajectory of their development. Perhaps most tellingly, they expanded sharply their utilization of resources obtained from elsewhere in the world.

The shift to heavy reliance on imported metals, fossil fuel, wood products, seafood, and other foodstuffs ended—for the moment at least—the overuse of most woodland, and in both Korea and Japan large areas of once-barren or clearcut hillside were reforested. Much of this reforestation, however, produced large sweeps of even-aged timber monocultures that were (and are) vulnerable to insects and blight and ill-suited to the present-day economics of the global forest trade. More worrisome in the long run, a gradually growing portion

of forest land was and still is being converted to urban uses as sites
for second homes, ski resorts, golf courses, and other recreational
activities, all of which disrupt and weaken local biomes as they further
extend the territory of the human-centered biological community at
the expense of native species.

The heavy reliance after 1960 on external sources of many primary
products not only spared woodland but also did much to distance
the two countries from the problems of pollution and/or resource
depletion that are universally associated with the production and
basic processing of raw materials. Nevertheless, the sharp acceleration
in industrial development from the 1960s onward, an acceleration
intended primarily to produce export goods to exchange for the
imports, was accompanied by a striking increase in environmental
pollution and deterioration. As conditions worsened, and especially
as chemical pollution struck segments of the human populace, small
environmental movements and rudimentary efforts at remediation
did appear. But to date they have proven almost powerless to stop
the outpouring of new chemicals and pharmaceuticals, whose longer-
term environmental effects mostly remain unknown. Nor have they
slowed appreciably the production of waste products—trash, garbage,
sewage, gaseous exhaust, and other effluents—that, unlike those of
pre-industrial days, are so laced with non-biodegradable materials and
poisonous substances as to constitute long-term menaces of unknown
magnitude to the biosystems of both countries and their nearby seas.

*   *   *

Today, at the dawning of the twenty first century, then, Korea and
Japan display most of the environment-related characteristics normal
to industrial society. Active exploitation of the global resource base
maximizes material standards of living while leaving others to face
the many problems of pollution and habitat injury and loss that are
associated with primary production. Biochemical management currently contains most microbial menaces to the general population,
although the global problem of resistance to antibiotics continues to
grow, as does the global capacity to engineer and deploy more dangerous microbes. Birth rates are much lower than before 1870, and
they continue to fall. And while average longevity has increased dramatically due to sharply reduced death rates, the overall rate of population growth has recently begun to slow perceptibly, especially in
Japan. Forest policy, for all it flaws, generally maintains woodland

in healthier condition than before 1870. Environmental movements are able to meliorate some forms of abuse to the human community, although concern for the broader biosystem remains largely undeveloped, in part perhaps because those lushly forested mountains help obscure problems of species endangerment and habitat loss.

Industrial pollution, however, continues unabated. The reduction in a few of the more visible forms is offset by continuing development of new pharmaceuticals, biocides, and other chemicals and their vigorous use, along with fossil fuels, by agriculture, industry, and the general public, even though the environmental effects of most new products are neither known nor adequately investigated. And the myriad forms of solid and fluid waste, with all their malign consequences, continue to be produced in growing volume and variety, accompanied by meliorative measures that mostly range from the inadequate to the disingenuous.

Finally, in Korea and Japan, as in all industrial societies, the short-term interests of all powerful interest groups are solidly bound to the ideology of progress with its unexamined faith in the merit of limitless linear expansion in human numbers and per-capita human consumption of goods, services, and space. When or whether society's ideals and the constraints of life on this little planet can be reconciled in a manner that enables an industrialized Korea and Japan—or anywhere else—to continue flourishing remains to be seen.

GLOSSARY*

akamai	"red rice" or Champa rice; an *indica* variety used in "medieval" southwest Japan because it was more hardy than *japonica* varieties of the day
Ashikaga	Japanese military family; operated second (Muromachi) *bakufu*, 1338–1573
Ashikaga Takauji	founder of Ashikaga (Muromachi) *bakufu* in 1338; lived 1305–58
bakufu	"tent government," meaning Japanese military ("shogunal") regimes (Minamoto, Ashikaga, Tokugawa) that dominated political life for most of 1185–1868
Buddhism	originally an Indian religion, later introduced to East Asia where it gained in richness and complexity; it reached Korea in the late 300s and Japan in the mid 500s, flourishing in both areas for a millennium or more
Champa	southern Vietnam; also a variety of rice (See *akamai*)
Chang Po-go	regional powerholder and merchant-shipping magnate in southwest Korea; flourished during 820s–840s, d. 846
Ch'ing	the Manchu dynasty in China, 1636–1910
Ch'oe	Korean family name; lineage of military commanders who dominated Koryŏ politics, 1196–1258
Ch'oe Ch'ung-hŏn	military figure of Koryŏ period; established Ch'oe dictatorship in 1196; lived 1149–1219
Chŏng Yag-yong	pen name Tasan; a Korean scholar of the Practical Learning school, who wrote widely on social issues; lived 1762–1836
Chosŏn	Korean dynasty, 1392–1910; also known as Yi

---

* of *Proper Nouns* and *Korean and Japanese terms* found in text (place names excepted)

chŭlmun	"comb-patterned" pottery; spread across Korea, ca. 4–2,000 BCE
Confucianism	Chinese social thought ascribed initially to Confucius (fl. ca. 500 BCE) but later developed into a highly complex, wide-ranging corpus of thought that influenced all of East Asia
daimyō	"great names," or regional barons in Japan; emerge in 1300s, consolidate in 1500s, stabilized as territorial lords during Tokugawa period
Daisen Tomb	or Nintokuryō; in Japan, a huge mounded earthen tomb south of Osaka, originally near the shore; said to be that of the Yamato monarch Nintoku, who probably reigned around 400 to 420 CE or so
Daoism	Chinese body of thought that dates from age of Confucius; rich with ideals of mysticism and self discipline
El Niño	El Niño-La Niña southern oscillation; the periodic fluctuation, every few years, of water circulation and temperature in the equatorial Pacific and Indian oceans, which causes wide-ranging fluctuations in global weather
Fossa Magna	the cordillera of towering mountain ranges in central Japan that separates the northeast from southwest regions of Honshu Island
Fujiwara	name of an early Japanese royal capital (Fujiwara-*kyō*) in southern Nara Basin, 680s; also name of a major group of aristocratic patrilineages that flourished ca. 700s–1000s and survived under various family names into twenty first century
Genmei	energetic woman monarch of Japan, r. 708–15; erected Nara as capital city; promoted use of money, expansion into northeast, development of elite culture and political legitimation; lived 661–721
Go-Daigo	monarch (*tennō*) of Japan; tried to restore power to his lineage during 1330s; lived 1288–1339
Han	Chinese dynasty, 195 BCE–221 CE
han'gŭl	the Korean alphabet; devised by his advisors and promulgated in 1446 by King Sejong (r. 1418–50) of the Chosŏn Dynasty; came into use very slowly due to *yangban* resistance; in use today
Heian	royal capital in central Japan; built in 794ff.; later

	called Miyako; remained site of royal lineage (*tennō:* emperor) until 1869; today's Kyoto
Himiko	woman ruler of Yamatai in Wa confederation, probably in northwest Kyushu; active during 230s–240s
Holocene	geological epoch within the Quarternary sub-era, from 10,000 years ago to the present; followed the terminal Pleistocene (final Würm) meltoff
Homo erectus	early, widespread type of human being; found in China roughly a million years ago, possibly in northeast Asia a half-million years ago.
Homo sapiens	more recent humans, including two sub-species, *H. s. Neanderthalis* and *H. s. sapiens*, the latter being ourselves.
hyangni	local officials in Korea during Chosŏn Dynasty
jitsugaku	"Practical Learning;" a body of critical social and political Confucian thought of the Tokugawa period in Japan
jōmon	Japanese "cord-marked" pottery; flourished ca. 10,000–200 BCE
kana	a syllabary to represent the sounds of Japanese; developed gradually from late eighth century onward by simplifying Chinese characters and employing them for their sound value; two types (*hiragana; katakana*) now exist
Kaya	cluster of small polities in south coastal Korea and Naktong River basin, between Silla and Paekche; overrun by Silla in stages, 530s–560s.
Koguryŏ	early kingdom in Korea-Manchuria region; destroyed by Silla-Tang forces in 668 CE
Kongmin	king of Koryŏ; r. 1351–74; revived the dynasty after ousting Mongols
Koryŏ	Korean kingdom, 935–1392; replaced by Chosŏn
Koryŏsa	or *History of Koryŏ*; an official history of the Koryŏ Dynasty; completed in 1451
Koryŏ Tripitaka	edition of the *Tripitaka*, a vast compendium of Buddhist writings; prepared in Korea, 1237–47
Kwanggaet'o	renowned king of Koguryŏ; r. 391–413; expanded his realm southward into central Korea
kye	communal arrangements of villages or other mutual-interest groups in Korea; proliferate from about 1500 onward

Lelang   commandery (frontier outpost) of Han
                             Dynasty in northwest Korea; ca. 75 BCE–
                             313 CE

Manchus   here, a political elite in the Liaodong region;
                             led by Nurhachi, who conquered China and
                             whose successors founded Ch'ing Dynasty
                             in 1636

Mesozoic   geological era; 230–65 million years ago

Minamoto   Japanese military lineage; founded first
                             (Kamakura) *bakufu*, 1185–1333

Minamoto no Yoritomo   founder of Kamakura *bakufu*; lived 1147–99

Ming   Chinese dynasty, 1368–1662

Mongols   nomadic tribal groups of central Asia, whose
                             leaders overran continental East Asia dur-
                             ing ca. 1200s–1260s; founded Yuan Dynasty
                             in China

mu   Korean measure of land area

mumun   "plain-style" pottery; spread across Korea
                             from ca. 2,000 BCE onward

Munmu   king of Silla, reigned 661–81; allied with
                             Tang to overrun Paekche and Koguryŏ

Muromachi   neighborhood in Kyoto; site of second *bakufu*
                             and hence a name given to it

nanbokuchō   "northern and southern courts" in Japan;
                             the period (1336–92) when two rival lin-
                             eages claimed the title of *tennō*, one resident
                             in Kyoto, one in the Yoshino Mountains
                             of Kii Peninsula

Neanderthalis   sub-species of *Homo sapiens* that lived widely
                             about Eurasia until about 30,000 years ago;
                             name derived from fossil site in Neanderthal
                             Valley of western Germany

Neo-Confucianism   or Ch'eng-Zhu thought; predominant Con-
                             fucian interpretations of the Sung Dynasty;
                             strongly influenced Korean and Japanese
                             Confucian thought thereafter

Nurhachi   founder of the Manchu or Ch'ing Dynasty
                             in China; lived 1559–1626

nyang   a Korean coin

Ōkura Nagatsune	Japanese writer of detailed, practical agronomic advice; lived 1768–1856?
Oligocene	geological epoch within the Tertiary sub-era, some 30 million years ago
Ōnin War	a conflict among *daimyō* in Japan; mostly fought in and around Kyoto, 1467–77
Paekche	early and affluent kingdom in southwest Korea; destroyed by Silla-Tang forces in 663 CE
Pangaea	name given to the assemblage of continental plates whose disaggregation, beginning some 200 million years ago, eventuated in today's global distribution of continents
Panthallasic Ocean	the large portion of earthly surface that was not occupied by Pangaea
Parhae	Manchuria-centered kingdom that controlled part of continental Korea, 713–926
p'il	Korean measure of cloth; a bolt or roll
Pleistocene	the "ice ages;" a geological epoch within the Quarternary sub-era, lasting from ca. 2 million down to ten thousand years ago
Pliocene	geological epoch within the Tertiary sub-era, lasting from 11 to 2 million years ago
Riss	stage of glaciation during the Pleistocene epoch, ca. 5–400,000 years ago
ritsuryō	Japanese "penal and civil codes;" law codes drafted in the years around 700 CE to guide the "aristocratic bureaucracy" that lasted through the Nara and Heian periods; used here to denote the regime so guided
samurai	in Japan, originally armed servants who, in late *ritsuryō* times acquired higher status, emerging as more or less hereditary warriors during the centuries of *bakufu* pre-eminence; ranging in rank from shogun to minor guardsmen
Shang	regime in north China, prior to ca. 1100 BCE
shōgun	Japanese military title; hereditary head of *bakufu* ("shogunate"); derived from *ritsuryō*-era military title *seiitaishōgun* or "barbarian subduing generalissimo"

Silla   kingdom in southeast Korea; later controlled
                         all peninsular Korea; overran Koguryŏ and
                         Paekche in 660s; replaced by Koryŏ in 935 CE
Sinjong   king of Koryŏ during early years of Ch'oe
                         dictatorship; r. 1197–1204
Sinmun   king of Silla, r. 681–92; erected the capital
                         city of Kyŏngju; consolidated kingly power
sirhak   "Practical Learning;" a body of critical social
                         and political Confucian thought of the later
                         Chosŏn period in Korea
sō   communal village associations in Japan; appear
                         from fourteenth century onward
sŏk   a measure of volume (koku in Japanese); used
                         for grain, timber, or freight volume
Song   Chinese dynasty, 960–1126
T'aejo   reign name of Yi Sŏng-gye, founder of Chosŏn
                         Dynasty, who reigned as its first king, 1392–98
Tang   Chinese dynasty, 618–907 CE
Tokugawa Ieyasu   Japanese military man; triumphed in 1600
                         and founded Tokugawa bakufu; lived 1542–
                         1616
Toyotomi Hideyoshi   Japanese military man and dictator; pacified
                         the realm in 1580s; failed to conquer China
                         in 1590s; lived 1536–98
Wa   name applied by Chinese and Korean ob-
                         servers to Japan or southwestern Japan and
                         the people thereof before ca. 700 CE; also a
                         polity or "confederation" in southwest Japan
                         prior to ca. 300 CE
waegu   or wakō in Japanese; "Wa pirates," mainly
                         meaning pirates from southwest Japan, ca.
                         1220–1400
Würm   stage of glaciation during the late Pleistocene
                         epoch, ca. 70,000 to 15,000 years ago, when
                         weather fluctuated between cool and severely
                         cold, prior to the final Würm melt-off
Yamatai   early polity in Japan, probably in northwest
                         Kyushu, ca. 200–250 CE; perhaps the core
                         unit of Wa

Yamato	name for Japan; also a province centered on the Nara Basin in central Japan; also a monarchial lineage in central Japan, ca. 300–700 CE
Yan	or Yen; a polity in the northeast China/Manchuria region; brought into reunifying China in 222 BCE
yang	(see *nyang*)
yangban	the "two orders" of civil and military officialdom in Korea; a Confucian formulation that prevailed in the Chosŏn Dynasty
Yayoi	Japanese pottery type; also early agricultural society in Japan, ca. 400 BCE–300 CE
Yi Sŏng-gye	founder of Chosŏn (Yi) Dynasty; reigned as King T'aejo, 1392–98
yin/yang	a Chinese system for dyadic categorizing of phenomena according to imputed gender and associated characteristics
Yuan	the Mongol dynasty in China, 1271–1368
yunkimun	"raised-design" pottery; present in Korea from ca. 12,000 yBP onward
za	guilds, in medieval Japan
Zhou	early dynasty in north China, ca. 1100–221 BCE

PLANT AND ANIMAL NAMES*

Given by common name:

barley	*Hordeum vulgare*
barnyard grass	*Echinochloa crus-galli*
birch	*Betula schmidtii Regel*
broomcorn millet	*Panicum miliaceum*
buckwheat	*Fagopyrum esculentum*
Chinese milk vetch	*Astradagus sinicus*
cotton	*Gossypium herbaceum*
egoma	in Japan, perilla; *Perilla ocimoides*
foxtail millet	*Setaria italica*
hemp	*Cannabis sativa*
Korean lespedeza	*Lespedeza stipulacea*
ramie	*Boehmeria nivea*
rice	*Oryza sativa*: "long grain" = *O. s. indica*; "short grain" = *O. s. japonica*; Javanese = *O. s. javanica*
shiso	in Japan, beefsteak plant; *Perilla nankinensis*
song choong	in Korea, the larval form of an insect, probably either the pine defoliator, *Dendrolimus spectabilis Butler*, or Gastropacha Pini L.
soya	soy bean; *Glycine soya* or *Glycine max*
unka	in Japan, the leaf hopper, *Cicadula sexnotata*; a recurrent pest on field crops

Given by Latin binomial:

Acanthopanax ricinifolia	??
Elæagnus	an oleaster or silverberry
Euonymous alatus	winged spindle tree
Rhus semipinnata	a sumac
Sophora Japonica	the Japanese Pagoda Tree
Thuja orientalis	an arbor vitae

---

* that are found in the text and notes

BIBLIOGRAPHICAL ESSAY*

Environmental topics are only beginning to receive attention from scholars of East Asian history. Consequently, although this bibliographical essay seeks to cover more exhaustively materials treating the ecosystem than other topics in the pre-industrial history of Korea and Japan, most of the entries in fact pertain to other aspects of the history.

Two basic criteria have guided the selection of titles for inclusion. Primarily, of course, I have tried to select works that are reliable and stimulating in their scholarship, but also I have given preference to those that offer readers the richest guidance to further English-language readings. This latter criterion has generally favored more recent works, and some older but excellent works of scholarship are, therefore, omitted. They can, however, be found in the bibliographies cited herein, as well as in the bibliographical sections of more recent books and articles. Most notably, perhaps, the recent appearance of Satomi Kurosu, "Studies in Historical Demography and Family in Early Modern Japan," with accompanying "Bibliography" in *Early Modern Japan, An Interdisciplinary Journal* 10/1 (Spring 2002): 3–21, 66–71, has enabled me to omit a large number of excellent essays on that topic, even though demography is a significant concern of this volume.

Following discussion of some general categories of works, materials are grouped in terms of the four chapters of the book. Within each group they are organized by topic and further broken down into the categories of (a) works *INCLUSIVE* of Korea and Japan (where appropriate), (b) works on *KOREA*, and (c) works on *JAPAN*.

---

* NOTES:

1. A number of valuable works on specific topics that are omitted here are cited, some with annotations, in the Footnotes of this volume.

2. Full publication information for volumes that consist of sets of essays appears in the Bibliography, where titles are listed in order of the identifiers used in both the Footnotes and here.

General Works

1. Bibliographies

INCLUSIVE. For decades the basic reference in the field of Asian Studies has been the annual *Bibliography of Asian Studies* (*BAS*) (Ann Arbor: Association for Asian Studies). *BAS* had its roots in the late 1930s in a set of thin, unbound publications that Earl Pritchard edited under the title *Bulletin of Far Eastern Bibliography* (Washington D.C.: American Council of Learned Societies, 1936–1940). After 1940 the *Bulletin* was incorporated into the scholarly journal, *Far Eastern Quarterly* (*FEQ*), but from 1946 onward it appeared as a separate bound volume, *Far Eastern Bibliography*. In 1956 *FEQ* was renamed the *Journal of Asian Studies*, and the annual bibliographical issues—which grew thicker and larger as decades advanced—appeared thereafter as *BAS*.

Two cumulative editions of *BAS* incorporate the issues for the three decades 1941–70: Association for Asian Studies, *Cumulative Bibliography of Asian Studies, 1941–1965*, 4 author vols. 4 subject vols. (1969–70); *Cumulative Bibliography of Asian Studies, 1966–1970*, 3 author vols. 3 subject vols. (1972–73). Although cumbersome to use in either its annual or cumulative version, *BAS* will enable the diligent student to conduct an exhaustive search for materials in English (and some other European languages) on any facet of Korean or Japanese history that has been treated by scholars.

As the quantity of scholarship on Asia grew from the 1960s onward, the difficulty and cost of preparing annual printed bibliographies became prohibitive, publication slipped ever farther behind schedule, and during the 1990s the Association for Asian Studies abandoned the published format in favor of an electronic bibliography. For information, visit www.aasianst.org, the web site of the Association.

Two other publications will assist the scholar in tracking down books and articles that antedate BAS: Bernard S. Silberman, *Japan and Korea, A Critical Bibliography* (Tucson: The University of Arizona Press, 1962), 120 pp.; Frank J. Shulman, ed., *Japan and Korea, An Annotated Bibliography of Doctoral Dissertations in Western Languages, 1877–1969* (Chicago: American Library Association, 1970), 340 pp. It is indicative of the imbalance in Korean and Japanese studies during those decades that about 80% of Silberman's pages and 80% of Shulman's entries deal with Japanese subjects, only about 20% with Korean.

For dissertations since 1969, see Shulman, *Doctoral Dissertations on Japan and Korea, 1969–1974* (Ann Arbor, MI: University Microfilms International, 1976), 78 pp. More recent dissertations on Korea and Japan are included in Shulman's periodic *Doctoral Dissertations on Asia*, also from Ann Arbor.

KOREA. Some older studies of Korea are included in the pre-1937 bibliography series on Japan that is cited below: namely, that by the German scholars Wenckstern, Nachod, Haenisch, and Praesent. The eruption of a major war in Korea in 1950, however, finally drew sustained Anglophone scholarly attention to the peninsula as a distinct realm. In response to the conflict, two bibliographies of Western-language materials were assembled: Helen D. Jones and Robin L. Winkler, comp., *Korea: An Annotated Bibliography of Publications in Western Languages* (Washington, D.C.: Library of Congress, 1950), 3 vols.; Shannon McCune, *Bibliography of Western Language Material on Korea*, rev. ed. (NY: Institute of Pacific Relations, 1950), 61 pp.

Later, these were supplemented by Kang Sang-un, *A List of Articles on Korea in the Western Languages, 1800–1964* (Seoul: Tangu-Dang Publication Co., 1967), 192 pp. Today the most substantial listing is Kim Han-Kyo, ed., *Studies on Korea: A Scholar's Guide* (Honolulu: University Press of Hawaii, 1980), 438 pp.

No comprehensive listing of more recent works yet exists. However, for over a decade now the National History Compilation Committee in Seoul has published the *Bulletin for Historical Studies*, a serialized publication arranged by period and discipline that covers Korean-language books and articles thoroughly, together with some English- and Japanese-language materials.

JAPAN. For Japan the major compilation of early Western-language scholarship is the Wenckstern-Nachod-Haenisch/Praesent series, as follows. Frederick von Wenckstern compiled *A Bibliography of the Japanese Empire, 1859–1906*, 2 vols. (Leiden: E. J. Brill, 1895 for Vol. 1) (Tokyo: Maruzen, 1907 for Vol. 2). Volume 1 includes a reprint of a sixty-eight-page French bibliography of Western-language works published before 1859. Wenkstern was followed by Oskar Nachod, who compiled *A Bibliography of the Japanese Empire, 1906–1926*, 2 vols. (London: Goldston, 1928), and subsequently *Bibliographie von Japan, 1927–1932*, 2 vols. (Leipzig: Hiersemann Verlag, 1931, 1935). Subsequently Wolf Haenisch and Hans Praesent prepared *Bibliographie von Japan 1933–1937*, 2 vols. (Leipzig: Hiersemann Verlag, 1937, 1940).

In 1970 the publisher Anton Hiersemann of Stuttgart reissued in a single six-volume edition the compilations by Nachod and Haenisch/Praesent. Although this newer edition is in German, most of its titles are in English, making the volumes quite easy for the reader of English to use with the aid of a simple German-English dictionary.

Much as the outbreak of war in 1950 put Korea on the Anglophone mental map, so the earlier eruption of global war in the late 1930s spurred scholars writing in English to take over the bibliographical work that German academics were less and less able to pursue. Reflected in the editorial work of Earl Pritchard in his *Bulletin of Far Eastern Bibliography*, the impetus was more overtly evident in Hugh Borton et al., comps., *A Selected List of Books and Articles on Japan in English, French, and German* (Washington D.C.: American Council of Learned Societies, 1940), 142 pp. In 1954 Borton et al. issued a revised and enlarged edition of 272 pp. that was published by Harvard University Press.

Since then bibliographies relating to Japan, mostly selective and specialized, have proliferated, and they now are innumerable. At present the most useful and current general bibliography on Japanese history—to which reference will be made hereafter as Dower & George, *op. cit.*—is John W. Dower with T. S. George, *Japanese History & Culture from Ancient to Modern Times: Seven Basic Bibliographies*, 2d ed. (Princeton, N.J.: Markus Wiener Publishing, 1995), 459 pp. It will lead one to more specialized bibliographies as well as to reference works, journals, and secondary sources.

2. *Other Reference Works*

By their nature, perhaps, general reference works tend to focus on either Korea or Japan (cf. p. 201, l. 9–10).

KOREA. A useful reference work with basic information on Korean (mainly South) society, economy, and affairs—which is updated and reissued every few years—is *A Handbook of Korea* (Seoul: Korean Overseas Information Service, various editions), 592 pp. A richer introduction to topics in Korean culture, society, and history is *Introduction to Korean Studies* (Seoul: National Academy of Sciences, 1986), 849 pp., which consists of 33 essays by recognized scholars. A major collection of translations from Korean cultural history is Peter H. Lee, ed., *Sourcebook of Korean Civilization*, Vol. 1 (NY: Columbia University Press, 1993), 750 pp., or the newer, two-volume publication edited by Lee et al., *Sources of Korean Tradition* (NY: Columbia University Press, 1996, 2000), 480, 448 pp.

JAPAN. There are several English-language encyclopedias on the history, society, and culture of Japan. Of them the most valuable for study of history remains the *Kōdansha Encyclopedia of Japan* (Tokyo: Kōdansha, 1983), 9 vols. Although dated in priorities and perspectives, and not very helpful in environmental matters, it contains the mother lode of reliable detail on innumerable historical topics. A newer and more concise work that contains myriad short entries is Louis Frédéric, *Japan Encyclopedia* (Cambridge, MA: Harvard University Press, 2002), 1102 pp., a translation of a 1996 work in French.

A valuable collection of translations on Japanese political and socioeconomic history is David J. Lu, *Japan: A Documentary History* (Armonk, NY: M. E. Sharpe, Inc., 1996), 2 vols. Similar to Peter Lee's translations for Korea is Ryusaku Tsunoda et al., *Sources of the Japanese Tradition* (NY: Columbia University Press, 1958), 928 pp., a new 2-volume edition of which is currently in preparation by Wm. Theodore de Bary and others. The titles of other, more specialized reference works can be gleaned from Dower & George, *op. cit.*, pp. 417–24.

3. *Journals*

INCLUSIVE. The fields of Korean and Japanese history are blessed with good scholarly journals. Many of them specialize on recent affairs or on facets of higher culture. But *The Journal of Asian Studies* covers history broadly, devoting a portion of its space to Korea and Japan. *Acta Asiatica* and the *Harvard Journal of Asiatic Studies* also cover these fields. *Asian Perspectives* specializes in archaeology and prehistory, and some of its articles are on northeast Asia. From time to time valuable essays also appear in non-regional journals such as *American Historical Review, Journal of World History, Past and Present*, or *Peasant Studies*, or in journals in other disciplines of science, social studies, and the humanities, as evidenced in this volume's Bibliography.

KOREA. A good number of the concise essays in *Korea Journal* proved particularly useful in this project. *Korean Studies*, the *Journal of Korean Studies*, and the *Seoul Journal of Korean Studies* regularly carry solid and usually longer articles on Korean history, while the venerable *Transactions of the Korea Branch of the Royal Asiatic Society* contains shorter, often less scholarly pieces.

JAPAN. The *Journal of Japanese Studies* and *Monumenta Nipponica* regularly contain solid articles on aspects of Japan's history. *Transactions of the Asiatic Society of Japan*, rather like the journal of the *Korea Branch*, offers generally short pieces on diverse topics, as does the *Japan Quarterly*. See Dower & George, *op. cit.*, pp. 427–30, for an extensive listing of other, more specialized journals.

4. *General Texts*

INCLUSIVE. Texts that treat Korean and Japanese history together are not available, but a few do treat them in the context of "East Asia." The finest of these is the venerable work by Edwin O. Reischauer and John K. Fairbank, *East Asia, The Great Tradition* (Boston: Houghton Mifflin Company, 1958), 739 pp., and its companion volume, *East Asia, The Modern Transformation* (Boston: Houghton Mifflin Company, 1965), 955 pp. Even *The Great Tradition*, however, which covers the story from "pre-history" down to the mid-1800s, treats East Asia not as an entity but as an assemblage of discrete, interacting states or societies, with eight chapters devoted to China, one to Korea, and three to Japan.

KOREA. The first major history of Korea in English was Homer B. Hulbert, *The History of Korea* (Seoul: The Methodist Publishing House, 1905), 2 vols. Despite its scholarly shortcomings, it remained the pre-eminent work until after the Korean War. Today, however, a number of good general histories of Korea exist in English. In this study I relied primarily on Lee Ki-baik (Edward W. Wagner, tr.), *A New History of Korea* (Cambridge, MA: Harvard University Press, 1984), 474 pp., and its revised version by Carter J. Eckert et al., *Korea Old and New, A History* (Seoul: Ilchokak Publishers, 1990), 454 pp., which provides a richer treatment of the recent history. The Lee text merits particular note for its excellent bibliography and index-glossary. Also helpful was Andrew C. Nahm, *Korea, Tradition and Transformation. A History of the Korean People* (Elizabeth, NJ: Hollym International Corporation, 1988), 582 pp.

JAPAN. Japan's pre-industrial history, too, is well served by general texts. The finest early work, which initially appeared in 1932 and was revised and republished in later years, was George B. Sansom, *Japan, A Short Cultural History* (NY: Appleton-Century-Crofts, 1943), 554 pp. Since then history texts have proliferated, as Dower & George, *op. cit.*, pp. 5–7, indicate. Dated, but still serviceable in many areas, particularly its second volume, is Sansom's more recent *History of Japan*, 3 vols. (Stanford: Stanford University Press, 1958–63), which follows the story from Japan's origins to the mid-nineteenth century. A rambling discussion of various topics in Japanese cultural, social, and political history is S. N. Eisenstadt, *Japanese Civilization, A Comparative View* (Chicago: University of Chicago Press, 1996), 581 pp.

Today *The Cambridge History of Japan*, ed. by John Whitney Hall et al. (Cambridge: Cambridge University Press, 1988–99), 6 vols., is by far the most detailed overall history, with rich treatment of political, socio-economic, and cultural topics. For this volume, however, I have relied heavily on Conrad Totman, *A History of Japan* (Oxford: Blackwell Publishers, 2000), 620 pp., which examines environmental issues.

Chapter 1. Paleogeography and Pre-Agricultural Society (to 1000 BCE)

The works relevant to this chapter seem to categorize as geography, geology and paleogeology, and forager society.

1. *Geography*

INCLUSIVE. Select chapters in Norton Ginsburg, ed., *The Pattern of Asia* (Englewood, NJ: Prentice-Hall, 1958), 929 pp., place Korea and Japan in a broader Asian context, even though the work depicts the Asia of a half-century ago. On pre-historic vegetation in northeast Asia, see Song Zhichen et al., "The Miocene Floristic Regions of East Asia," in Whyte, 1984, Vol. II, pp. 448–59. On the role of monsoons in the region's human history, see Yasuda Yoshinori, "Monsoon Fluctuations and Cultural Changes During the Last Glacial Age in Japan," *Japan Review* 1 (1990): 113–51, whose arguments are relevant to Korea as well as Japan.

KOREA. Visitors to Korea have provided scattered accounts of what they saw, as evidenced, for example, in Isabella Bird Bishop, *Korea and Her Neighbors* (NY: Fleming H. Revell Co., 1897), 480 pp., and Gari Ledyard, *The Dutch Come to Korea* (Seoul: Royal Asiatic Society Korea Branch, 1971), 231 pp. On Korean perceptions of geography during the Chosŏn period, see Yang Bo-Kyung, "Perceptions of Nature in the Chosŏn Period, *Korea Journal* 37/4 (Winter 1997): 134–55. The first full treatment of Korea's geography in the modern manner, a work that is concise, readable, and richly illustrated, is Shannon McCune, *Korea's Heritage: A Regional and Social Geography* (Rutland, VT: Charles E. Tuttle Co., 1956), 250 pp. A more up-to-date and more richly detailed collection of essays is Kim Doo-jung and Yoo Jea-taik, coordinators, *Korea: Geographical Perspectives* (Seoul: Korean Educational Development Institute, 1988), 464 pp.

JAPAN. Indigenous writings on the realm date to early times, as evidenced in Michiko Y. Aoki, *Records of Wind and Earth* (Ann Arbor, MI: Association for Asian Studies, 1997), 347 pp., which is a translation of seventh-century *fudoki* or gazetteers. As in Korea, visitors have recorded their observations, as seen, for example, in Ryūsaku Tsunoda, tr. and L. Carrington Goodrich, ed., *Japan in the Chinese Dynastic Histories* (South Pasadena: P. D. and Ione Perkins, 1951), 187 pp. Also, Isabella L. Bird, *Unbeaten Tracks in Japan* (NY: G. P. Putnam & Sons, 1881), 2 vols., and Engelbert Kaempfer (ed., & trans. by Beatrice Bodart-Bailey), *Kaempfer's Japan, Tokugawa Culture Observed* (Honolulu: University of Hawai'i Press, 1999), 545 pp. A particularly valuable collection of observations on Japan around 1600 CE is Michael Cooper, comp., *They Came to Japan, An Anthology of European Reports on Japan, 1543–1640* (Berkeley: University of California Press, 1965), 459 pp. An early but still useful work by a professional geographer is Glenn Thomas Trewartha, *Japan, A Physical, Cultural, and Regional Geography* (Madison: The University of Wisconsin Press, 1963, 1978), 607 pp. It is a skillfully updated and expanded version of a work originally published in 1934 as *A Reconnaissance Geography of Japan*. For more detail on select topics, see the collection of essays by the Association of Japanese Geographers, ed., *Geography of Japan* (Tokyo: Teikoku-Shoin, 1980), 440 pp.

2. *Geology and Paleogeology*

INCLUSIVE. A concise, nicely illustrated treatment of Earth's early geological history is Richard K. Bambach, et al., "Before Pangaea: The Geographies of the Paleozoic World," in Skinner, 1980, pp. 86–98. On the later, post-Pangaea story, see Robert S. Dietz and John C. Holden, "The Breakup of Pangaea," *Scientific American* 223/4 (1970): 30–41. B. C. Burchfiel, "Evolution of Continental and Oceanic Crust," *Proceedings of the American Philosophical Society* 137/1 (March 1993): 1–29, provides both a useful update and guidance to the earlier specialized literature. On the India-Eurasia collision in particular, see the brief comments in Burchfiel and the works he cites, including Peter Molnar and Paul Tapponnier, "Cenozoic Tectonics of Asia: Effects of a Continental Collision," *Science* 189/4201 (8 August 1975): 419–26, and C. J. Allègre et al., "Structure and Evolution of the Himalaya-Tibet Orogenic Belt," *Nature* 307 (5 January 1984): 17–22. A handy reference for geological terminology is Alec Watt, *Barnes & Noble Thesaurus of Geology* (NY: Barnes & Noble, 1982), 192 pp.

An attempt to determine the paleogeological relationship of the Korean and Japanese land masses is Hiroi Yoshikuni, "Subdivision of the Hida Metamorphic Complex, Central Japan, and its Bearing on the Geology of the Far East in Pre-Sea of Japan Time," *Tectonophysics* 76 (1981): 317–33. Formation of the Sea of Japan is illuminated by Mitsuo Shimazu et al., "Tectonics and Volcanism in the Sado-Pohang Belt from 20 to 14 Ma and Opening of the Yamato Basin of the Japan Sea," *Tectonophysics* 181 (1990): 321–30, and Y. Otofuji et al., "Brief Review of Miocene Opening of the Japan Sea: Paleomagnetic Evidence from the Japan Arc," *Journal of Geomagnetism and Geoelectricity* 38 (1986): 287–94.

KOREA. Lee, Dai-sung, ed., *Geology of Korea* (Seoul: Kyohak-sa, 1987), 514 pp., offers a richly detailed, beautifully illustrated treatment of Korea's geology. Sung Kwun Chough, *Marine Geology of Korean Seas* (Boston: International Human Resources Development Corporation, 1983), 157 pp., discusses the geology of coastal seas.

JAPAN. Although dated, Yoshida Takashi, ed., *Outline of the Geology of Japan* (Kawasaki: Geological Survey of Japan, 1976), 61 pp., is a concise and useful report on the geology of Japan. For more recent scholarship, see the highly detailed technical studies in Toshio Kimura et al., *Geology of Japan* (Tokyo: University of Tokyo Press, 1991), 287 pp.

3. *Forager Society*

There exists a rich literature, mainly archaeological, on many aspects of Korean and Japanese pre-agricultural history. A number of titles are listed in the Bibliography; many more appear in the bibliographies of recent works.

INCLUSIVE. A valuable introduction to scholarship on the archaeology of the region is Gina L. Barnes, ed., *Hoabinhan, Jōmon, Yayoi, Early Korean States: Bibliographic Reviews of Far Eastern Archaeology* (Oxford: Oxbow Books for East Asian Archaeology Network, 1990), 162 pp.

For society at the depths of the final glaciation, see T. E. G. Reynolds and S. C. Kaner, "Japan and Korea at 18,000 BP," in Soffer and Gamble, 1990, pp. 296–311. A recent, broadly arched, richly illustrated interpretive overview of forager and early agricultural society in East Asia is Gina L. Barnes, *China, Korea and Japan: The Rise of Civilization in East Asia* (London: Thames and Hudson, 1993), 288 pp. An older study of the region's prehistory that gives good attention to Siberian connections is Chester S. Chard, *Northeast Asia in Prehistory* (Madison: University of Wisconsin Press, 1974), 212 pp. Kikuchi Toshihiko, "Continental Culture and Hokkaido," in Pearson, 1986, pp. 149–62, also treats Siberian influence.

KOREA. A rich recent treatment of Korean archaeology is Sarah Milledge Nelson, *The Archaeology of Korea* (Cambridge: Cambridge University Press, 1993), 307 pp., which will lead one to earlier works. Among these, a work to note is the detailed, highly descriptive presentation of archaeological sites by Kim Jeong-hak, *The Prehistory of Korea* (Honolulu: University Press of Hawaii, 1978), 237 pp., which is translated by Richard and Kazue Pearson from a 1972 Japanese edition. A thoughtful discussion of incipient agriculture is Choe Chong Pil, "Origins of Agriculture in Korea," *Korea Journal* 30/11 (November-December 1990): 4–14. A valuable recent discussion of the archaeological scholarship, particularly that in Korean, is Choi Mong-lyong and Rhee Song-nai, "Korean Archaeology for the 21st Century: From Prehistory to State Formation," *Seoul Journal of Korean Studies* 14 (December 2001): 117–47.

JAPAN. A recent general text is Keiji Imamura, *Prehistoric Japan, New Perspectives on Insular East Asia* (Honolulu: University of Hawai'i Press, 1996), 246 pp. An outstanding collection of essays is Richard J. Pearson, ed., *Windows on the Japanese Past: Studies in Archaeology and Prehistory* (Ann Arbor: Center for Japanese Studies, The University of Michigan, 1986), 629 pp. See also J. Edward Kidder, Jr., "The Earliest Societies in Japan," *Cambridge History* 1, pp. 48–107.

On subsistence practices, see these three items: the thoughtful essay by Hiroko Koike, "Exploitation Dynamics During the Jomon Period," in Aikens and Rhee, 1992, pp. 53–57; the lively attempt by Sasaki Kōmei, "The Wa People and Their Culture in Ancient Japan: The Culture of Swidden Cultivation and Padi-Rice Cultivation," *Acta Asiatica* 61 (1991): 24–46, to link developments in Japan to those on the continent, and the meticulous examination of stone tool usage by Kaoru Yamamoto, "Space-time Analysis of Raw Material Utilization for Stone Implements of the Jomon Culture in Japan," *Antiquity* 64/245 (December 1990): 868–89. For population estimates, see Shūzō Koyama, "Jōmon Subsistence and Population," *Senri Ethnological Studies* 2 (1978): 1–65.

Chapter 2. The Rise of Early Agrarian Regimes (1000 BCE–700 CE)

Works on these centuries are organized here in terms of general texts, agriculture and metallurgy, and politics and society.

1. *General Texts*

INCLUSIVE. The earlier-noted work by Gina L. Barnes, *China, Korea and Japan, op. cit.*, treats this topic.

KOREA. A pioneer study is Kenneth J. H. Gardiner, *The Early History of Korea* (Honolulu: University Press of Hawaii, 1969), 78 pp. On Paekche, Jonathan Best has a full-length study and translation currently in press. Gina L. Barnes, *State Formation in Korea, Historical and Archaeological Perspectives* (Richmond, Surrey: Curzon Press, 2001), 245 pp., a collection of her essays, includes a splendid bibliography of relevant works. An extremely thoughtful historiographical study of "national identity" issues in shaping our understanding of this early Korean history is Hyung Il Pai, *Constructing "Korean" Origins* (Cambridge, MA: Harvard University Asian Center, 2000), 543 pp.

JAPAN. William Wayne Farris, *Sacred Texts and Buried Treasures: Issues in the Historical Archaeology of Ancient Japan* (Honolulu: University of Hawai'i Press, 1998), 333 pp., examines major aspects of this topic, and his bibliography will lead readers to the rich earlier literature. Gina Lee Barnes, *Protohistoric Yamato: Archeology of the First Japanese State* (Ann Arbor, MI: Center for Japanese Studies, University of Michigan, 1988), 473 pp., is a careful study of the Yamato Basin. See also the revealing essay by Mark Hudson and Gina Barnes, "Yoshinogari: A Yayoi Settlement in Northern Kyushu," *Monumenta Nipponica* 46/2 (Summer 1991): 211–35. "National identity" issues are addressed by Mark J. Hudson, *Ruins of Identity, Ethnogenesis in the Japanese Islands* (Honolulu: University of Hawai'i Press, 1999), 323 pp. Dower & George, *op. cit.*, pp. 12–24, list many other works by topic.

2. *Agriculture and Metallurgy*

INCLUSIVE. On rice culture, a richly informative collection of essays is that of The Association of Japanese Agricultural Scientific Societies, ed., *Rice in Asia* (Tokyo: University of Tokyo Press, 1975), 600 pp. Young-nai Chon, "Introduction of Rice Agriculture into Korea and Japan: From the Perspective of Polished Stone Implements," in Aikens and Rhee, 1992, pp. 161–69, examines the emergence of rice tillage in the two societies.

KOREA. On the introduction of rice to Korea, see the seminal discussion, Sarah M. Nelson, "The Origins of Rice Agriculture in Korea—A Symposium," *Journal of Asian Studies* 41/3 (May 1982): 511–48. It contains essays by Won-yong Kim and Chong-pil Choe, as well as Nelson. Also see Hyo-jae Im, "Prehistoric Rice Agriculture in Korea," in Aikens and Rhee, 1992, pp. 157–60. Two very good essays on metallurgy are Yoon Dong Suk "Early Iron Metallurgy in Korea," *Archaeological Review from Cambridge* 8/1 (1989): 92–99, and Sarah Taylor, "The Introduction and Development of Iron Production in Korea: a Survey," *World Archaeology* 20/3 *Archaeometallurgy* (1989): 422–34, which list earlier studies.

JAPAN. On the development of agriculture in central Japan, see C. Melvin Aikens and Takeru Akazawa, "Fishing and Farming in Early Japan: Jomon Littoral Tradition Carried into Yayoi Times at the Miura Caves on Tokyo Bay," in Aikens and Rhee, 1992, pp. 75–82. And for the northeast, these two essays: Gary W. Crawford and Hirota Takamiya, "The Origins and Implications of Late Prehistoric Plant Husbandry in Northern Japan," *Antiquity* 64/245 (December 1990): 889–911, and Gary W. Crawford, "The Transitions to Agriculture in Japan," in Gebauer and Price, 1992, pp. 117–32. Also Yasuda Yoshinori, "Early Historic Forest Clearance around the Ancient Castle Site of Tagajo, Miyagi Prefecture, Japan," *Asian Perspectives* 19/1 (1978): 42–58. On the use of iron, see Ch. 2 of Farris, *Sacred Texts, op. cit.*

3. *Politics and Society*

INCLUSIVE. See Barnes, *China, Korea and Japan, op. cit.,* especially Chs. 13–15. An attempt to compare the process of elite consolidation in Korea and Japan is Yi Ki-dong, "Shilla's Kolp'um System and Japan's Kabane System," *Korean Social Science Journal* 11 (1984):

7–24. Several other works on early Korea-Japan relations are cited in Dower & George, *op. cit.*, pp. 21–22.

KOREA. The bibliography in Barnes, *State Formation in Korea, op. cit.*, will guide one to works on this topic. Regarding the Lelang commandery, in particular, see Pai, *Constructing "Korean" Origins, op. cit.*, and Richard Pearson, "Lelang and the Rise of Korean States and Chieftains," *Journal of the Hong Kong Archaeological Society* 7 (1976–1978): 77–90. On Kaya, see Ch. 7 of Barnes, *State Formation in Korea, op. cit.*, and Kwon Oh-young, "The Recent Trends and Problems in the Studies of Kaya History," *Seoul Journal of Korean Studies* 7 (December 1994): 187–200.

JAPAN. Highly revealing of society in ancient southwestern Japan are the translated Chinese sources in the earlier-cited Tsunoda and Goodrich, *Japan in the Chinese Dynastic Histories.* Joan R. Piggott, *The Emergence of Japanese Kingship* (Stanford: Stanford University Press, 1997), 434 pp., is the richest scholarly study of political process, and its fine bibliography will lead one to earlier works. See also these three essays in *Cambridge History* 1: Delmer M. Brown, "The Yamato Kingdom," pp. 108–62; Inoue Mitsusada, "The Century of Reform," pp. 163–220, and Okazaki Takashi, "Japan and the Continent," pp. 268–316. Hanihara Kazuro, "Estimations of the Number of Early Migrants to Japan: A Simulative Study," *Journal of the Anthropological Society of Nippon* 95/3 (July 1987): 391–403, addresses the thorny question of migration from Korea to Japan during these centuries.

Chapter 3. The Early Agricultural Order (700–1350)

The scholarship on these centuries seems to categorize nicely as general texts, political history, and works on society, commerce, and environmental issues.

1. General Texts

Substantial segments of standard "national" histories treat these centuries, covering political, social, cultural, and economic developments. These include, for *KOREA,* the aforementioned Lee Ki-baik, *A New History of Korea,* and Andrew C. Nahm, *Korea, Tradition and Transformation.* And for *JAPAN, The Cambridge History,* vols. 1–3, and Totman, *A History of Japan.* Pierre François Souyri, *The World Turned Upside Down:*

Medieval Japanese Society (NY: Columbia University Press, 2001), 280 pp., translated from a 1998 work in French, is a broadly arched study of "medieval" Japan, meaning in this case the centuries ca. 1200–1600.

2. *Political History*

KOREA. Because of insufficient records, Silla politics has been little studied. But see Lee [Yi] Ki-dong, "Bureaucracy and Kolp'um System in the Middle Age of Silla," in *Journal of Social Sciences and Humanities* 52 (December 1980): 31–58. Silla's collapse is treated by Ellen Salem Unruh, "Reflections of the Fall of Silla," *Korea Journal* 15/5 (May 1975): 54–62, and Kenneth H. J. Gardiner, "Korea in Transition: Notes on the Three Later Kingdoms (900–36)," *Papers on Far Eastern History* 36 (September 1987): 139–61.

On Parhae, see three essays by Song Ki-ho: "Several Questions in Studies of the History of Palhae," *Korea Journal* 30/6 (June 1990): 4–20; his "Current Trends in the Research of Palhae History," *Seoul Journal of Korean Studies* 3 (1990): 157–74, and his more recent "The Dual Structure of Parhae: Kingdom and Empire," *Seoul Journal of Korean Studies* 12 (December 1999): 104–23.

On Koryŏ, two fine recent studies are John B. Duncan, *The Origins of the* Chosŏn *Dynasty* (Seattle: University of Washington Press, 2000), 395 pp., and Edward J. Shultz, *Generals and Scholars, Military Rule in Medieval Korea* (Honolulu: University of Hawai'i Press, 2000), 254 pp. Both carry good bibliographies that list the many solid earlier studies. Two scholarly articles that study the examination system as mechanism for selecting government officials are H. W. Kang, "Institutional Borrowing: The Case of the Chinese Civil Service Examination System in Early Koryŏ," *Journal of Asian Studies* 34/1 (November 1974): 109–25, and Yi Sŏng-mu, "Kwagŏ System and Its Characteristics: Centering on the Koryŏ and Early Chosŏn Periods, *Korea Journal* 21/7 (July 1981): 4–19. Lee Ki-baik, "Korea—The Military Tradition," in Kang H, 1975, pp. 1–42, places the rise of military rulership in the longer-term context of the role of military men in Korean history. Park Yong-woon studies the Koryŏ capital city in "Kaegyŏng in the Age of Koryŏ," *Seoul Journal of Korean Studies* 11 (December 1998): 79–106.

On Koryŏ relations with neighboring continental polities see, among several titles, William Ellsworth Henthorn, *Korea, The Mongol Invasions*

(Leiden: E. J. Brill, 1963), 252 pp.; Kim Tang-Taek, "Im Yon's Regime and Koryŏ's Return of the Capital to Kaesŏng," in *Korean Social Science Journal* 23 (1997): 103–12, and Michael C. Rogers, "The Regularization of Koryŏ-Chin Relations (1116–1131), *Central Asiatic Journal* 6/1 (1961): 51–84.

JAPAN. The politics of the centuries 700–1350 has received much attention, as evidenced by several of the essays in Jeffrey P. Mass., ed., *The Origins of Japan's Medieval World* (Stanford: Stanford University Press, 1997), 504 pp.; volumes 1–3 of *The Cambridge History*, and the entries in Dower & George, *op. cit.*, pp. 24–27, 37–42. Among recent studies, Andrew Edmund Goble, *Kenmu, Go-Daigo's Revolution* (Cambridge, MA: Harvard University Press, 1996), 390 pp., and Mikael S. Adolphson, *The Gates of Power: Monks, Courtiers, and Warriors in Premodern Japan* (Honolulu: University of Hawai'i Press, 2000), 456 pp., provide thoughtful analyses of inter-elite relations during these centuries.

On aspects of cross-Straits relations, see Tōno Haruyuki, "Japanese Embassies to T'ang China and Their Ships," *Acta Asiatica* 69 (1995): 39–62; Charlotte von Verschuer, "Japan's Foreign Relations 600 to 1200 AD, A Translation from *Zenrin Kokuhōki*," *Monumenta Nipponica* 54/1 (Spring 1999): 1–39, and her follow-up essay on the years 1200–1392 in MN 57/4 (Winter 2002): 413–45; Kawazoe Shōji, "Japan and East Asia," in *Cambridge History* 3, pp. 396–446; and Thomas Conlan, *In Little Need of Divine Intervention, Scrolls of the Mongol Invasions of Japan* (Ithaca, NY: Cornell East Asia Series, 2001), 320 pp. For relations with the northeast, see Karl F. Friday, "Pushing Beyond the Pale: The Yamato Conquest of the Emishi and Northern Japan," in *Journal of Japanese Studies* 23/1 (Winter 1997): 1–24, and Mimi Hall Yiengpruksawan, *Hiraizumi, Buddhist Art and Regional Politics in Twelfth-Century Japan* (Cambridge, MA: Harvard University Press, 1998), 263 pp.

3. *Society*

KOREA. An attempt to reconstruct Silla society is Chin Kim, "The Silla Village Registers and Korean Legal History: a Preliminary Inquiry," *Korean Journal of Comparative Law* 7 (November 1979): 99–120. On elite structure, see Yi [Lee] Ki-baek, "Formation and Development of the Lineage Aristocratic Society of Koryŏ," in *Introduction*, pp. 71–88. The thorny issue of social organization and land control in Koryŏ is addressed in these three essays: Kang Chinch'ol, "Traditional

Land Tenure Relations in Korean Society: Ownership and Management," in Kang H, 1975, pp. 43-l04; Kim Yong-sŏp, "The Land Tenure in Premodern Korea," in *Introduction*, pp. 527–62, and James B. Palais, "Land Tenure in Korea: Tenth to Twelfth Centuries." *Journal of Korean Studies* 4 (1982–83): 73–205. For late Koryŏ, see Yi T'ae-jin, "Social Changes in Late Koryŏ to Early Chosŏn Period," *Korea Journal* 23/5 (May 1983): 32–44.

The social role (among other topics) of Buddhism is examined by articles in The Korean Buddhist Institute, ed., *The History and Culture of Buddhism in Korea* (Seoul: Dongguk University Press, 1993), 294 pp., and by articles in Lewis R. Lancaster and C. S. Yu, *Introduction of Buddhism to Korea: New Cultural Patterns* (Berkeley: Asian Humanities Press, 1989), 229 pp.; Lancaster, *Assimilation of Buddhism in Korea: Religious Maturity and Innovation in the Silla Dynasty* (Berkeley: Asian Humanities Press, 1991), 250 pp., and Lancaster et al., eds., *Buddhism in Koryŏ: A Royal Religion* (Berkeley: Institute of East Asian Studies, University of California, 1996), 211 pp.

Slavery has received considerable attention, as in these several essays: Seung-ki Hong, "A Study of Slave Policies in Early Koryŏ," *Journal of Social Science and Humanities* 53 (June 1981): 79–114; Chong Sun Kim, "Slavery in Silla and its Sociological and Economic Implications," in Nahm, 1974, pp. 29–39; James B. Palais, "Slavery and Slave Society in the Koryŏ Period," *Journal of Korean Studies* 5 (1984): 173–90; Mark Peterson, "Slaves and Owners; or Servants and Masters? A Preliminary Examination of Slavery in Traditional Korea," *Transactions of the Korea Branch of the Royal Asiatic Society* 60 (1985): 31–41; Ellen Salem, "The Utilization of Slave Labor in the Koryŏ Period," in *Papers*, 1979, pp. 630–42, and Ellen Salem Unruh, "The landowning Slave: a Korean Phenomenon," *Korea Journal* 16/4 (April 1976): 27–34.

JAPAN. On *ritsuryō* cities and urbanization, see Farris, *Sacred Texts and Buried Treasures, op. cit.*, Ch. 3, and William H. McCullough, "The Capital and its Society," in *Cambridge History* 2, pp. 97–182. On hinterland society and agriculture, see William Wayne Farris, *Population, Disease, and Land in Early Japan, 645–900* (Cambridge, MA: Harvard University Press, 1985), 235 pp., and Dana Morris, "Land and Society," in *Cambridge History* 2, pp. 183–235.

On "medieval" centuries, see Hitomi Tonomura, "Black Hair and Red Trousers: Gendering the Flesh in Medieval Japan," *American Historical Review* 99/1 (February 1994): 129–54; Kristina Kade Troost,

"Peasants, Elites, and Villages in the Fourteenth Century," in Mass, 1997, pp. 91–109, and two essays in *Cambridge History* 3: Nagahara Keiji, "The Medieval Peasant," pp. 301–43, and Barbara Ruch, "The Other Side of Culture in Medieval Japan," pp. 500–43.

Elite culture, the warrior "class," and institutional religion have been examined at great length, as evidenced by titles in Dower & George, *op. cit.*, pp. 27–37, 62–84.

4. *Commerce*

The scholarship treating commerce falls into three categories: that on piracy, maritime trade and technology, and domestic trade.

INCLUSIVE. On piracy see three essays by Benjamin H. Hazard: "The Wakō and Korean Responses," in Parsons, 1976, pp. 15–28; "The Formative Years of the *Wakō*, 1223–63," *Monumenta Nipponica* 22/3–4 (1967): 260–77, and "The Creation of the Korean Navy During the Koryŏ Period," *Transactions of the Korea Branch of the Royal Asiatic Society* 48 (1973): 10–28. Also see Jurgis Elisonas, "The Inseparable Trinity: Japan's Relations with China and Korea", in *Cambridge History* 4, pp. 235–300.

KOREA. On maritime trade and technology, see Hazard, "The Creation of the Korean Navy During the Koryŏ Period," cited above, and Shee Sung, "The Contributions of Chinese Merchants to the Trade Relations between Sung China and Koryo," in *Chinese Culture* 18/4 (December 1977): 1–18. Information on domestic trade in Korea is thin, as Lee Hyoun-young, "A Geographic Study of the Korean Periodic Markets," *Korea Journal* 15/8 (August 1975): 12–24, reveals.

JAPAN. On maritime trade and technology, consult the above-noted works by Tōno Haruyuki, "Japanese Embassies to T'ang China and Their Ships," and Verschuer, "Japan's Foreign Relations 600 to 1200 AD" and "1200 to 1392 AD." See also William Wayne Farris, "Shipbuilding and Nautical Technology in Japan, 1100–1640," a ms. currently in preparation.

On *ritsuryō* domestic trade, see Farris, "Trade, Money, and Merchants in Nara Japan," *Monumenta Nipponica* 53/3 (Fall 1998): 303–34; Sakaehara Towao, "Coinage in the Nara and Heian Periods," *Acta Asiatica* 39 (1980): 1–20, and Torao Yoshiya, "Nara Economic and Social Institutions," in *Cambridge History* 1, pp. 415–52. For later centuries, see Janet R. Goodwin, "Shadows of Transgression: Heian and

Kamakura Constructions of Prostitution," *Monumenta Nipponica* 55/3 (Autumn 2000): 327–68, and Kozo Yamamura, "The Growth of Commerce in Medieval Japan," in *Cambridge History* 3, pp. 344–95.

5. *Environmental Issues*

INCLUSIVE. For preliminary population estimates, see Colin McEvedy and Richard Jones, *Atlas of World Population History* (NY: Penguin Books, 1978), 368 pp.

KOREA. For population estimates of late Koryŏ, see Yi Tae-Jin, "The Influence of Neo-Confucianism on 14th–16th Century Korean Population Growth," *Korea Journal* 37/2 (Summer 1997): 5–23.

JAPAN. On *ritsuryō* demographics, see Farris, *Population, Disease, and Land in Early Japan, op. cit.*, and his forthcoming essay, "The Population of Ancient Japan: New Estimates and Fresh Approaches." He is also currently studying population trends from about 1100 onward. On disease, see his *Population, Disease, and Land, op. cit.*, and also his "Diseases of the Premodern Period in Japan," in Kiple, 1993, pp. 376–85. On forests, see Ch. 1 of Conrad Totman, *The Green Archipelago, Forestry in Preindustrial Japan* (Berkeley: University of California Press, 1989; Athens, OH: Ohio University Press, 1998), 297 pp.

Chapter 4. The Later Agricultural Order (1350–1870)

As for Chapter 3, works on these centuries seem to categorize nicely as general texts, political history, and works on society, commerce, and environmental issues.

1. *General Texts*

The general texts cited for Chapter 3 are also useful for the period covered by this chapter, with vols. 3–5 of *The Cambridge History, op. cit.*, being the relevant ones on Japan. Also on Japan, Souyri, *The World Turned Upside Down, op. cit.*, surveys "late medieval" developments down to about 1570; and Totman, *Early Modern Japan* (Berkeley: University of California Press, 1993), 593 pp, treats the "early modern," from 1570 to 1870. A magisterial new text, Marius B. Jansen, *The Making of Modern Japan* (Cambridge, MA: Harvard University Press, 2000), 871 pp., devotes over 300 pages to the Tokugawa period, with chapters on society, economy, and culture fleshing out a centrally political narrative.

2. *Political History*

This is the predominant topic in the general texts cited above and the most extensively treated topic in monographic works.

INCLUSIVE. Korean-Japanese political relations of these centuries have received considerable attention. The fullest study of the diplomatic relationship, its ambiguities, vicissitudes, and ideological content is Etsuko Hae-Jin Kang, *Diplomacy and Ideology in Japanese-Korean Relations From the Fifteenth to the Eighteenth Century* (Houndmills, Hampshire: Macmillan, 1997), 312 pp. It contains an extensive bibliography of earlier works.

Viewed mainly from the Korean side, works of note include the pioneering study by George M. McCune, "The Exchange of Envoys between Korea and Japan during the Tokugawa Period," *Far Eastern Quarterly* 5/3 (May 1946): 308–25. More recent essays include James B. Lewis, "Beyond *Sakoku*: The Korean Envoy to Edo and the 1719 Diary of Shin Yu-han," *Korea Journal* 25/11 (November 1985): 22–41; Kenneth R. Robinson, "Centering the King of Chosŏn: Aspects of Korean Maritime Diplomacy, 1392–1592," *Journal of Asian Studies* 59/1 (February 2000): 109–25, Ronald P. Toby, "Korean-Japanese Diplomacy in 1711: Sukchong's Court and the Shogun's Title," *Chōsen gakuhō* 74 (January 1975): 231–56, and Yi Chin-hŏi, "Korean Envoys and Japan: Korean-Japanese Relations in the 17th to 19th Centuries, *Korea Journal* 25/12 (December 1985): 24–35.

On Korean military resistance to Hideyoshi, see the celebratory biography by Yune-hee Park, *Admiral Yi Sun-shin and his Turtleboat Armada*, rev. ed. (Seoul: Hanjin Publishing, 1978). For a brief review of the nineteenth century, see Ch. 1 of Key-Hiuk Kim, *The Last Phase of the East Asian World Order* (Berkeley: University of California Press, 1980), 414 pp.

Looking outward from Japan, an excellent new historiographical essay is Brett L. Walker, "Foreign Affairs and Frontiers in Early Modern Japan," with appended bibliography in *Early Modern Japan, An Interdisciplinary Journal* 10–2 (Fall 2002): 44–62, 124–28. A broad-ranging older work that still merits attention is Yoshi S. Kuno, *Japan's Expansion on the Asiatic Continent* (Berkeley: University of California, 1940), 2 vols.

A useful collection of more recent views is the five scholarly articles that comprise *Acta Asiatica* 67 (1994). Particularly relevant here is the essay by Tsuruta Kei, "The Establishment and Characteristics of the 'Tsushima Gate,'" *AA* 67, pp. 30–48. On Japan's relations with Korea before and during Hideyoshi's day, see the earlier-mentioned essay by Jurgis Elisonas, "The Inseparable Trinity: Japan's Relations with China and Korea." Later relations are treated in Ronald P. Toby, *State and Diplomacy in Early Modern Japan* (Princeton: Princeton University Press, 1984), 309 pp. See also Toby's "Carnival of the Aliens: Korean Embassies in Edo-Period Art and Popular Culture," *Monumenta Nipponica* 41/4 (Winter 1986): 415–56.

KOREA. A recent, richly discursive study is James B. Palais, *Confucian Statecraft and Korean Institutions, Yu Hyŏngwŏn and the Late Chosŏn Dynasty* (Seattle: University of Washington Press, 1996), 1279 pp., which is centrally an examination of the political thought of the scholar Yu Hyŏngwŏn (1622–72), secondarily a study of the historiography of the major topics in Chosŏn political history, and thirdly a review of much of the political and socio-economic history from early Chosŏn to late.

On the founding of Chosŏn, see Duncan, *The Origins of the Chosŏn Dynasty, op. cit.*, and its bibliography. Among earlier works, see Donald N. Clark, "Chosŏn's Founding Fathers: A Study of Merit Subjects in the Early Yi Dynasty," *Korean Studies* 6 (1982): 17–40; Park Won-ho, "The Liaotung Peninsula Invasion Controversy during the Early Years of the Yi Dynasty," *Social Science Journal* 6 (1979): 148–81, and Kenneth R. Robinson, "From Raiders to Traders: Border Security and Border Control in Early Chosŏn, 1392–1450," *Korean Studies* 16 (1992): 94–115. A study of seventeenth-century reform politics is Ching Young Choe, "Kim Yuk (1580–1658) and the Taedongbŏp Reform," *Journal of Asian Studies* 23/1 (November 1963): 21–35. On eighteenth-century royal politics, a close study is JaHyun Kim Haboush, *A Heritage of Kings* (NY: Columbia University Press, 1988), 322 pp., reissued in 2001 as *The Confucian Kingship in Korea, Yŏngjo and the Politics of Sagacity*. For the 1860s–1870s see James B. Palais, *Politics and Policy in Traditional Korea* (Cambridge, MA: Harvard University Press, 1975), 390 pp.

On *yangban* factionalism, see Edward W. Wagner, *The Literati Purges: Political Conflict in Early Yi Korea* (Cambridge, MA: Harvard University Press, 1974), 238 pp., and Sŏng-mu Lee [Yi], "On the Causes of Factional Strife in Late Chosŏn," in Suh, 1994, pp. 3–27.

On local political organization, see these essays by Fujiya Kawashima: "The Role and the Structure of the Local Gentry Association in Mid-Yi Dynasty Korea, *Papers*, 1979, pp. 655–72; "A Study of the Hyangan: Kin Groups and Aristocratic Localism in the Seventeenth- and Eighteenth-century Korean Countryside, *Journal of Korean Studies* 5 (1984): 3–38, and "The Local Yangban in Andong: Village Bureau Heads & Their Deputies in Late Chosŏn Dynasty Korea, in *Papers*, 1988, Vol. 1, pp. 209–52. Also see Dieter Eikemeier, "Villages and Quarters as Instruments of Local Control in Yi Dynasty Korea," *T'oung Pao* 62/1–3 (1976): 71–110.

For samples of political thought, see the translations in Peter H. Lee, et al., eds., *Sources of the Korean Tradition*, *op. cit.* A major collection of essays on intellectual life is Wm. Theodore de Bary and JaHyun Kim Haboush, eds., *The Rise of Neo-Confucianism in Korea* (NY: Columbia University Press, 1985), 551 pp.

Reformist Practical Learning (*sirhak*) thought has received much attention. Besides Palais, *Confucian Statecraft and Korean Institutions*, *op. cit.*, see Chŏng Yak-yong, "A Treatise on Land," *Korea Journal* 25/9 (September 1985): 37–42; Michael C. Kalton, "An Introduction to Silhak," *Korea Journal* 15/5 (May 1975): 29–46; Kang Man-gil, "Chŏng Yak-yong's Policy Proposals for Mining and Industry," *Korea Journal* 25/9 (September 1985): 17–24; Jang-tae Keum, "The Emergence and Evolution of Sirhak Thought," in *Introduction*, 1986, pp. 333–55; Kim Yong-sŏp, "Two Sirhak Scholars' Agricultural Reform Theories," *Korea Journal* 14/10 (October 1974): 13–26; Pak Sŏng-nae, "Western Science and *Shilhak* Scholars," *Korea Journal* 26/3 (March 1986): 4–24, and Shin Yong-ha, "On Tasan's Land Reform Thought," *Korea Journal* 26/2 (February 1986): 44–57.

JAPAN. Two recent studies of aspects of political history during the earlier centuries are Lee Butler, *Emperor and Aristocracy in Japan 1467–1680* (Cambridge, MA: Harvard University Press, 2002), 400 pp., and S. A. Thornton, *Charisma and Community Formation in Medieval Japan, The Case of the Yugyō-ha (1300–1700)* (Ithaca: Cornell University Press, 1999), 312 pp. Dower & George, *op. cit.*, pp, 37–41, will guide one to earlier works.

For later centuries, see Mark Ravina, *Land and Lordship in Early Modern Japan* (Stanford: Stanford University Press, 1999), 278 pp., and Luke S. Roberts, *Mercantilism in a Japanese Domain* (Cambridge: Cambridge University Press, 1998), 251 pp. Their bibliographies and those in Jansen, *The Making of Modern Japan, op. cit.*, and in Totman,

Early Modern Japan and *A History of Japan, op. cit.*, discuss the rich earlier literature. A dated but more complete listing of older English-language works on political history can be found in Totman, *Politics in the Tokugawa Bakufu, 1600–1843* (Berkeley: University of California Press, 1988), 354 pp.

On political thought, see Tsunoda, et al., eds., *Sources of the Japanese Tradition, op. cit.*, for select translations. The bibliographical essays and bibliographies by James McMullin and Janine Anderson Sawada in *Early Modern Japan, An Interdisciplinary Journal* 10/1 (Spring 2002): 22–64, 72–85, offer excellent guidance to the extensive English-language corpus on political, philosophical, and religious thought. On Practical Learning (*jitsugaku*) in Japan, see the excellent essays in Wm. Theodore de Bary and Irene Bloom, eds., *Principle and Practicality, Essays in Neo-Confucianism and Practical Learning* (NY: Columbia University Press, 1979), 543 pp.

3. Society

KOREA. On basic issues of demography, see Donald L. Baker, "Diseases and Deities in Eighteenth Century Korea," in *Papers*, 1988, Vol. 1, pp. 152–68; Tony Mitchell, "Fact and Hypothesis in Yi Dynasty Economic History: The Demographic Dimension," *Korean Studies Forum* 6 (Winter-Spring 1979–80): 65–93; and Jin Young Ro, "Demographic and Social Mobility Trends in Early Seventeenth-century Korea: An Analysis of Sanŭm County Census Registers," *Korean Studies* 7 (1983): 77–113. On disease, see the essay by Baker cited above and the two essays by Lois N. Magner, "Diseases of Antiquity in Korea" and "Diseases of the Premodern Period in Korea" in Kiple, 1993, pp. 389–400.

On cities and urbanization, see Kim Dong Uk, "The City and Architecture of Seoul During the Late Chosŏn Period," *Korea Journal* 34/3 (Autumn 1994): 54–68; Hung-Tak Lee, "A Socio-Economic Analysis of the Pre-Modern Urban Areas in Korea," *Korea & World Affairs* 1/3 (Fall 1977): 321–46; and Yi Tae-jin, "The Nature of Seoul's Modern Urban Development during the 18th and 19th Centuries," *Korea Journal* 35/3 (Autumn, 1995): 5–30.

The thorny issue of land control is addressed in several essays: Kang Chinch'ol, "Traditional Land Tenure Relations in Korean Society: Ownership and Management," in Kang H, 1975, pp. 43–104; Kim Yong-sŏp, "The Land Tenure in Premodern Korea," in

Introduction, pp. 527–62; Park Byoung-ho, "The Legal Nature of Land Ownership in the Yi Dynasty, *Korea Journal* 15/10 (October 1975): 4–10, and Shin Yong-ha, "Landlordism in the Late Yi Dynasty" (1) (2), *Korea Journal* 18/6 and 18/7 (June, July 1978): 25–32, 22–29.

On *kye*, see Young-iob Chung, "Kye: A Traditional Economic Institution in Korea," in Nahm, 1974, pp. 89–112, and Ko Sung-je, "The Cooperative Practice of the Korean Village Community," in *Introduction*, 1986, pp. 697–727.

On outcastes, see Dae-hong Chang, "A Study of Korean Cultural Minority: The Paekchong," in Nahm, 1974, pp. 155–87. On slavery, besides the earlier-cited works on the Koryŏ period, see Kwon Yon-ung, "Studies in Chosŏn Slavery: A Review," in *Papers*, 1988, Vol. 1, pp. 253–67.

A major study of the way Confucian thought was expressed in family structure and process is Martina Deuchler, *The Confucian Transformation of Korea: A Study of Society and Ideology* (Cambridge, MA: Harvard University Press, 1992), 439 pp. Also on the concept of family see the long essay by Dae-hong Chang, "The Historical Development of the Korean Socio-Family System Since 1392—A Legalistic Interpretation," *Journal of East Asiatic Studies* (Manila) 11/2 (March 1967): 1–124.

The literature on *yangban* is relatively extensive. On their education, see Kim Tong-wook, "The Life of the Literati in the Sŏnggyun'gwam," in *Upper-class Culture in Yi-dynasty Korea* (Korean Culture Series 2) (Seoul: International Cultural Foundation, 1973), pp. 41–65. On social mobility and access to *yangban* status, see the careful study of the examination system by Yŏng-ho Ch'oe, *The Civil Examinations and the Social Structure in Early Yi Dynasty Korea: 1392–1600* (Seoul: The Korean Research Center, 1987), 179 pp. Also see Ch'oe Yŏng-ho, "Commoners in Early Yi Dynasty Civil Examinations: An Aspect of Korean Social Structure, 1392–1600," *Journal of Asian Studies* 33/4 (August 1974): 611–31; Mark Peterson, "Hyong ban and Merchant in Kaesŏng," *Korea Journal* 19/10 (October 1979): 4–18; Edward W. Wagner, "The Civil Examination Process as Social Leaven," *Korea Journal* 17/1 (January 1977): 22–27, and two works cited earlier: Jin Young Ro, "Demographic and Social Mobility Trends in Early Seventeenth-century Korea," and Yi Sŏng-mu, "Kwagŏ System and Its Characteristics."

On Chosŏn's social structure and status system more broadly, see several essays, including Yoo Seung-won, "The Status System in the

Early Chosŏn Period," *Seoul Journal of Korean Studies* 1 (1988): 69–99; and three that appear in *Introduction*, 1986: Kim Yŏng-mo, "Social Status and Social Class," pp. 751–69; Pak Wŏn-sŏn, "Traditional Korean Commercial and Industrial Institutions and Thought," pp. 563–601, and Yi Su-gŏn, "The Formation and Development of Yangban Society," pp. 89–112. Also see three essays in *Social Science Journal* 6 (1979): 90–147: Hahn Young-woo, "An Interpretation of Social Stratification and Social Mobility in the Early Yi Dynasty," Kim Young-mo, "The Conceptualization of Social Strata and its Changing Structure during the Later Yi Dynasty," and Park Yŏng-sin "Social Movements and Social Change at the End of the Yi Dynasty—A Sociological Approach."

For aspects of social change, see Kim Yong-dŏk, "The New Cultural Trend," in *Introduction*, 1986, pp. 163–91; Mark A. Peterson, *Korean Adoption and Inheritance: Case Studies in the Creation of a Classic Confucian Society* (Ithaca, NY: Cornell University East Asian Program, 1996), 267 pp., the earlier-cited Jin Young Ro, "Demographic and Social Mobility Trends in Early Seventeenth-century Korea," and Susan S. Shin, "Economic Development and Social Mobility in Pre-Modern Korea: 1600–1860," *Peasant Studies* 7/3 (Summer 1978): 187–97.

Two broader examinations of socio-economic change are essays by Sung-jae Koh: "Studies of Korean Economic History—in the First Stage of the Yi Dynasty," *Journal of Social Sciences and Humanities* 40 (December 1984): 119–38, and "Study of Socio-economic History of the Later Yi Dynasty Period and its Prospects," *Journal of Social Sciences and Humanities* 42 (December 1975): 71–86.

Social unrest of the nineteenth century, which culminated in major outbursts late in the century, is examined in several essays. Besides Park Yŏng-sin's 1979 essay cited above, see An Pyŏng-uk, "The Growth of Popular Consciousness and Popular Movement in the 19th Century," *Korea Journal* 28/4 (April 1988): 4–19; Lee Young-ho, "The Socioeconomic Background and the Growth of the New Social Forces of the 1894 Peasant War," *Korea Journal* 34/4 (Winter 1994): 90–100, and Yi I-hwa, "People's Movements During the Chosŏn Period," *Korea Journal* 25/5 (May 1985): 4–17. Several aspects of late Chosŏn culture and society are also treated in the six essays in JaHyun Kim Haboush and Martina Deuchler, eds., *Culture and the State in Late Chosŏn Korea* (Cambridge, MA: Harvard University Press, 1999), 304 pp.

JAPAN. On basic issues of demography up to 1600, see William Wayne Farris, whose study on "medieval" demographic trends, "Population, Famine, and War in Japan, 1100–1600," is currently in progress. On post-1600 trends, see the aforementioned bibliographical work by Satomi Kurosu, "Studies in Historical Demography and Family in Early Modern Japan," and "Bibliography" in *Early Modern Japan, An Interdisciplinary Journal, op. cit.* with its extremely thorough and well organized listing of books and articles. Also valuable for its bibliography, as well as its contents, is Laurel L. Cornell, "Infanticide in Early Modern Japan: Demography, Culture, and Population Growth," *Journal of Asian Studies* 55/1 (February 1996): 22–50.

On disease prior to 1600, see Farris, "Diseases of the Premodern Period in Japan," in Kiple, 1993, pp. 376–85. On post-1600 developments, see three works by Ann Bowman Jannetta: *Epidemics and Mortality in Early Modern Japan* (Princeton: Princeton University Press, 1987), 224 pp.; "Diseases of the Early Modern Period," in Kiple, 1993, pp. 385–93, and "Public Health and the Diffusion of Vaccination in Japan," in Liu, 2001, pp. 292–305.

On urbanization, an older, broadly arched, and richly detailed work that follows the story of Japan's city development from origins to the 1920s is Takeo Yazaki, *Social Change and the City in Japan* (Tokyo: Japan Publications, Inc., 1968), 549 pp. Two rich studies of late medieval Kyoto are Mary Elizabeth Berry, *The Culture of Civil War in Kyoto* (Berkeley: University of California Press, 1994), 373 pp., and Suzanne Gay, *The Moneylenders of Late Medieval Kyoto* (Honolulu: University of Hawai'i Press, 2001), 301 pp.

For post-1600 Kyoto, and urban life more generally, see two essays in Vol. 4 of *Cambridge History*: Nakai Nobuhiko, "Commercial Change and Urban Growth in Early Modern Japan," pp. 519–95, and Donald H. Shively, "Popular Culture," pp. 706–69. On Osaka, see the fine essays on that city in James L. McClain and Wakita Osamu, eds., *Osaka, The Merchants' Capital of Early Modern Japan* (Ithaca: Cornell University Press, 1999), 295 pp. For Edo, see James L. McClain et al., eds., *Edo and Paris, Urban Life & the State in the Early Modern Era* (Ithaca: Cornell University Press, 1994), 483 pp., and Nishiyama Matsunosuke (Gerald Groemer, tr.), *Edo Culture, Daily Life and Diversions in Urban Japan, 1600–1868* (Honolulu: University of Hawai'i Press, 1997), 309 pp., whose bibliography is particularly helpful.

On outcastes before 1600, see Nagahara Keiji, "The Medieval Origins of the *Eta-Hinin*," *Journal of Japanese Studies* 5/2 (Summer 1979): 385–403. On their post-1600 situation, see Ch. 5 of Herman Ooms, *Tokugawa Village Practice: Class, Status, Power, Law* (Berkeley: University of California Press, 1996), 425 pp., and two articles by Gerald Groemer: "The Creation of the Edo Outcaste Order," *Journal of Japanese Studies* 27/2 (Summer 2001): 263–93, and "The Guild of the Blind in Tokugawa Japan," *Monumenta Nipponica* 56/3 (Autumn 2001): 349–80.

Most people, of course, were villagers during these centuries. *Sō* village organization and peasant circumstances before 1600 are examined in Souyri, *The World Turned Upside Down, op. cit.*; Kristina Kade Troost, "Peasants, Elites, and Villages in the Fourteenth Century," in Mass, 1997, pp. 91–109, and two essays by Nagahara Keiji, "The Decline of the *Shōen* System" and "The Medieval Peasant," in *Cambridge History* 3, pp. 260–343. On the rise of rural commerce, see Hitomi Tonomura, *Community and Commerce in Late Medieval Japan, The Corporate Villages of Tokuchin-ho* (Stanford: Stanford University Press, 1992), 285 pp., and on changing rural culture, Barbara Ruch, "Medieval Jongleurs and the Making of a National Literature," in Hall and Toyoda, 1977, pp. 279–309.

Post-1600 rural society has been studied at length, most famously in Thomas C. Smith, *The Agrarian Origins of Modern Japan* (Stanford: Stanford University Press, 1959), 250 pp. Many fine, pre-1985 works are listed and discussed in Conrad Totman, "Tokugawa Peasants: Win, Lose, or Draw?," *Monumenta Nipponica* 41/4 (Winter 1986): 457–76, while the earlier-mentioned Satomi Kurosu, "Studies in Historical Demography and Family," offers a more up-to-date listing. Recent works to note are Susan Hanley, *Everyday Things in Premodern Japan*, (Berkeley, University of California Press, 1997), 213 pp.; Ooms, *Tokugawa Village Practice, op. cit.*; Brian W. Platt, "Elegance, Prosperity, Crisis: Three Generations of Tokugawa Village Elites," *Monumenta Nipponica* 55/1 (Spring 2000): 45–81; and Edward E. Pratt, *Japan's Protoindustrial Elite, The Economic Foundations of the Gōnō* (Cambridge, MA: Harvard University Press, 1999), 260 pp., as well as Furushima Toshio, "The Village and Agriculture During the Edo period," in *Cambridge History* 4, pp. 478–518.

4. *Commerce*

The sustained economic growth of the centuries after 1350 is reflected in a much expanded scholarly literature on maritime and domestic production and trade.

INCLUSIVE. Aspects of Korean-Japanese trade relations are treated in Sung Jae Koh, "A History of the Cotton Trade between Korea and Japan, 1423–1910," *Asian Economies* 12 (March 1975): 5–16; Park Seong-Rae, "Korea-Japan Relations and the History of Science and Technology," *Korea Journal* 32/4 (Winter 1992): 80–88 and in the earlier-noted essays by Kenneth R. Robinson, "Centering the King of Chosŏn: Aspects of Korean Maritime Diplomacy, 1392–1592," and Yi Chin-hŭi, "Korean Envoys and Japan: Korean-Japanese Relations in the 17th to 19th Centuries."

Looking from the other direction, for the "late medieval" centuries see Tanaka Takeo, "Japan's Relations with Overseas Countries," in Hall and Toyoda, eds., *Japan in the Muromachi Age, op. cit.*, pp. 159–78, and the earlier-cited essay by Elisonas, "The Inseparable Trinity: Japan's Relations with China and Korea." For later centuries, see Robert Leroy Innes, *The Door Ajar: Japan's Foreign Trade in the Seventeenth Century*, 2 vols. (Ann Arbor: University Microfilms, 1980); and two essays from the earlier-noted *Acta Asiatica* 30 (1976): Tashiro Kazui, "Tsushima han's Korean Trade, 1684–1710," pp. 85–105, and Iwao Seiichi, "Japanese Foreign Trade in the 16th and 17th Centuries", pp. 1–18.

On pirates, Kwan-wai So, *Japanese Piracy in Ming China During the 16th Century* (East Lansing: Michigan State University Press, 1975), 251 pp., touches Korea briefly.

KOREA. Domestic commercial activity during the Chosŏn Dynasty is treated in several essays: Baek Seung-ch'ŏl, "The Development of Local Markets and the Establishment of a New Circulation System in Late Chosŏn Society," *Seoul Journal of Korean Studies* 12 (1999): 152–76; Lee Hyoun-young, "A Geographic Study of the Korean Periodic Markets," *Korea Journal* 15/8 (August 1975): 12–24; Mark Peterson, "Hyong ban and Merchant in Kaesŏng," *Korea Journal* 19/10 (October 1979): 4–18; Yi Tae-jin, "The Nature of Seoul's Modern Urban Development During the 18th and 19th Centuries," *Korea Journal* 35/3 (Autumn, 1995): 5–30; and two essays by Kang Man-gil: "Research on Han River Merchants," *Korea Journal* 19/3 (March 1979): 21–32, and "The Relations between Artisans and

Merchants in the Latter Period of the Yi Dynasty," *Journal of Asiatic Studies* 9/3 (1966): 45–47 (English summary).

On commercial thought, see the two long essays by Pak Wŏn-sŏn, "Traditional Korean Commercial and Industrial Institutions and Thought," and Zo Ki-jun, "Economic Thought of the Late Chosŏn Period: Modern Economic Concepts in Sirhak," in *Introduction*, 1986, pp. 563–638.

JAPAN. On "late medieval" commercial development, see three earlier-cited works: Berry, *The Culture of Civil War in Kyoto*; Gay, *The Moneylenders of Late Medieval Kyoto*; and Tonomura, *Community and Commerce in Late Medieval Japan*. Also see Wakita Haruko, "Towards a Wider Perspective on Medieval Commerce," *Journal of Japanese Studies* 1/2 (Spring 1975): 321–45, and her "Ports, Markets, and Medieval Urbanism in the Osaka Region," in McClain and Wakita, 1999, cited above. Also Andrew M. Watsky, "Commerce, Politics and Tea: The Career of Imai Sōkyū," *Monumenta Nipponica* 50/1 (Spring 1995): 46–65; Toyoda Takeshi et al., "The Growth of Commerce and the Trades," in Hall and Toyoda, 1977, pp. 129–44, and Kozo Yamamura, "The Growth of Commerce in Medieval Japan, in *Cambridge History* 3, pp. 344–95.

On "early modern" commercial development, titles are numerous. See Kozo Yamamura, "Returns on Unification: Economic Growth in Japan, 1550–1650," in Hall, 1981; Nakai Nobuhiko, "Commercial Change and Urban Growth in Early Modern Japan," in *Cambridge History* 4, pp. 519–95, and Sydney Crawcour, "Economic Change in the Nineteenth Century," in Vol. 5, pp. 569–617. For further titles, see Dower and George, *op. cit.*, pp. 105–110, and also the pertinent pages of William D. Wray, *Japan's Economy: A Bibliography of its Past and Present* (Princeton, NJ: Markus Wiener, 1989), 303 pp.

On rural commercial development, see the above-noted work by Pratt, *Japan's Protoindustrial Elite*, and also Platt, "Elegance, Prosperity, Crisis," *loc. cit.*, which lists earlier works. On the cotton industry in particular, see William B. Hauser, *Economic Institutional Change in Tokugawa Japan: Osaka and the Kinai Cotton Trade* (Cambridge: Cambridge University Press, 1974), 239 pp. On fisheries, see David L. Howell, *Capitalism from Within: Economy, Society, and the State in a Japanese Fishery* (Berkeley: University of California Press, 1995), 246 pp., and Arne Kalland, *Fishing Villages in Tokugawa Japan* (Honolulu: University of Hawai'i Press, 1995), 355 pp. On mining, see Kozo Yamamura, "Returns on Unification: Economic Growth in Japan," cited above, and Patricia G. Sippel, "Re-usable Solutions: Copper Mines and Water Pollution in the Early Modern Era," a paper delivered at the 2002 Annual Meeting of the Association for Asian Studies. On forest industries, see Conrad Totman, *The Lumber Industry in Early Modern Japan* (Honolulu: University of Hawai'i Press, 1995), 159 pp.

On commercial thought, see Janine Anderson Sawada, *Confucian Values and Popular Zen, Sekimon Shingaku in Eighteenth-Century Japan* (Honolulu: University of Hawai'i Press, 1993), 256 pp., and Eiji Takemura, *The Perception of Work in Tokugawa Japan* (Lanham, MD: University Press of America, 1997), 229 pp., which will also guide one to several fine earlier works, including the seminal study by Robert Bellah, *Tokugawa Religion: The Values of Pre-Industrial Japan* (Glencoe, IL: The Free Press, 1957), 259 pp.

5. *Environmental Issues*

INCLUSIVE. Works treating demographics and disease are discussed above, under Society. A careful examination of volcanism as an influence on climate in East Asia before 1700 is William S. Atwell, "Volcanism and Short-Term Climatic Change in East Asian and World History, ca. 1200–1699," *Journal of World History* 12/1 (Spring 2001): 29–98.

KOREA. Apart from observations made by commentators of the day, environmental issues await scholarly treatment. An examination of *sirhak* thought on matters geographical is Yang Bo-Kyung, "Perceptions of Nature in the Chosŏn Period," *Korea Journal* 37/4 (Winter 1997): 134–55.

JAPAN. For introductory comments, see Totman, *A History of Japan, op. cit.*, pp. 150–52, 247–59. For somewhat fuller treatment of post–1600 trends, see Ch. 11–13 of his *Early Modern Japan, op. cit.* Footnotes in that volume will guide readers to a number of additional sources on weather, geography, and other matters environmental. On geographical perceptions, and further references, see Kären Wigen, "The Geographic Imagination in Early Modern Japanese History: Retrospect and Prospect," *Journal of Asian Studies* 51/1 (February 1992): 3–29.

An investigation of climate is A. Murata, "Reconstruction of Rainfall Variations of the *Baiu* in Historical Times," in Bradley and Jones, 1992, pp. 224–45. See also William S. Atwell, "Some Observations on the 'Seventeenth-Century Crisis' in China and Japan," *Journal of*

Asian Studies 45/2 (Summer 1985): 369–99, and Takeo Yamamoto, "On the Nature of the Japanese Climate in So-called 'Little Ice Age' between 1750 and 1850," *Geophysical Magazine* 35/2 (January 1971): 165–85. The tricky issue of climate's relationship to famine and demography is addressed in Osamu Saito, "The Frequency of Famines as Demographic Correctives in the Japanese Past," in Dyson and O Grada, 2002, pp. 218–39.

On water management, see William W. Kelly, *Water Control in Tokugawa Japan: Irrigation Organization in a Japanese River Basin, 1600–1870* (Cornell University East Asia Papers No. 31) (Ithaca, NY: China-Japan Program, Cornell University, 1982), 260 pp., and Totman, "Preindustrial River Conservancy, Causes and Consequences," *Monumenta Nipponica* 47/1 (Spring 1992): 59–76. On water pollution, see Sippel, "Re-usable Solutions: Copper Mines and Water Pollution in the Early Modern Era," cited above.

The role of geography in shaping regional experience is nicely illustrated in Kären Wigen, *The Making of a Japanese Periphery, 1750–1920* (Berkeley: University of California Press, 1995), 336 pp. On forestry and deforestation, see Totman, *The Green Archipelago, op. cit.* On aspects of wildlife's experience during the early modern period, see Brett Walker, *The Conquest of Ainu Lands* (Berkeley: University of California Press, 2001), 332 pp., and his essay, "Commercial Growth and Environmental Change in Early Modern Japan: Hachinohe's Wild Boar Famine of 1749," *Journal of Asian Studies* 60/2 (May 2001): 329–51. Most importantly, watch for his forthcoming study of wolves.

BIBLIOGRAPHY*

This alphabetically arranged bibliography lists only books and articles cited in the footnotes and illustrations. A number of works mentioned in the bibliographical essay (see p. 181) do not appear here. Sources used solely in preparing maps are cited in the Acknowledgements.

Each entry is preceded by the identifier used in the notes—such as "Ahn, 1991"—and the works are alphabetized accordingly. Authorial names are then given as they appear in the works: European surnames generally appear last; Japanese surnames usually first; Korean usage varies. The complete citations for volumes that consist of assembled articles appear separately from those of the individual articles. Thus the essay entered as "Aikens and Akazawa, 1992" appears in the volume listed as "Aikens and Rhee, 1992."

Ahn, 1991. Ahn Kye-hyŏn, "Introduction of Buddhism to Korea," in Lancaster, 1989, pp. 1–28.
Aikens and Akazawa, 1992. C. Melvin Aikens and Takeru Akazawa, "Fishing and Farming in Early Japan: Jomon Littoral Tradition Carried into Yayoi Times at the Miura Caves on Tokyo Bay," in Aikens and Rhee, 1992, pp. 75–82.
Aikens and Rhee, 1992. C. Melvin Aikens and Song Nai Rhee, *Pacific Northeast Asia in Prehistory* (Pullman, WA: Washington State University Press, 1992), 223 pp.
Allègre, 1984. C. J. Allègre et al., "Structure and Evolution of the Himalaya-Tibet Orogenic Belt," *Nature* 307 (5 January 1984): 17–22.
Alley, 2000. Richard B. Alley, *The Two-Mile Time Machine: Ice Cores, Abrupt Climate Change, and Our Future* (Princeton: Princeton University Press, 2000), 229 pp.
Association of Japanese Agricultural Scientific Societies, 1975. [AJASS], ed., *Rice in Asia* (Tokyo: University of Tokyo Press, 1975), 600 pp.
Association of Japanese Geographers, 1980. [AJG], ed., *Geography of Japan* (Tokyo: Teikoku-Shoin, 1980), 440 pp.
Atwell, 1986. William S. Atwell, "Some Observations on the 'Seventeenth-Century Crisis' in China and Japan," *Journal of Asian Studies* 45/2 (February 1986): 223–44.
———, 1990. William S. Atwell, "A Seventeenth-Century 'General Crisis' in East Asia?" *Modern Asian Studies* 24/4 (October 1990): 661–82.
———, 2001. William S. Atwell, "Volcanism and Short-Term Climatic Change in East Asian and World History, ca. 1200–1699," *Journal of World History* 12/1 (Spring 2001): 29–98.
Baek, 1999. Baek Seung-ch'ŏl, "The Development of Local Markets and the Establishment of a New Circulation System in Late Chosŏn Society," *Seoul Journal of Korean Studies* 12 (1999): 152–76.
Baker, 1988. Donald L. Baker, "Diseases and Deities in Eighteenth Century Korea," in *Papers*, 1988, Vol. 1, pp. 152–68.
Bambach, 1980. Richard K. Bambach, et al., "Before Pangaea: The Geographies of the Paleozoic World," in Skinner, 1980, pp. 86–98.
Barnes, 1993. Gina L. Barnes, *China, Korea and Japan: The Rise of Civilization in East Asia* (London: Thames and Hudson, 1993), 288 pp.

---

* Of works cited in text.

——, 2001. Gina L. Barnes, *State Formation in Korea, Historical and Archaeological Perspectives* (Richmond, Surrey: Curzon Press, 2001), 245 pp.

Batten, 1986. Bruce L. Batten, "Foreign Threat and Domestic Reform: The Emergence of the *Ritsuryō* State," *Monumenta Nipponica* 41/2 (Summer 1986): 199–219.

——, 2003. Bruce L. Batten, *To the Ends of Japan: Premodern Frontiers, Boundaries, and Interactions* (Honolulu: University of Hawai'i Press, 2003), 337 pp.

Berry, 1982. Mary Elizabeth Berry, *Hideyoshi* (Cambridge, MA: Harvard University Press, 1982), 293 pp.

Bird, 1881. Isabella L. Bird, *Unbeaten Tracks in Japan* (NY: G.P. Putnam & Sons, 1881), 2 vols.

Bishop, 1897. Isabella Bird Bishop, *Korea and Her Neighbors* (NY: Fleming H. Revell Co., 1897), 480 pp.

Bleed, 1992. Peter Bleed, "Ready for Anything: Technological Adaptations to Ecological Diversity at Yagi, an Early Jomon Community in Southwestern Hokkaido, Japan," in Aikens and Rhee, 1992, pp. 47–52.

Bodart-Bailey, 1999 (see Kaempfer, 1999).

Bodart-Bailey and Massarella, 1995. Beatrice M. Bodart-Bailey and Derek Massarella, *The Furthest Goal, Engelbert Kaempfer's Encounter with Tokugawa Japan* (Folkestone, Kent: Japan Library, 1995), 204 pp.

Bradley and Jones, 1992. Raymond S. Bradley and Philip D. Jones, eds., *Climate Since A.D. 1500* (London: Routledge, 1992), 679 pp.

Breen and Teeuwen, 2000. John Breen and Mark Teeuwen, eds., *Shinto in History: Ways of the Kami* (Honolulu: University of Hawai'i Press, 2000), 368 pp.

Brown, 1951. Delmer M. Brown, *Money Economy in Medieval Japan: A Study in the Use of Coins* (New Haven: Yale University Press, 1951), 128 pp.

Burchfiel, 1993. B. C. Burchfiel, "Evolution of Continental and Oceanic Crust," *Proceedings of the American Philosophical Society* 137/1 (March 1993): 1–29.

Cambridge History, 1, 2, 3, 4, 5. John Whitney Hall, et al., general editors, *The Cambridge History of Japan*, 6 vols. (Cambridge: Cambridge University Press, 1988–99).
  Vol. 1, Delmer M. Brown, ed., *Ancient Japan* (1993), 602 pp.
  Vol. 2, Donald H. Shively & William H. McCullough, eds., *Heian Japan* (1999), 754 pp.
  Vol. 3, Kozo Yamamura, ed., *Medieval Japan* (1990), 712 pp.
  Vol. 4, John Whitney Hall, ed., *Early Modern Japan* (1991), 831 pp.
  Vol. 5, Marius B. Jansen, ed., *The Nineteenth Century* (1989), 828 pp.

Chard, 1974. Chester S. Chard, *Northeast Asia in Prehistory* (Madison: University of Wisconsin Press, 1974), 212 pp.

Chew, 2001. Sing C. Chew, *World Ecological Degradation: Accumulation, Urbanization, and Deforestation 3000 B.C.–A.D. 2000* (Lanham, MD: Rowman & Littlefield, 2001), 216 pp.

Choe C-p, 1990. Choe Chong Pil, "Origins of Agriculture in Korea," *Korea Journal* 30/11 (November–December 1990): 4–14.

Ch'oe Y-h, 1974. Yŏng-ho Ch'oe, "Commoners in Early Yi Dynasty Civil Examinations: An Aspect of Korean Social Structure, 1392–1600," *Journal of Asian Studies* 33/4 (August 1974): 611–31.

Ch'oe Y-h, 1987. Yŏng-ho Ch'oe, *The Civil Examinations and the Social Structure in Early Yi Dynasty Korea: 1392–1600* (Seoul: The Korean Research Center, 1987), 179 pp.

Ch'oi, 1992. Mong-lyong Ch'oi, "Trade in Wiman State Formation," in Aikens and Rhee, 1992, pp. 185–89.

Chon, 1992. Young-nai Chon, "Introduction of Rice Agriculture into Korea and Japan: From the Perspective of Polished Stone Implements," in Aikens and Rhee, 1992, pp. 161–69.

Chŏng, 1985. Chŏng Yak-yong, "A Treatise on Land," *Korea Journal* 25/9 (September 1985): 37–42.

Chough, 1983. Sung Kwun Chough, *Marine Geology of Korean Seas* (Boston: International Human Resources Development Corporation, 1983), 157 pp.

Chung, 1974. Young-iob Chung, "Kye: A Traditional Economic Institution in Korea," in Nahm, 1974, pp. 89–112.

Clark, 1982. Donald N. Clark, "Chosŏn's Founding Fathers: A Study of Merit Subjects in the Early Yi Dynasty," *Korean Studies* 6 (1982): 17–40.

Craig and Shively, 1970. Albert M. Craig and Donald H. Shively, eds., *Personality in Japanese History* (Berkeley: University of California Press, 1970), 481 pp.

Crawford, 1992. Gary W. Crawford, "The Transitions to Agriculture in Japan," in Gebauer and Price, 1992, pp. 117–32.

Crawford & Takamiya, 1990. Gary W. Crawford and Hirota Takamiya, "The Origins and Implications of Late Prehistoric Plant Husbandry in Northern Japan," *Antiquity* 64/245 (December 1990): 889–911.

Dietz and Holden, 1970. Robert S. Dietz and John C. Holden, "The Breakup of Pangaea," *Scientific American* 223/4 (1970): 30–41.

Duncan, 2000. John B. Duncan, *The Origins of the Chosŏn Dynasty* (Seattle: University of Washington Press, 2000), 395 pp.

Dyson and O'Grada, 2002. Tim Dyson and Cormac O'Grada, eds., *Famine Demography: Perspectives from the Past and the Present* (Oxford: Oxford University Press, 2002), 264 pp.

Eckert, 1990. Carter J. Eckert et al., *Korea Old and New, A History* (Seoul: Ilchokak Publishers, 1990), 454 pp.

Edwards, 1996. Walter Edwards, "In Pursuit of Himiko: Postwar Archaeology and the Location of Yamatai," *Monumenta Nipponica* 51/1 (Spring 1996): 53–79.

Elisonas, 1991. Jurgis Elisonas, "The Inseparable Trinity: Japan's Relations with China and Korea," in *Cambridge History* 4, pp. 235–300.

Farris, 1985. William Wayne Farris, *Population, Disease, and Land in Early Japan, 645–900* (Cambridge, MA: Harvard University Press, 1985), 235 pp.

———, 1993. W. Wayne Farris, "Diseases of the Premodern Period in Japan," in Kiple, 1993, pp. 376–85.

———, 1998a. William Wayne Farris, *Sacred Texts and Buried Treasures: Issues in the Historical Archaeology of Ancient Japan* (Honolulu: University of Hawai'i Press, 1998), 333 pp.

———, 1998b. William Wayne Farris, "Trade, Money, and Merchants in Nara Japan," *Monumenta Nipponica* 53/3 (Fall 1998): 303–34.

———, pending-I. William Wayne Farris, "Shipbuilding and Nautical Technology in Japan, 1100–1640," a ms. currently in press.

———, pending-II. William Wayne Farris, "Climate, Farming, and Famine in Early Japan, 670–1100," a ms. currently in preparation.

Gay, 2001. Suzanne Gay, *The Moneylenders of Late Medieval Kyoto* (Honolulu: University of Hawai'i Press, 2001), 301 pp.

Gebauer and Price, 1992. Anne Birgitte Gebauer and T. Douglas Price, eds., *Transitions to Agriculture in Prehistory* (Monographs in World Archaeology, No. 4) (Madison, WI: Prehistory Press, 1992), 180 pp.

Geological Survey of Japan, "Fact Sheet D-3," (February 1998), 2 pp.

Gillet, 1913. Philip L. Gillet, "The Village Gilds of Old Korea," *Transactions of the Korea Branch of the Royal Asiatic Society* 4/2 (1913): 13–44.

Goble, 1996. Andrew Edmund Goble, *Kenmu, Go-Daigo's Revolution* (Cambridge, MA: Harvard University Press, 1996), 390 pp.

Goodwin, 2000. Janet R. Goodwin, "Shadows of Transgression: Heian and Kamakura Constructions of Prostitution," *Monumenta Nipponica* 55/3 (Autumn 2000): 327–68.

Groemer, 2001a. Gerald Groemer, "The Creation of the Edo Outcaste Order," *Journal of Japanese Studies* 27/2 (Summer 2001): 263–93.

Groemer, 2001b. Gerald Groemer, "The Guild of the Blind in Tokugawa Japan," *Monumenta Nipponica* 56/3 (Autumn 2001): 349–80.

Hall, 1981. John Whitney Hall et al., eds., *Japan Before Tokugawa, Political Consolidation and Economic Growth, 1500 to 1650* (Princeton: Princeton University Press, 1981), 392 pp.

Hall and Toyoda, 1977. John Whitney Hall and Toyoda Takeshi, eds., *Japan in the Muromachi Age* (Berkeley: University of California Press, 1977), 376 pp.

Hamilton, 1904. Angus Hamilton, *Korea* (NY: Charles Scribner's Son, 1904), 313 pp.

Handbook, 1993. *A Handbook of Korea* (Seoul: Korean Overseas Information Service, 1993), 592 pp.

Hanihara, 1987. Hanihara Kazuro, "Estimations of the Number of Early Migrants to Japan: A Simulative Study," *Journal of the Anthropological Society of Nippon* 95/3 (July 1987): 391–403.

Hanley, 1997. Susan Hanley, *Everyday Things in Premodern Japan* (Berkeley, University of California Press, 1997), 213 pp.

Hayami, 2001. Akira Hayami, *The Historical Demography of Pre-modern Japan* (Tokyo: University of Tokyo Press, 2001), 191 pp.

Hazard, 1967. Benjamin H. Hazard, "The Formative Years of the *Wakō*, 1223–63," *Monumenta Nipponica* 22/3–4 (1967): 260–77.

———, 1973. Benjamin H. Hazard, "The Creation of the Korean Navy During the Koryŏ Period," *Transactions of the Korea Branch of the Royal Asiatic Society* 48 (1973): 10–28.

———, 1976. Benjamin H. Hazard, "The Wakō and Korean Responses," in Parsons, 1976, pp. 15–28.

Henthorn, 1963. William Ellsworth Henthorn, *Korea, The Mongol Invasions* (Leiden: E. J. Brill, 1963), 252 pp.

Hiroi, 1981. Hiroi Yoshikuni, "Subdivision of the Hida Metamorphic Complex, Central Japan, and its Bearing on the Geology of the Far East in Pre-Sea of Japan Time," *Tectonophysics* 76 (1981): 317–33.

Holcombe, 2001. Charles Holcombe, *The Genesis of East Asia, 221 B.C.–A.D. 907* (Honolulu: University of Hawai'i Press, 2001), 332 pp.

Hong, 1981. Seung-ki Hong, "A Study of Slave Policies in Early Koryŏ," *Journal of Social Science and Humanities* 53 (June 1981): 79–114.

Howell, 1995. David L. Howell, *Capitalism from Within: Economy, Society, and the State in a Japanese Fishery* (Berkeley: University of California Press, 1995), 246 pp.

Hudson, 1989. Mark Hudson, "Ethnicity in East Asian Archaeology: Approaches to the Wa," *Archaeological Review from Cambridge* 8 (Spring 1989): 51–63.

———, 1999. Mark J. Hudson, *Ruins of Identity, Ethnogenesis in the Japanese Islands* (Honolulu: University of Hawai'i Press, 1999), 323 pp.

Im, 1992. Hyo-jae Im, "Prehistoric Rice Agriculture in Korea," in Aikens and Rhee, 1992, pp. 157–60.

Introduction, 1986. *Introduction to Korean Studies* (Seoul: National Academy of Sciences, 1986), 849 pp.

Jamieson, 1970. John C. Jamieson, "Collapse of the T'ang Silla Alliance—Chinese and Korean Accounts Compared," in Frederic Wakeman, Jr. *"Nothing Concealed," Essays in Honor of Liu Yü-Yün* (San Francisco: Chinese Materials and Research Aids Service Center, Inc., 1970), pp. 83–94.

Jannetta, 1987. Ann Bowman Jannetta, *Epidemics and Mortality in Early Modern Japan* (Princeton: Princeton University Press, 1987), 224 pp.

———, 1993. Ann Bowman Jannetta, "Diseases of the Early Modern Period," in Kiple, 1993, pp. 385–93.

———, 2001. Ann Bowman Jannetta, "Public Health and the Diffusion of Vaccination in Japan," in Liu, 2001, pp. 292–305.

Jeon, 1974. Sang-woon Jeon [Chon Sang-un], *Science and Technology in Korea, Traditional Instruments and Techniques* (Cambridge MA: The MIT Press, 1974), 383 pp.

Kaempfer, 1999. Engelbert Kaempfer (ed., & trans. by Beatrice Bodart-Bailey),

Kaempfer's Japan, Tokugawa Culture Observed (Honolulu: University of Hawai'i Press, 1999), 545 pp.

Kalland, 1995. Arne Kalland, *Fishing Villages in Tokugawa Japan* (Honolulu: University of Hawai'i Press, 1995), 355 pp.

Kalton, 1975. Michael C. Kalton, "An Introduction to Silhak," *Korea Journal* 15/5 (May 1975): 29–46.

Kamata, 1996. Shigeo Kamata, "Buddhism During Koryŏ," in Lancaster, 1996, pp. 35–66.

Kamiya, 1994. Kamiya Nobuyuki, "Japanese Control of Ezochi and the Role of Northern Koryŏ," *Acta Asiatica* 67 (1994): 49–68.

Kang C-c, 1975. Kang Chinch'ol, "Traditional Land Tenure Relations in Korean Society: Ownership and Management," in Kang H, 1975, pp. 43–104.

Kang E. H-j, 1997, Etsuko Hae-Jin Kang, *Diplomacy and Ideology in Japanese-Korean Relations From the Fifteenth to the Eighteenth Century* (Houndmills, Hampshire: Mcmillan, 1997), 312 pp.

Kang H., 1974. H. W. Kang, "Institutional Borrowing, The Case of the Chinese Civil Service Examination System in Early Koryŏ," *Journal of Asian Studies* 34/1 (November 1974): 109–25.

——, 1975. Hugh H. W. Kang, ed., *The Traditional Culture and Society of Korea: Thought and Institutions* (Honolulu: University of Hawai'i Press, 1975), 176 pp.

——, 1977. H. W. Kang, "The First Succession Struggle of Koryŏ, in 945: a Reinterpretation," *Journal of Asian Studies* 36/3 (May 1977): 411–28.

Kang M-g, 1979. Kang Man-gil, "Research on Han River Merchants," *Korea Journal* 19/3 (March 1979): 21–32.

——, 1985. Kang Man-gil, "Chŏng Yak-yong's Policy Proposals for Mining and Industry," *Korea Journal* 25/9 (September 1985): 17–24.

Katsu, 1988. Katsu Kokichi (tr. Teruko Craig), *Musui's Story, The Autobiography of a Tokugawa Samurai* (Tucson: The University of Arizona Press, 1991), 178 pp.

Kawashima, 1979. Fujiya Kawashima, "The Role and the Structure of the Local Gentry Association in Mid-Yi Dynasty Korea," in *Papers*, 1979, pp. 655–72.

——, 1988. Fujiya Kawashima, "The Local Yangban in Andong: Village Bureau Heads & Their Deputies in Late Chosŏn Dynasty Korea," in *Papers*, 1988, Vol. 1, pp. 209–52.

Kelly, 1982. William W. Kelly, *Water Control in Tokugawa Japan: Irrigation Organization in a Japanese River Basin, 1600–1870* (Cornell University East Asia Papers No. 31) (Ithaca, NY: China-Japan Program, Cornell University, 1982), 260 pp.

Kikuchi, 1986. Kikuchi Toshihiko, "Continental Culture and Hokkaido," in Pearson, 1986, pp. 149–62.

Kim B-m, 1987. Kim Byong-mo, "Archaeological Fruits since Liberation and Reconstruction of Ancient History," *Korea Journal* 27/12 (December 1987): 50–56.

Kim C, 1979. Chin Kim, "The Silla Village Registers and Korean Legal History: a Preliminary Inquiry," *Korean Journal of Comparative Law* 7 (November 1979): 99–120.

Kim C-s, 1974. Chong Sun Kim, "Slavery in Silla and its Sociological and Economic Implications," in Nahm, 1974, pp. 29–39.

Kim D-u, 1994. Kim Dong Uk, "The City and Architecture of Seoul During the Late Chosŏn Period," *Korea Journal* 34/3 (Autumn 1994): 54–68.

Kim H-k, 1990. Han-Kyo Kim, "Shannon McCune and his Korean Studies," *The Journal of Modern Korean Studies* 4 (May 1990): 9–12.

Kim-Renaud, 1997. Young-Key Kim-Renaud, *The Korean Alphabet, Its History and Sructure* (Honolulu: University of Hawai'i Press, 1997), 317 pp.

Kim Y-s, 1974. Kim Yong-sŏp, "Two Sirhak Scholars' Agricultural Reform Theories," *Korea Journal* 14/10 (October 1974): 13–26.

——, 1986. Kim Yong-sŏp, "The Land Tenure in Premodern Korea," in *Introduction*, pp. 527–62.

Kim and Yoo, 1988. Kim Doo-jung and Yoo Jea-taik, coordinators, *Korea: Geographical Perspectives* (Seoul: Korean Educational Development Institute, 1988), 464 pp.

King, 1911. F. H. King, *Farmers of Forty Centuries or Permanent Agriculture in China, Korea and Japan* (Emmaus, PA: Rodale Press Inc., n.d.) (orig. printing 1911), 441 pp.

Kiple, 1993. Kenneth F. Kiple, ed., *The Cambridge World History of Human Disease* (Cambridge: Cambridge University Press, 1993), 1176 pp.

Kirkland, 1981. J. Russell Kirkland, "The Horseriders in Korea: A Critical Evaluation of a Historical Theory," *Korean Studies* 5 (1981): 109–28.

Ko S-j, 1986. Ko Sung-je, "The Cooperative Practice of the Korean Village Community," in *Introduction*, 1986, pp. 697–727.

Koh S-j, 1975. Sung Jae Koh [Ko Sung-je], "A History of the Cotton Trade between Korea and Japan, 1423–1910," *Asian Economies* 12 (March 1975): 5–16.

Koike, 1992. Hiroko Koike, "Exploitation Dynamics During the Jomon Period," in Aikens and Rhee, 1992, pp. 53–57.

Korea Journal 27/12 (December 1987): 23–56.

Koyama, 1978. Shūzō Koyama, "Jōmon Subsistence and Population," *Senri Ethnological Studies* 2 (1978): 1–65.

Kurosu, 2002. Satomi Kurosu, "Studies in Historical Demography and Family in Early Modern Japan," and "Bibliography" in *Early Modern Japan, An Interdisciplinary Journal* 10/1 (Spring 2002): 3–21, 66–71.

Kwon T-h, 1975. Tai Hwan Kwon et al., *The Population of Korea* (Seoul: Seoul National University Population and Development Studies Center, 1975), 154 pp.

Kwon Y-g, 1990. Kwon Yigu, "The Population of Ancient Korea in Physical Anthropological Perspective," *Korea Journal* 30/10 (October 1990): 4–12.

Kwon Y-u, 1988. Kwon Yon-ung, "Studies in Chosŏn Slavery: A Review," in *Papers*, 1988, Vol. 1, pp. 253–67.

Lancaster, 1989. Lewis R. Lancaster and C. S. Yu, *Introduction of Buddhism to Korea: New Cultural Patterns* (Berkeley: Asian Humanities Press, 1989), 229 pp.

——, 1996. Lewis R. Lancaster et al., eds., *Buddhism in Koryŏ: A Royal Religion* (Berkeley: Institute of East Asian Studies, University of California, 1996), 211 pp.

Ledyard, 1971. Gari Ledyard, *The Dutch Come to Korea* (Seoul: Royal Asiatic Society Korea Branch, 1971), 231 pp.

Lee D-s, 1987. Lee, Dai-sung, ed., *Geology of Korea* (Seoul: Kyohak-sa, 1987), 514 pp.

Lee H-k, 1936. Hoon K. Lee, *Land Utilization and Rural Economy in Korea* (Chicago: University of Chicago Press, 1936), 302 pp.

Lee H-t, 1977. Hung-Tak Lee, "A Socio-Economic Analysis of the Pre-Modern Urban Areas in Korea," *Korea & World Affairs* 1/3 (Fall 1977): 321–46.

Lee H-y, 1975. Lee Hyoun-young, "A Geographic Study of the Korean Periodic Markets," *Korea Journal* 15/8 (August 1975): 12–24.

Lee J, 1999. John Lee, "Trade and Economy in Preindustrial East Asia, c. 1500–c. 1800: East Asia in the Age of Global Integration," *Journal of Asian Studies* 58/1 (February 1999): 2–26.

Lee K-b, 1984. Lee Ki-baik (Edward W. Wagner, tr.), *A New History of Korea* (Cambridge, MA: Harvard University Press, 1984), 474 pp.

Lee S-y, 1960. Sung Yoon Lee, ed., *Forestry of Korea, 1960* (Seoul: Bureau of Forestry, Ministry of Agriculture and Forestry, ROK, 1960), 142 pp.

Leupp, 1992. Gary P. Leupp, *Servants, Shophands, and Laborers in the Cities of Tokugawa Japan* (Princeton: Princeton University Press, 1992), 237 pp.

Lewis, 1985. James B. Lewis, "Beyond *Sakoku*: The Korean Envoy to Edo and the 1719 Diary of Shin Yu-han," *Korea Journal* 25/11 (November 1985): 22–41.

Liu, 2001. Liu, Ts'ui-jung et al., eds., *Asian Population History* (Oxford: Oxford University Press, 2001), 451 pp.

Magner, 1993. Lois N. Magner, "Diseases of Antiquity in Korea," "Diseases of the Premodern Period in Korea," in Kiple, 1993, pp. 389–400.

Mass, 1997. Jeffrey P. Mass., ed., *The Origins of Japan's Medieval World* (Stanford: Stanford University Press, 1997), 504 pp.

McCann, 1979. David R. McCann et al., eds., *Studies on Korea in Transition* (Occasional Papers No. 9) (Honolulu: Center for Korean Studies, 1979), 245 pp.

McClain and Wakita, 1999. James L. McClain and Wakita Osamu, eds., *Osaka, The Merchants' Capital of Early Modern Japan* (Ithaca: Cornell University Press, 1999), 295 pp.

McCullough, 1980. William H. and Helen McCullough, *A Tale of Flowering Fortunes*, (Stanford: SUP, 1980), 2 vols.

———, 1999a. William H. McCullough, "The capital and its society," in *Cambridge History* 2, pp. 97–182.

———, 1999b. William H. McCullough, "The Heian Court, 794–1070," in *Cambridge History* 2, pp. 20–96.

McCune, 1956. Shannon McCune, *Korea's Heritage: A Regional and Social Geography* (Rutland, VT: Charles E. Tuttle Co., 1956), 250 pp.

———, 1980. Shannon McCune, *Views of the Geography of Korea 1935–1960* (Seoul: The Korean Research Center, 1980), 227 pp.

McEvedy and Jones, 1978. Colin McEvedy and Richard Jones, *Atlas of World Population History* (NY: Penguin Books, 1978), 368 pp.

Mitchell, 1979–80. Tony Mitchell, "Fact and Hypothesis in Yi Dynasty Economic History: The Demographic Dimension," *Korean Studies Forum* 6 (Winter-Spring 1979–80): 65–93.

Molnar & Tapponnier, 1975. Peter Molnar and Paul Tapponnier, "Cenozoic Tectonics of Asia: Effects of a Continental Collision," *Science* 189/4201 (8 August 1975): 419–26.

Morris, 1999. Dana Morris, "Land and Society," in *Cambridge History* 2, pp. 183–235.

Muntschick, 1995. Wolfgang Muntschick, "The Plants that Carry his Name: Kaempfer's Study of the Japanese Flora," in Bodart-Bailey and Massarella, 1995, pp. 71–95.

Murata, 1992. A. Murata, "Reconstruction of Rainfall Variations of the *Baiu* in Historical Times," in Bradley and Jones, 1992, pp. 224–45.

Nahm, 1974. Andrew C. Nahm, ed., *Traditional Korea—Theory and Practice* (Kalamazoo, MI: Western Michigan University Center for Korean Studies, 1974), 159 pp.

———, 1988. Andrew C. Nahm, *Korea, Tradition and Transformation. A History of the Korean People* (Elizabeth, N.J.: Hollym International Corporation, 1988), 582 pp.

Najita, 1987. Tetsuo Najita, *Visions of Virtue in Tokugawa Japan: The Kaitokudō, Merchant Academy of Osaka* (Chicago: The University of Chicago Press, 1987), 334 pp.

Nakai, 1991. Nakai Nobuhiko, "Commercial Change and Urban Growth in Early Modern Japan," in *Cambridge History* 4, pp. 519–95.

Nelson, 1982. Sarah M. Nelson, "The Origins of Rice Agriculture in Korea—A Symposium," *Journal of Asian Studies* 41/3 (May 1982): 511–48.

———, 1990. Sarah M. Nelson, "The Neolithic in Northwestern China and Korea," *Antiquity* 64/243 (June 1990): 234–48.

———, 1993. Sarah Milledge Nelson, *The Archaeology of Korea* (Cambridge: Cambridge University Press, 1993), 307 pp.

Nishida, 1983. Nishida Masaki, "The Emergence of Food Production in Neolithic Japan," *Journal of Anthropological Archaeology* 2/4 (December 1983): 305–22.

Ooms, 1996. Herman Ooms, *Tokugawa Village Practice: Class, Status, Power, Law* (Berkeley: University of California Press, 1996), 425 pp.

Oppert, 1880. Ernest Oppert, *A Forbidden Land: Voyages to the Corea* (NY: G. P. Putnam's Sons, 1880), 349 pp.

Pai, 1989. Pai Hyung Il, "Lelang and the 'Interaction Sphere:' An Alternative Approach to Korean State Formation," *Archaeological Review from Cambridge* 8/1 (1989): 64–75.

———, 2000. Hyung Il Pai, *Constructing "Korean" Origins* (Cambridge, MA: Harvard University Asian Center, 2000), 543 pp.

Pak S-n, 1986. Pak Sŏng-nae, "Western Science and *Shilhak* Scholars," *Korea Journal* 26/3 (March 1986): 4–24.

Palais, 1982–83. James B. Palais, "Land Tenure in Korea: Tenth to Twelfth Centuries." *Journal of Korean Studies* 4 (1982–83): 73–205.
——, 1996. James B. Palais, *Confucian Statecraft and Korean Institutions, Yu Hyŏngwŏn and the Late Chosŏn Dynasty* (Seattle: University of Washington Press, 1996), 1279 pp.
Papers, 1979. *Papers of the 1st International Conference of Korean Studies* (Seoul: Academy of Korean Studies, 1979), 1,457 pp.
——, 1988. *Papers of the 5th International Conference of Korean Studies* (Seoul: Academy of Korean Studies, 1988), 2 vols.
Park S-r, 1992. Park Seong-Rae [Pak Sŏng-nae], "Korea-Japan Relations and the History of Science and Technology," *Korea Journal* 32/4 (Winter 1992): 80–88.
Park Y-w, 1998. Park Yong-woon, "Kaegyŏng in the Age of Koryŏ," in *Seoul Journal of Korean Studies* 11 (December 1998): 79–106.
Parsons, 1976. James B. Parsons, ed., *Papers in Honor of Professor Woodbridge Bingham*. (San Francisco: Chinese Materials Center, Inc., 1976), 302 pp.
Pearson, 1986. Richard J. Pearson, ed., *Windows on the Japanese Past: Studies in Archaeology and Prehistory* (Ann Arbor: Center for Japanese Studies, The University of Michigan, 1986), 629 pp.
——, 1990. Richard Pearson, "Chiefly Exchange Between Kyushu and Okinawa, Japan, in the Yayoi Period," *Antiquity* 64/245 (December 1990): 912–22.
——, 1992. Richard Pearson, *Ancient Japan* (NY: George Braziller, 1992), 324 pp.
Peterson, 1979. Mark Peterson, "Hyong ban and Merchant in Kaesŏng," *Korea Journal* 19/10 (October 1979): 4–18.
Piggott, 1990. Joan R. Piggott, "*Mokkan*: Wooden Documents from the Nara Period," *Monumenta Nipponica* 45/4 (Winter 1990): 449–70.
——, 1997. Joan R. Piggott, *The Emergence of Japanese Kingship* (Stanford: Stanford University Press, 1997), 434 pp.
——, 1999. Joan R. Piggott, "Chieftain Pairs and Co-rulers: Female Sovereignty in Early Japan," in Tonomura, 1999, pp. 17–52.
Platt, 2000. Brian W. Platt, "Elegance, Prosperity, Crisis: Three Generations of Tokugawa Village Elites," *Monumenta Nipponica* 55/1 (Spring 2000): 45–81.
Pratt, 1999. Edward E. Pratt, *Japan's Protoindustrial Elite, The Economic Foundations of the Gōnō* (Cambridge, MA: Harvard University Press, 1999), 260 pp.
Reischauer, 1955. Edwin O. Reischauer, *Ennin's Travels in T'ang China* (NY: The Ronald Press, 1955), 341 pp.
Reischauer and Fairbank, 1958. Edwin O. Reischauer and John K. Fairbank, *East Asia, The Great Tradition* (Boston: Houghton Mifflin Company, 1958), 739 pp.
Reynolds and Kaner, 1990. T. E. G. Reynolds and S. C. Kaner, "Japan and Korea at 18,000 BP," in Soffer and Gamble, 1990, pp. 296–311.
Rhee, 1992. Song Nai Rhee, "Secondary State Formation: The Case of Koguryo State," in Aikens and Rhee, 1992, pp. 191–96.
Ro J-y, 1983. Jin Young Ro, "Demographic and Social Mobility Trends in Early Seventeenth-century Korea: An Analysis of Sanŭm County Census Registers," *Korean Studies* 7 (1983): 77–113.
Robinson, 1992. Kenneth R. Robinson, "From Raiders to Traders: Border Security and Border Control in Early Chosŏn, 1392–1450," *Korean Studies* 16 (1992): 94–115.
——, 2000. Kenneth R. Robinson, "Centering the King of Chosŏn: Aspects of Korean Maritime Diplomacy, 1392–1592," *Journal of Asian Studies* 59/1 (February 2000): 109–25.
Rogers, 1961. Michael C. Rogers, "The Regularization of Koryŏ-Chin Relations (1116–1131)," *Central Asiatic Journal* (Weisbaden) 6/1 (1961): 51–84.
——, 1983. Michael C. Rogers, "National Consciousness in Medieval Korea: The Impact of Liao and Chin on Koryŏ," in Rossabi, 1983, pp. 151–72.
Rossabi, 1983. Morris Rossabi, ed., *China among Equals, The Middle Kingdom and its Neighbors, 10th–14th Centuries* (Berkeley: University of California Press, 1983), 419 pp.

Saito, 2002. Osamu Saito, "The Frequency of Famines as Demographic Correctives in the Japanese Past," in Dyson and O'Grada, 2002, pp. 218–39.

Sakaehara, 1980. Sakaehara Towao, "Coinage in the Nara and Heian Periods," *Acta Asiatica* 39 (1980): 1–20.

Salem, 1975, 1976. (*See* Unruh.)

——, 1979. Ellen Salem, "The Utilization of Slave Labor in the Koryŏ Period," in *Papers*, 1979, pp. 630–42.

Sasaki, 1991. Sasaki Kômei, "The Wa People and Their Culture in Ancient Japan: The Culture of Swidden Cultivation and Padi-Rice Cultivation," *Acta Asiatica* 61 (1991): 24–46.

Sawada, 1993. Janine Anderson Sawada, *Confucian Values and Popular Zen, Sekimon Shingaku in Eighteenth-Century Japan* (Honolulu: University of Hawai'i Press, 1993), 256 pp.

Science News (Washington D.C.: Science Service, published weekly): 160/11 (September 15, 2001): 168–70; 160/13 (Sepember 29, 2001): 199.

Seeley, 1991. Christopher Seeley, *A History of Writing in Japan* (Leiden: Brill, 1991), 243 pp.

Shimazu, 1989. Mitsuo Shimazu, Sun Yoon and Masaaki Tateishi, "Tectonics and Volcanism in the Sado-Pohang Belt from 20 to 14 Ma and Opening of the Yamato Basin of the Japan Sea," *Tectonophysics* 181 (1990): 321–30.

Shin, 1978. Susan S. Shin, "Economic Development and Social Mobility in Pre-Modern Korea: 1600–1860," *Peasant Studies* 7/3 (Summer 1978): 187–97.

Shin and Robinson, 2000. Gi-Wook Shin and Michael Robinson, eds., *Colonial Modernity in Korea* (Cambridge, MA: Harvard University Press, 2000), 466 pp.

Shultz, 1979. Edward J. Shultz, "The Military-Civilian Conflict of the Koryŏ Dynasty," in McCann, 1979, pp. 5–16.

——, 2000. Edward J. Shultz, *Generals and Scholars, Military Rule in Medieval Korea* (Honolulu: University of Hawai'i Press, 2000), 254 pp.

Sippel, 1972. Patricia Sippel, "Aoki Kon'yō (1698–1769) and the Beginnings of *Rangaku*," *Japanese Studies in the History of Science* 11 (1972): 127–62.

——, 1998. Patricia Sippel, "Abandoned Fields: Negotiating Taxes in the Bakufu Domain," *Monumenta Nipponica* 53/2 (Summer 1998): 197–223.

——, 2002. Patricia G. Sippel, "Re-usable Solutions: Copper Mines and Water Pollution in the Early Modern Era," a paper delivered at the 2002 Annual Meeting of the Association for Asian Studies.

Skinner, 1980. Brian J. Skinner, ed., *Earth's History, Structure and Materials* (Los Altos, CA: William Kaufmann, Inc., 1980), 179 pp.

Smith, 1959. Thomas C. Smith, *The Agrarian Origins of Modern Japan* (Stanford: Stanford University Press, 1959), 250 pp.

——, 1970. Thomas C, Smith, "Ōkura Nagatsune and the Technologists," in Craig and Shively, 1970, pp. 127–54.

Social Science Journal (Seoul: Korean Social Science Research Council) 6 (1979): 90–147.

Soffer and Gamble, 1990. Olga Soffer and Clive Gamble, *The World at 18,000 BP (Vol. One, High Latitudes)* (London: Unwin Hyman, 1990), 353 pp.

Song K-h, 1990a. Song Ki-ho, "Several Questions in Studies of the History of Palhae," *Korea Journal* 30/6 (June 1990): 4–20.

——, 1990b. Song Ki-ho, "Current Trends in the Research of Palhae History," *Seoul Journal of Korean Studies* 3 (1990): 157–74.

Song Z, 1984. Song Zhichen et al., "The Miocene Floristic Regions of East Asia," in Whyte, 1984, Vol. II, pp. 448–59.

Souyri, 2001. Pierre François Souyri, *The World Turned Upside Down: Medieval Japanese Society* (NY: Columbia University Press, 2001), 280 pp.

Suh, 1994. Dae-Sook Suh, *Korean Studies: New Pacific Currents* (Honolulu: Center for Korean Studies, University of Hawaii, 1994), 305 pp.

Sung, 1977. Shee Sung, "The Contributions of Chinese Merchants to the Trade Relations between Sung China and Koryo," in *Chinese Culture* 18/4 (December 1977): 1–18.

Tabata, 1999. Tabata Yasuko, "Women's Work and Status in the Changing Medieval Economy," in Tonomura, 1999, pp. 99–118.

Takeda, 1989. Takeda Yukio, "Studies on the King Kwanggaito Inscription and Their Basis," *Memoirs of the Research Department of the Toyo Bunko* 47 (1989): 57–87.

Takemura, 1997. Eiji Takemura, *The Perception of Work in Tokugawa Japan* (Lanham, MD: University Press of America, 1997), 229 pp.

Taylor, 1989. Sarah Taylor, "The Introduction and Development of Iron Production in Korea: a Survey," *World Archaeology* 20/3 Archaeometallurgy (1989): 422–34.

Tōno, 1995. Tōno Haruyuki, "Japanese Embassies to T'ang China and Their Ships," *Acta Asiatica* 69 (1995): 39–62.

Tonomura, 1992. Hitomi Tonomura, *Community and Commerce in Late Medieval Japan, The Corporate Villages of Tokuchin-ho* (Stanford: Stanford University Press, 1992), 285 pp.

——, 1994. Hitomi Tonomura, "Black Hair and Red Trousers: Gendering the Flesh in Medieval Japan," *American Historical Review* 99–1 (February 1994): 129–54.

——, 1999. Hitomi Tonomura et al., eds., *Women and Class in Japanese History* (Ann Arbor, MI: Center for Japanese Studies, 1999), 330 pp.

Torao, 1993. Torao Yoshiya, "Nara Economic and Social Institutions," in *Cambridge History* 1, pp. 415–52.

Totman, 1986. Conrad Totman, "Tokugawa Peasants: Win, Lose, or Draw?" *Monumenta Nipponica* 41/4 (Winter 1986): 457–76.

——, 1989. Conrad Totman, *The Green Archipelago, Forestry in Preindustrial Japan* (Berkeley: University of California Press, 1989; Athens, OH: Ohio University Press, 1998), 297 pp.

——, 1992. Conrad Totman, "Preindustrial River Conservancy, Causes and Consequences," *Monumenta Nipponica* 47/1 (Spring 1992): 59–76.

——, 1993. Conrad Totman, *Early Modern Japan* (Berkeley: University of California Press, 1993), 593 pp.

——, 1995. Conrad Totman, *The Lumber Industry in Early Modern Japan* (Honolulu: University of Hawai'i Press, 1995), 159 pp.

——, 2000. Conrad Totman, *A History of Japan* (Oxford: Blackwell Publishers, 2000), 620 pp.

Trewartha, 1978. Glenn Thomas Trewartha, *Japan, A Physical, Cultural, and Regional Geography* (Madison: The University of Wisconsin Press, 1963, 1978), 607 pp.

Troost, 1990. Kristina Kade Troost, "Common Property and Community Formation: Self-Governing Villages in Late Medieval Japan, 1300–1600" (PhD Dissertation, Harvard University, 1990).

——, 1997. Kristina Kade Troost, "Peasants, Elites, and Villages in the Fourteenth Century," in Mass, 1997, pp. 91–109.

Unruh, 1975. Ellen Salem Unruh, "Reflections of the Fall of Silla," *Korea Journal* 15/5 (May 1975): 54–62.

——, 1976. Ellen Salem Unruh, "The Landowning Slave: A Korean Phenomenon," *Korea Journal* 16/4 (April 1976): 27–34.

Uyeda and Miyashiro, 1974. S. Uyeda and A. Miyashiro, "Plate Tectonics and the Japanese Islands: A Synthesis," *Geological Society of America Bulletin* 85 (July 1974): 1159–70.

Vaporis, 1994. Constantine Vaporis, *Breaking Barriers, Travel and the State in Early Modern Japan* (Cambridge, MA: Harvard University Press, 1994), 372 pp.

Verschuer, 1999. Charlotte von Verschuer, "Japan's Foreign Relations 600 to 1200 A.D.: A Translation from *Zenrin Kokuhōki*," *Monumenta Nipponica* 54/1 (Spring 1999): 1–39.

——, 2002. Charlotte von Verschuer, "Japan's Foreign Relations 1200 to 1392

A.D.: A Translation from *Zenrin Kokuhōki*," *Monumenta Nipponica* 57/4 (Winter 2002): 413–45.

Wa, 1992. Ye Wa, "Neolithic Tradition in Northeast China," in Aikens and Rhee, 1992. pp. 139–56.

Wagner, 1974. Edward W. Wagner, *The Literati Purges: Political Conflict in Early Yi Korea* (Cambridge, MA: Harvard University Press, 1974), 238 pp.

——, 1977. Edward W. Wagner, "The Civil Examination Process as Social Leaven," *Korea Journal* 17/1 (January 1977): 22–27.

Walker, 1999. Brett L. Walker, "The Early Modern Japanese State and Ainu Vaccination: Redefining the Body Politic 1799–1868," *Past and Present* 163 (May 1999): 121–60.

——, 2001a. Brett Walker, "Commercial Growth and Environmental Change in Early Modern Japan: Hachinohe's Wild Boar Famine of 1749," *Journal of Asian Studies* 60/2 (May 2001): 329–51.

——, 2001b. Brett Walker, *The Conquest of Ainu Lands* (Berkeley: University of California Press, 2001), 332 pp.

Walker, pending. Brett Walker, "Creating and Killing the Wolves of Japan," book ms. currently in press.

Wang, 1984. Wang Pinxian, "Progress in Late Cenozoic Palaeoclimatology of China: a Brief Review," in Whyte, 1984, Vol. I, pp. 165–87.

Watt, 1982. Alec Watt, *Barnes & Noble Thesaurus of Geology* (NY: Barnes & Noble, 1982), 192 pp.

Whyte, 1984. Robert Orr Whyte, *The Evolution of the East Asian Environment* (Hong Kong: Centre of Asian Studies, University of Hong Kong, 1984), 2 vols.

Yamamoto, 1990. Kaoru Yamamoto, "Space-time Analysis of Raw Material Utilization for Stone Implements of the Jomon Culture in Japan," *Antiquity* 64/245 (December 1990): 868–89.

Yamamura, 1981. Kozo Yamamura, "Returns on Unification: Economic Growth in Japan," in Hall, 1981, pp. 327–72.

Yang B-k, 1997. Yang Bo-Kyung, "Perceptions of Nature in the Chosŏn Period, *Korea Journal* 37/4 (Winter 1997): 134–55.

Yasuda, 1990. Yasuda Yoshinori, "Monsoon Fluctuations and Cultural Changes During the Last Glacial Age in Japan," *Japan Review* 1 (1990): 113–51.

Yi C-h, 1985. Yi Chin-hŏi, "Korean Envoys and Japan: Korean-Japanese Relations in the 17th to 19th Centuries," *Korea Journal* 25/12 (December 1985): 24–35.

Yi K-d, 1984. Yi Ki-dong, "Shilla's Kolp'um System and Japan's Kabane System," *Korean Social Science Journal* 11 (1984): 7–24.

Yi S-m, 1981. Yi Sŏng-mu, "Kwagŏ System and Its Characteristics: Centering on the Koryŏ and Early Chosŏn Periods," *Korea Journal* 21/7 (July 1981): 4–19.

Yi T-j, 1983. Yi T'ae-jin, "Social Changes in Late Koryŏ to Early Chosŏn Period," *Korea Journal* 23/5 (May 1983): 32–44.

——, 1995. Yi Tae-jin, "The Nature of Seoul's Modern Urban Development During the 18th and 19th Centuries," *Korea Journal* 35/3 (Autumn, 1995): 5–30.

——, 1997. Yi Tae-Jin, "The Influence of Neo-Confucianism on 14th–16th Century Korean Population Growth," *Korea Journal* 37/2 (Summer 1997): 5–23.

Yiengpruksawan, 1998. Mimi Hall Yiengpruksawan, *Hiraizumi, Buddhist Art and Regional Politics in Twelfth-Century Japan* (Cambridge, MA: Harvard University Press, 1998), 263 pp.

Yoo, 1988. Yoo Seung-won, "The Status System in the Early Chosŏn Period," *Seoul Journal of Korean Studies* 1 (1988): 69–99.

Yoon, 1989. Yoon Dong Suk, "Early Iron Metallurgy in Korea," *Archaeological Review from Cambridge* 8/1 (1989): 92–99.

Yoshida, 1976. Yoshida Takashi, ed., *Outline of the Geology of Japan* (Kawasaki: Geological Survey of Japan, 1976), 61 pp.

INDEX

Agriculture 1–3; beginnings, 27–9, 31–7; early in Korea, 37–42; early in Japan, 42–5; intensification of, 66, 81, 124–8, 142–6, 166–7; intensive in Japan, 103–4, 153–4; intensive in Korea, 105; environmental effects of, 64, 88–91, 108–9, 112, 166–7. *See also* cultivators, fertilizer, rice

Art 22, 28, 59, 76

Artisans: early, 79, 104; later, 131, 133–4, 137–8, 150, 162. *See also* commerce, technology

Ashikaga: politics, 100–1, 112; compared to Korea, 117–9, 120n10; and society, 134, 138

Ashikaga Takauji 100

bakufu. See shogunate

Bishop, Isabella (Bird) 155, 158

bronze. *See* metallurgy

Buddhism: introduced to northeast Asia, 58; role of institutions, 70, 72, 81, 93, 96, 101; and commerce, 79, 134; cultural influence of, 76, 101–3, 122; environmental impact of, 87

burial 28, 37, 41, 56

ceramics. *See* pottery

Chang Po-go 78

Ch'eng-Zhu. *See* Neo-Confucianism

China: agriculture in, 1, 31, 33, 34, 39; influence on northeast Asia, general, 3, 5, 83; influence of politics, 37, 39–53, 98, 106, 114, 116, 119; influence of agriculture, 39, 40, 105; influence of metallurgy, 41, 130; trade with northeast Asia, 46, 59, 77–8, 104, 131, 134–5; influence of culture, 55–6, 58, 73, 75–6, 86

Ch'ing Dynasty 116

Ch'oe 96, 98, 105

Ch'oe Ch'ung-hŏn 96, 100

Chŏng Yag-yong 143–4, 148

Chosŏn: founding of, 94, 101, 106; politics of, 112, 114–9, 121–3, 134

chŭlmun 26, 37, 38

cities: early cities, 58, 73–5, 85–8, 109; environmental impact of, 108–9, 139–40; later cities, 131–3, 135, 149–50, 152. *See also* Edo, Heian, Kaesŏng, Kyŏngju, Kyoto, Nara, Osaka, Pusan, P'yŏngyang, Seoul, Taegu

climate 16–8; and forager society, 22–3, 28, 165; and agriculture, 34, 38, 91, 139

clothing 22, 26, 59, 126

coal 159–60, 163, 167

commerce: in forager society, 26–8, 58–9; among regimes, 46, 49–50, 59–60, 77–8; in early agricultural society, 78–9, 92–3; in later agricultural society, 112, 129–36, 143–4, 146–9

Confucianism 58, 71, 76, 99, 122, 133

cotton 126, 143–5, 148

cultivators: incipient, 27–9; early, 36, 38–9, 66, 77, 81, 103–4, 107; intensive, 123–8, 138, 141, 143–5, 148, 153, *See also* agriculture, rice, villages

daimyō 118–20, 121, 135

Daisen Tomb. *See* Nintokuryō

Daoism 76

diet. *See* food

disease: in early agricultural society, 55, 61–2, 81–4, 107–8; in later agricultural society, 112, 139, 143, 150, 157, 160

Edo 119, 129, 135, 148, 149

El Nino 91, 139

famine: in forager society, 28; in agricultural society, 44, 62, 83, 91, 108, 142

fertilizer 36; in early agriculture, 90–1, 108; in intensive agriculture, 125, 127–8, 141, 145–7, 163

fisheries 17; in forager society, 21,

PLATES

Plate 1. Korea's mountains and lower, rounded hills are visible from most areas, including the sedimentary flatlands of the Seoul vicinity, as seen here.

Plate 2. Japan's mountains are highly incised by millennia of upthrust and erosional wearing. Many are so steep that landslides are frequent, and they can be logged or otherwise disturbed only with great care.

Plate 3. In this picture of ripening rice southwest of Tokyo, the adjoining hillsides host a richly varied growth. Besides diverse woody shrubs, at right rear is a persimmon orchard with an understory of dwarf bamboo. Beyond it in center rear is a stand of large bamboo and, on the edges of the paddy fields, various small grasses and forbs. The farmer has strung up lines of reflective tape to scare away birds that otherwise would feed on his ripening rice.

Plate 4. The small port of Hirado in southwest Japan exemplifies the many small ports that have sustained waterborne traffic for millennia, enabling residents of Japan to bypass the mountains that obstruct much land travel.

Plate 5. In January the accumulated snow atop Mt. Kwanak, across the Han River south of Seoul, is modest, and in this cold clear air adjacent valleys and hills are readily visible. A small temple sanctifies the mountaintop.

Plate 6. Monsoon rains can overload Japan's rivers, as even here in the Edogawa, a man-made channel northeast of Tokyo. It incorporates on its near bank a broad overflow area that is bounded, off-camera left, by a dike. Farmers till the nutrient-rich overflow area, mostly growing crops that can withstand temporary immersion.

Plate 7. This lowland area west of Seoul once supported a diverse woodland biosystem, remnants of which are visible on the far hills. In the 1950s it supported domesticated rice and diversified grain and vegetable production, as well as spreading human settlement.

Plate 8. This aerial view of an upper valley entering low hills in northeast Japan suggests how land clearance created miles of forest edge and placed humans and wildlife in closer contact.

Plate 9. This aerial view of the Sendai Plain in northeast Japan suggests the complexity of large-scale wet-rice cultivaton. Three main irrigation ditches snake across the plain, running from foreground left, center, and right, upward into the distance, wiggling about as required by surface contour. The paddy fields, similarly, are shaped to fit the land's gradient. The light brown fields are still in winter dormancy; the dark brown ones have been tilled and prepared for flooding; the glassy blue ones are flooded, enabling the water to warm in preparation for the transplanting of seedlings.

Plate 10. The aristocratic elegance of Paekche was sustained by the rich agricultural lowlands of southwest Korea. This picture shows rice fields being harvested, and in the background, beyond the electric lines that parallel the railroad, the slopes that support dryfield cropping and the low hills whose forest cover yields mulch, fuel, and construction timber.

Plate 11. The Hōryūji, whose main hall is shown here, is a seventh-century Buddhist temple that still stands near Nara. It exemplifies the architectural style that sharply increased the demand for construction timber and for fuel wood used in the production of roof tiles.

Plate 12. North of Seoul in early August, wet rice ripens on the lowland while slopes and low hills support mixed cropping, and higher, sharply etched mountains retain deteriorated forest cover.

Plate 13. West of Tokyo in the autumn, the brushy hillside above a village sports bright colors while winter crops begin to grow, scattered among the remnants of summer garden crops and a few dry-grain and paddy fields.

Plate 14. Insofar as minor *yangban* lived in villages such as this one southwest of Seoul, which is seen here in mid-November, they would have experienced considerable contact with commoners in the course of their daily lives.

Plates 15, 16. In the castle town of Shimabara in southwest Japan, samurai lived in a small neighborhood of streets such as this, with drainage ditches in the center, and thatch-roofed houses set behind heavy stone walls and gates. The walls were intended to function as layers of fortification shielding the castle proper from attack, but they also served to isolate samurai from the broader society.

Plate 17. This farm house southwest of Seoul, seen here in November, is tucked into the edge of the low hill, leaving flatter foreground parcels for tillage. A small area to the rear holds the mounded tombs of ancestors, while the house's immediate surroundings are used for equipment storage and other purposes.

Plate 18. This larger-scale farm household near Sendai in northeast Japan, seen here in mid-May, has storage and work sheds laid out around a central area devoted to garden crops. Trees shelter the homestead and its work areas against winter winds. Rice seed-beds are situated adjacent the household plot, while other paddy fields are in varying stages of preparation for the seedling trans-plant.

Plate 19. Rows of winter wheat ripen on a warm spring day northwest of Tokyo.

Plate 20. A farmer west of Tokyo double-crops his field. As his winter grain crop is maturing, he starts a summer crop of cucumbers. Later he harvests his grain, leaves the cut fodder to suppress weeds and rot into mulch between the rows of cucumber, and installs bamboo poles for the cucumber vines to ascend, thereby increasing his yield-per-acre.

Plate 21. In May a farmer west of Tokyo prepares his wet-rice seedbed and strings reflective tape to repel birds. While the seed sprouts, he goes about the tasks of cleaning and repairing irrigation ditches, plowing and smoothing paddy fields, and flooding them preparatory to planting. This particular site, adjacent International Christian University, grew rice for centuries, became a golf course in the 1970s, and a section of divided highway during the 1980s.

Plate 22. The huge main hall of the Kyŏngbok Palace in Seoul, shown here in autumn, exemplifies the heavy demand for timber, fuel wood, masonry stone, and human labor that urban construction, particularly that of the ruling elite, entailed.

Plate 23. The gigantic castle at Kumamoto in southwest Japan, seen here in spring, consumed immense amounts of labor, masonry stone, timber, and fuel wood when constructed around 1600.

Plate 24. During the 1960s the spiny peninsula adjacent Nagasaki Harbor in southwest Japan, off-camera to the left, supported a few terraced fields, patches of scrub woodland, and extensive areas of deteriorated soil.

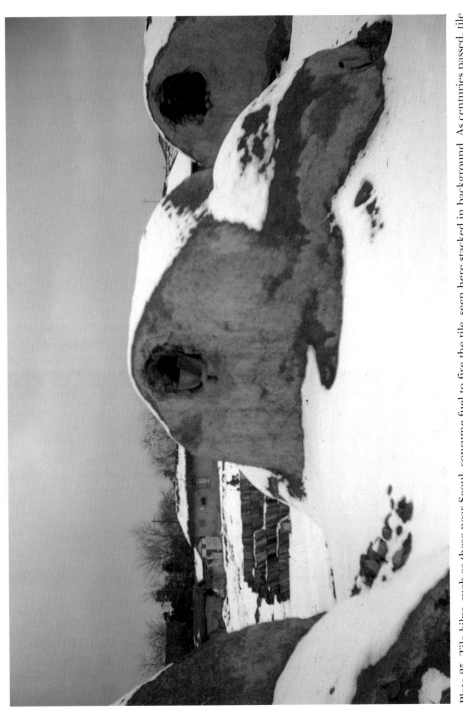

Plate 25. Tile kilns, such as these near Seoul, consume fuel to fire the tile, seen here stacked in background. As centuries passed, tile replaced thatch roofing in more and more construction in both Korea and Japan.

Plate 26. Giant buildings, such as the Honganji in Kyoto, shown here, required immense amounts of fuel wood to produce their expanses of tile roofing, not to mention the metal work used within.

Plate 27. The four men on the barren skyline, pausing to rest and enjoy the crystalline winter view, are carrying A-frame loads of fuel and fodder that they raked together on the far side of the mountain. They still have miles to go, descending the mountain and travelling across the lowlands, to reach their homes west of Seoul.

Plate 28 In south central Korea lowlands fit for wet-rice culture are ready for harvest in October, while side hills yield such other crops and woodland produce as they can. Coal smoke from the passing train casts a shadow over the crop.

Plate 29. In southwestern Japan high levels of rainfall that are spread broadly throughout the year enable farmers to grow wet rice and dry field crops as far up hillsides as gradient allows. A winter crop of mustard is in yellow bloom; steep slopes remain in scrub woodland.

Plate 30. In north central Japan, where heavy snow still blankets the landscape in March, wet and dry fields rise as far as water and gradient allow. On higher, steeper slopes, residents harvest forests for their yield of fuel, timber, and other usables.

Plate 31. A man laden with fodder and fuel material on a crisp January day nears his home west of Seoul after traveling miles from where he obtained it in the vicinity of Mt. Kwanak. He has lost part of his load but for the moment has no way to recover it.

Plate 32. West of Seoul on a late autumn day a man gathers night soil, which his patient bullock will haul to a storage pit for months of bacterial processing before application to the field in the following spring.

Plate 33. West of Tokyo on a warm spring day a woman applies to her cabbage crop night soil she has retrieved from the processing pit.

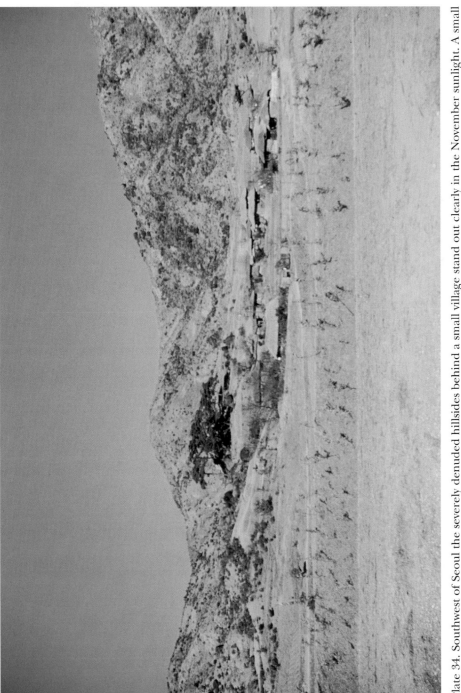

Plate 34. Southwest of Seoul the severely denuded hillsides behind a small village stand out clearly in the November sunlight. A small village temple is surrounded by a handful of scraggly pine trees.

Plate 35. Southwest of Tokyo in early October a comfortable farm homestead stands amidst handsome fields of ripening rice, persimmon trees, a bamboo grove, and forested hillsides.

Plate 36. In Korea, as here seen southwest of Seoul, the reforesting of dessicated hillsides was proving a difficult task in 1954-55. Government foresters test various species of pine and other trees, and plantings are made. On more rounded hills the seedlings are planted in contoured rows; on steeper slopes workers assemble stones to form walls that will hold the soil while the hardy young trees establish themselves.

Plate 37. Legend see plate 36.

Plate 38. West of Seoul a man makes good use of the sedimentary deposits produced by centuries of erosion. He wets the soil and stirs it to proper consistency, packs it into his wooden box-frame, and when it is firm tips the box over, unlatches its sides, and leaves the block to harden in the dry, wintry air. Later his creations will be hauled by bullock cart to the construction site.

Plate 39. These parcels of even-aged monoculture evergreen forest, planted on low hills hard by cultivated fields in central Japan, were approaching harvest age in the spring of 1955. A central section had recently been clearcut while several other small parcels nearby had been cleared, replanted, and were starting a new generation of timber stands.